JOHN HICK'S PLURALIST PHILOSOPHY OF WORLD RELIGIONS

One of the most fascinating and controversial interpretations of religious diversity is 'religious pluralism.' According to John Hick's model of religious pluralism, all the world's great religions are equally valid ways of understanding and responding to the ultimate spiritual reality.

This book offers an exposition of, and critical response to, John Hick's model. Introducing the various interpretations of religious diversity being discussed today, this book presents constructive suggestions as to how things could be further developed to offer a more accurate, less confusing presentation of the various options in theology of religions. The standard threefold typology of responses to religious diversity - exclusivism, inclusivism, and pluralism - are explained and defended. Hick's pluralist interpretation of religious diversity is traced, culminating in a critical assessment of Hick's pluralistic model and an up-to-date summary of a variety of critiques directed toward Hick's proposal. Paul Rhodes Eddy concludes that Hick's present model is ultimately unsuccessful in retaining both of his long-cherished goals, a robust religious realism and a consistent religious pluralism, whilst overcoming the most difficult problem for the pluralist, the fact that the world's religions understand the divine in often contradictory ways.

ASHGATE NEW CRITICAL THINKING IN RELIGION, THEOLOGY & BIBLICAL STUDIES

The *Ashgate New Critical Thinking in Religion, Theology and Biblical Studies* series brings high quality research monograph publishing back into focus for authors, international libraries, and student, academic and research readers. Headed by an international editorial advisory board of acclaimed scholars spanning the breadth of religious studies, theology and biblical studies, this open-ended monograph series presents cutting-edge research from both established and new authors in the field. With specialist focus yet clear contextual presentation of contemporary research, books in the series take research into important new directions and open the field to new critical debate within the discipline, in areas of related study, and in key areas for contemporary society.

Other Titles in the Series:

The Rhetorical Word
Theo Hobson
Feminist Biblical Interpretation in Theological Context
J'annine Jobling

John Hick's Pluralist
Philosophy of World Religions

PAUL RHODES EDDY
Bethel College, USA

ASHGATE

Published by
Ashgate Publishing Limited
Gower House
Croft Road
Aldershot
Hampshire GU11 3HR
England

Ashgate Publishing Company
131 Main Street
Burlington, VT 05401-5600 USA

Ashgate website: http://www.ashgate.com

British Library Cataloguing in Publication Data
Eddy, Paul Rhodes
    John Hick's pluralist philosophy of world religions. -
    (Ashgate new critical thinking in religion, theology and
    biblical studies)
    1. Hick, John, 1922- 2. Religious pluralism 3. Religions -
    Philosophy
    I. Title
    291.1'72'01

Library of Congress Cataloging-in-Publication Data
Eddy, Paul Rhodes, 1959-
    John Hick's pluralist philosophy of world religions/Paul Rhodes Eddy.
      p.cm. – (Ashgate new critical thinking in religion, theology and biblical studies)
    Includes bibliographical references.
    ISBN 0-7546-0512-4 (alk. paper)
      1.Hick, John. 2.Religious pluralism. 3.Religion – Philosophy. I. Title.II Series.

BL51 .E37 2002
291.1'72–dc21
                                                                    2002016329

ISBN 0 7546 0512 4
Printed and bound by Athenaeum Press, Ltd.,
Gateshead, Tyne & Wear.

Dedicated to my parents,
my life-long encouragers:

To my Mother, Donna Eddy and in
loving memory of my Father, Delbert Eddy

Contents

Preface

This book represents a revision of my doctoral dissertation, "John Hick's Pluralist Philosophy of World Religions: An Exposition and Response" (Marquette University, 1999). The seeds of this project began in the winter of 1989, during my time at Bethel Theological Seminary (St. Paul, Minn.), as a cafeteria conversation with my theological mentor and friend, Dr. David K. Clark. His insight and encouragement throughout this project have been substantial. My time at Bethel also put me in contact with Dr. Robert Rakestraw and Dr. Bruce Reichenbach, both of whom have offered continual support.

During my doctoral studies at Marquette University, this project developed and matured under the supervision of my dissertation director, Dr. Brad Hinze, whose insight and suggestions have shaped the outcome in many important ways. I am also grateful for having had the opportunity to work with the other members of my committee. Dr Michel Barnes, Dr. Lyle Dabney, Dr. Robert Masson, and Fr. Gerald O'Collins have each, in their own way, contributed to the growth and maturity of this project. I cannot imagine a more supportive committee.

This undertaking has benefited from my interaction with a number of scholars currently involved with the theology of religions discussion. First and foremost, I must express my great appreciation for the interaction with and support of Professor John Hick. Professor Hick has graciously encouraged this project since its early stages. His willingness to dialogue with me through personal correspondence, face to face interaction, and publication, has added a depth and dimension to this project that would have been otherwise sorely missing. The project has also benefited from the insights of and personal interaction and/or correspondence with Jim Beilby, Greg Boyd, Gavin D'Costa, Doug Geivett, Chester Gillis, Paul Griffiths, Paul Knitter, James Lewis, Randy Nelson, Harold Netland, Clark Pinnock, and John Sanders.

With regard to the final phase of this project—from dissertation to published volume—I am indebted to Sarah Lloyd of Ashgate Publishing for accepting the manuscript for publication, and to Chelsea DeArmond for her invaluable assistance in preparing it in final form. I would also like to thank *Religious Studies* journal for permission to use a substantial amount of material from my previously published article, "Religious Pluralism and the Divine."

My final word of appreciation goes to my family. Throughout this project, my wife and best friend, Kelly, offered me nothing but tireless love, support, and no small amount of patience. And over the course of this project—as through my entire life—my parents, Delbert and Donna Eddy, demonstrated to me their endless love, encouragement and support. It is to them that I dedicate this book.

Introduction

A number of factors have converged during the 20th century resulting in a heightened awareness of religious diversity in many quarters of the globe. This growing awareness of the fact of religious diversity has brought with it new interpretations of this fact. More specifically, something of a revolution has taken place within some sectors of Christianity regarding the assessment of other religions and religious persons. The various contemporary options of Christian response to religious diversity have come to be classified under three general rubrics: exclusivism, inclusivism, and pluralism.[1] Forms of Christian exclusivism and inclusivism have been a part of the church since its early days. However, what is now being referred to as the 'pluralist' interpretation of religious diversity represents a substantially new perspective *vis-à-vis* traditional Christian approaches to the question.

Since the early 1970s, John Hick has been at the vanguard of the rapidly developing pluralist perspective. He has produced one of the most sophisticated and influential pluralist philosophies of world religions currently available. In barest terms, Hick's pluralist hypothesis proposes that:

> the great world faiths embody different perceptions and conceptions of, and correspondingly different responses to, the Real from within the major variant ways of being human; and that within each of them the transformation of human existence from self-centeredness to Reality-centeredness is taking place.[2]

From the beginning, Hick's pluralist hypothesis has faced a variety of criticisms. Over the last two decades, critiques of Hick's pluralism have tended to focus on two broad issues: (1) the philosophical viability of Hick's hypothesis, and (2) the problematic ramifications of his proposal for Christian theology. More recently, a third line of critique has arisen out of our 'postmodern' context: the ironic charge that Hick's proposal is fundamentally 'totalizing,' 'imperialistic,'—even 'exclusivistic'—in nature.

Hick has, generally speaking, been willing to listen and learn from his critics. He has continued to rework and modify his thesis over the years, often times in ways that dramatically affected his over-all proposal. It is just because of Hick's willingness to modify his proposal over the years that a number of his critics' charges from the past (sometimes from the very recent past) have been rendered partially—if not wholly—obsolete and thus largely irrelevant. More recently, Hick has published several works which serve to develop and/ or clarify his ideas in the midst of focused responses to a wide variety of his critics. An in-depth re-assessment of Hick's most current pluralist model is thus called for.

With others, I will argue that the most critical conceptual problem facing the pluralist hypothesis in general—and Hick's model in particular—involves the *de facto* existence of the often radically conflicting conceptions of divine reality throughout the world religions. The heart of the problem is this. Given Hick's pluralist model, one would prima facie expect human perceptions of the single divine Reality to be relatively similar, or at least not mutually exclusive, in nature. Phenomenologically, of course, this is anything but the case. The most obvious—and problematic—of these differences is the radical conceptual dichotomy between those religions that view the Real as a personal Being, and those that view it in terms of a non-personal principle, force, or 'absolute.' Thus, to survive the day, it is clear that Hick's pluralist philosophy of religions must include a viable solution to this problem of apparently contradictory conceptions of the divine.

The primary purpose of this study is threefold. First, a description and fresh analysis of the rise and subsequent development of Hick's pluralist hypothesis will be presented. The central lens through which this development is viewed will be the 'conflicting conceptions' problematic and Hick's various responses to it. Second, a discussion and evaluation of the most challenging criticisms that have been leveled against Hick's mature model of religious pluralism will be provided. Practically, this catalogue of critiques could be used to serve several different purposes. On one hand, it could function as a summary outline for those seeking to construct a sustained argument against John Hick's model of religious pluralism. On the other hand, it could assist in flagging the crucial issues that must be addressed by those who would wish to clarify, develop, and/or defend Hick's pluralist hypothesis. Third and finally, a philosophical critique of Hick's mature pluralist model is offered from an 'immanent,' internal perspective by asking the question: 'Does it work'? That is, does Hick's pluralist philosophy/theology of world religions deliver the conceptual goods required of it? Again, the primary touchstone that will be used to answer this general query will be the question of just how successful Hick's current response to the 'conflicting conceptions' problem actually is.

Finally, a word on perspective is in order. There is a new awareness in our 'postmodern' world of 'historical consciousness,' and of the fact that every perspective is embedded in a concrete socio-cultural context that sheds light upon its genesis, motives, and nature. Forthrightness with regard to the 'place' wherein one stands and from which one launches out into conceptual description and assessment is an important step toward facilitating mutual understanding and honest dialogue in our diverse world. To this end, it should be understood that this study is offered by one whose philosophical perspective is primarily indebted to the western analytic tradition, and whose theological commitments have been predominately shaped within an evangelical Christian context. While consciousness of the 'place' that grounds this study is important, my hope is that those who stand elsewhere, philosophically and/or theologically, will nonetheless find it useful.

Notes

1   See chapter one for definition and discussion of these three positions.
2   Hick, *An Interpretation of Religion: Human Responses to the Transcendent* (New Haven: Yale University Press, 1989), 240.

1 Christian Responses to Religious Diversity

This chapter will begin by explicating the conceptual stage upon which the contemporary Christian theology of religions debate is being played out. Along the way, constructive proposals will be made as to the manner in which certain concepts and terms could be more precisely defined and/or developed to offer a more accurate presentation of the various options in Christian theology of religions today. The pluralist paradigm will eventually take the spotlight in this discussion. Here, it will be suggested that the most pressing conceptual problem facing proponents of the pluralist approach today involves the conflicting conceptions of the divine found within the various world religions. Finally, the discussion will narrow toward the focus of this dissertation: John Hick's religious pluralism.

The Problem of Religious Diversity for Contemporary Christian Theology

It is rare that one finds contemporary Christian theologians across the spectrum agreeing on any one thing. However, it appears that Christian thinkers of virtually every persuasion concur that the phenomenon of religious diversity and the issues it raises must be at the forefront of the theological agenda as Christianity moves into the 21st century. This recognition permeates a wide array of Christian denominations.[1] If literary output is any measure, it is a sentiment that is shared by theological radicals, liberals, moderates, and conservatives alike.[2] The importance of this subject is highlighted by the fact that a growing number of contemporary Christian systematic theologians and philosophers of religion feel compelled to include substantial discussions on the matter when canvassing their respective domains.[3]

It is not as if religious diversity itself is a new phenomenon to be faced by Christians. This simple fact does seem to be overlooked in too many contemporary discussions. Chronocentrism can rob us of an historical awareness of the rich and varied resources available in the Christian tradition for addressing these issues. For much of the early church, religious diversity, in the form of various philosophies, pagan cults, mystery religions, popular superstition, etc., was an ever-present given. As Robert Wilken has noted, the "oldest and most enduring criticism of Christianity is an appeal to religious [diversity]."[4] John North has argued that it was during the time of the early church that 'religious pluralism,' which he describes as "a system of interacting competing religions between which the individual could, even in a sense had to, choose," actually developed in the Mediterranean world.[5] In any case, the earliest Christian theologians were forced to wrestle with a variety of problems that stemmed from the religious diversity of the world surrounding them.[6]

What then, if anything, is new about the contemporary situation of religious diversity? The answer to this question is complex and not uncontroversial. According to many, it is simply the growing *awareness* of religious diversity in much of the contemporary world that constitutes a new state of affairs. Kenneth Cragg captures this sensibility when he writes, "[p]luralisms, of course, there have always been....The contemporary difference is that pluralisms are conscious."[7] Some would add to this and say that the newness is not simply a matter of awareness, but of unavoidable mutual contact in what is quickly becoming, through modern technology, a virtual 'global village.' Thus, M. M. Thomas writes, "There have always been a plurality of religions and cultures in the world....What is new today is that they have moved from their separate, isolated existence to what may be called a dialogical existence."[8] Others, however, would go a step further and identify the new moment as the embracing of a distinct *attitude* toward religious diversity. Langdon Gilkey nicely summarizes this view:

> Plurality is not new; there have always been other religions. What is new is the dawning recognition of what I have come to call the 'rough parity' between them, and so a new relation of *dialogue*, of mutual respect, of the recognition of truth, of some sort of truth, in the Other, and thus a stance of listening as well as of proclaiming and instructing.[9]

For Gilkey and others, this sense of the "rough parity" of the world's great religions—the sense that many religions offer "the presence of truth and grace"—is so basic as to be "assumed" as the "common consciousness" within our contemporary world.[10] With respect to the American religious scene in particular, Richard Wenty has recently argued for a similar interpretation of religious diversity:

> the transformation of diversity into pluralism is a religious phenomenon that serves as a prevailing factor in the development of American culture. Pluralism denotes the ac-

ceptance of diversity; and this acceptance, we have observed, always works within some perception of ultimate order and meaning not confined to traditional religions.[11]

I have, to this point, consciously chosen to talk of religious 'diversity' rather than religious 'pluralism.' A chief concern of this chapter shall be to assist in clarifying several terminological issues that have served to cloud the discussion of religious diversity. The first concerns the word 'pluralism.' As Francis Clooney has remarked, 'pluralism' is "a word of many meanings."[12] Some simply use the term *descriptively* as a synonym for 'diversity.' Here religious 'pluralism' is intended to denote the fact that a plurality of religions exists, or, perhaps, that they exist in mutual contact with each other. Some scholars are careful to designate this use of the term as "descriptive pluralism," or "phenomenological pluralism."[13] Others, however, use the term *normatively* to denote a particular intellectual and/or attitudinal response to religious diversity. In this case, 'pluralism' refers to "an interpretation of plurality, an evaluation of religious and cultural diversity."[14] Specifically, a pluralist interpretation of religious diversity would, with Gilkey, affirm the 'rough parity' of the world's religious traditions. The terms "normative pluralism," "philosophical pluralism," "dogmatic pluralism," and "extramural pluralism" have all been used to describe this perspective.[15]

Clearly, terminological equivocation within the field at this point can lead to miscommunication and misunderstanding. Some, conflating and confusing the two distinct issues, have pointed to the "fact of religious pluralism," by which they mean both that the world is religiously diverse and that an interpretation of 'rough parity' is thus in order.[16] To avoid any such confusions in this study, I shall reserve use of the term religious 'pluralism' for the normative judgment that there is a rough parity among the world's religions. I shall use the term religious 'diversity' to signal the fact that a plurality of religions exist in the world, often in conscious contact with each other.[17]

Christian Responses to Religious Diversity: Types of Theology of Religions

Over the last several decades, a variety of ideal-typical schemas have been proposed by which to classify the various Christian theological responses to religious diversity. In the early 1960s, Hans Küng could be found contrasting an "ecclesiocentric" approach (i.e., "No salvation outside the Church") with a "theocentric" perspective, wherein he emphasized the "great and gracious, all-embracing *intra*" that is God's desire to save all humanity.[18] In 1969, Owen

Thomas offered ten models by which to classify different approaches that Christians had taken to the question of other religions. These included: rationalism (Herbert of Cherbury), romanticism (Schleiermacher), Relativism (Troeltsch), Exclusivism (Barth), Dialectic (Brunner), Reconception (Hocking), Tolerance (Toynbee), Dialogue (Tillich), Catholicism (Küng), and Presence (M. Warren and John Taylor).[19] By the early 1970s, John Hick had made a move to a pluralist interpretation of religious diversity. At this time he presented something of a threefold typology built around an astronomical analogy: an ecclesiocentric 'Ptolemaic' view, various Christocentric 'epicycles' (developed to be sure, but Ptolemaic nonetheless), and a theocentric 'Copernican' perspective that represented a "revolution" in Christian theology of religions.[20]

In a seminal article in 1976, J. Peter Schineller proffered a fourfold typology that revolved around the intersection of Christology and ecclesiology. The following options emerged: (1) "Ecclesiocentric universe, exclusive Christology" (i.e., Jesus and the church as the constitutive and exclusive way of salvation); (2) "Christocentric universe, inclusive Christology" (i.e., Jesus and church as constitutive but not exclusive way of salvation, *or* Jesus as constitutive but church nonconstitutive way of salvation); (3) "Theocentric universe, normative Christology" (i.e., Jesus and church normative but not constitutive way of salvation); and (4) "Theocentric universe, nonnormative Christology" (i.e., Jesus one of many ways of salvation).[21] A key to understanding the significance of Schineller's classifications is the distinction between 'constitutive' and 'normative.' Schineller explains:

> To say that Jesus is the constitutive mediator of salvation is to say that he is not only normative but the indispensable one. Without him there would be no salvation.... 'Constitutive,' therefore, means that without this historical incarnation, life, death, and resurrection, no person would be saved.[22]

In a 'normative Christology,' on the other hand, Jesus functions as the 'norm' or standard by which to measure various soteriological aspects in other religions.

In his important 1985 volume, *No Other Name?*, Paul Knitter proposed a fourfold typology that mirrors Schineller's in significant ways: (1) The "Conservative Evangelical" model (i.e., "one true religion"); (2) the "Mainline Protestant" model (i.e., "salvation only in Christ"); (3) the "Catholic" model (i.e., "many ways, one norm"; this model represents a Rahnerian-like, post-Vatican II perspective); and (4) the "Theocentric" model (i.e., "many ways to the center").[23] Unfortunately, Knitter chose rubrics for his models that identified a particular form of Christianity with a certain view of other religions. The fact that each of these forms contained within them adherents of at least one of the other perspectives practically ruled against the widespread adoption of Knitter's typology.

The Standard Threefold Typology: Exclusivism, Inclusivism, Pluralism

In 1983, Alan Race advanced a new threefold typology.[24] This schema was quickly adopted by leading scholars in the field, including Hick and Knitter.[25] His three types—'exclusivism,' 'inclusivism,' and 'pluralism' (Race himself argues for the pluralist perspective)—would soon become the three standard paradigms by which to discuss the basic options in Christian theology of religions.[26] It is worth noting that, although these terms were finally given schematic permanence by Race, the essence of these conceptual paradigms were effectively delineated by Hick a decade earlier under his Copernican analogy. It is also interesting to note that, within a few years, Race himself was already developing his threefold typology in a manner not unlike Schineller by distinguishing an "inclusivism from above" from an "inclusivism from below."[27]

In the mid-1980s, Gavin D'Costa emerged as one of the most consistent and influential proponents of the threefold typology. He offers the following as definitions: (1) *Exclusivism* - "only those who hear the Gospel proclaimed and explicitly confess Christ are saved." (2) *Inclusivism* - "Christ is the normative revelation of God, although salvation is possible outside of the explicit Christian Church, but this salvation is always from Christ." (3) *Pluralism* - "all religions are equal and valid paths to the one divine reality and Christ is one revelation among many equally important revelations."[28] It is important to note here that D'Costa's definitions remained quite fixed for at least a decade; the significance of this fact will be made clear below.[29]

Criticisms of the Standard Typology

It seems clear that the standard threefold typology has been a generally helpful schematic, at one level or another. Minimally, it has provided a common vocabulary by which the Christian theology of religions discussion has been able to progress over the last few years. This is not to say that this typology has not had its critics. Criticisms have come from several different directions.

Against A Priori Typologies in General First, there are those who argue that any theology of religions that is primarily driven by an *a priori* typology rooted in theological presuppositions is anathema to honest and open engagement with, and assessment of, other religious traditions. These critics argue that Christians must enter into study of, and dialogue with, another religion before they can legitimately claim to have categorized or appropriately responded to that religion. A leading voice in this respect is that of Paul Griffiths, whose work revolves around the emerging field of the comparative philosophy of religion (Griffiths, himself a Christian, specializes in Buddhist studies).[30] Griffiths writes of the "burgeoning industry" wherein Christian theologians offer theologies of other religions. Here:

> we find the more or less obligatory discussions of Karl Barth's and Hendrik Kraemer's word-centered exclusivism; of Karl Rahner's hierarchical inclusivism;...and of John Hick's radical theocentric pluralism. There is usually comparatively little discussion of what any non-Christian tradition actually asserts, values, and practices....Christian theologians, whose major specialty is theologizing about non-Christian religions...[do so as] a purely abstract *a priori* intra-Christian enterprise, constrained not by the religions themselves, as they impinge upon and make claims upon members of the Christian community, but rather by presuppositions drawn only from some particular reading of the Christian tradition.[31]

Griffiths rues the fact that there are "relatively few Christian theologians with the knowledge or interest to undertake an a posteriori theology whose object is some specific non-Christian religious community or communities."[32] Using his own area of expertise as an example, Griffiths writes:

> A proper theological encounter with Buddha cannot occur if it has already been decided, on an *a priori* basis, what will issue from the encounter. If I already know that my Buddhist interlocutors are anonymous Christians; or that their faithful appropriation of their tradition relates them to the same transcendent reality as does my appropriation of mine; or that they are part of the *massa perditionis*, outside the elect group of the saved—if I know any of these things before I begin, I will neither be able to hear clearly nor respond theologically to what my interlocutors are saying.[33]

It should be noted that this sort of criticism poses a challenge to any typology that primarily derives from theological *a prioris*.

While Griffiths' concerns are worthy of attention, this criticism should not, in and of itself, cause one to abandon the use of ideal-typical schemas with respect to Christian theology of religions. To do so would be to allow an important warning that should lead one to a balanced approach to become an extreme over-reaction. Even Griffiths himself has acknowledged that there are theological *a prioris* that must play a role in guiding a Christian approach to religious diversity.[34] There will always be a legitimate place for some typology of views on these matters. What Griffiths and others demonstrate is that any typology that is informed only by deductive theological *a prioris*, to the neglect of the inductive study of the religions themselves, will most likely prove to be less than satisfactory.

Against the Standard Typology's Categories Another series of critics has taken the standard typology to task for its inability to accurately capture the actual variety of Christian positions with respect to a theology of religions. In this vein, David Burrell writes of the "singularly unilluminating categories of *exclusivism, inclusivism*, and *pluralism*."[35] The expression of this concern takes various forms. Some argue that the three ideal-types—exclusivism, inclusivism, and pluralism—must be supplemented with one or more types in order to accurately reflect the breadth of available options.[36]

Others go further to suggest that an entirely new typology of positions is needed. E. L. Copeland, for example, offers a tenfold typology. Paul Varo Martinson ignores the standard approach, proposing instead a threefold typology drawn from George Lindbeck's schema of approaches to religious doctrine. James Kraft has argued that Ted Peter's threefold typology—'confessional exclusivism', 'confessional universalism', and 'supra-confessional universalism'— is a more helpful approach to Christian questions of inter-religious dialogue.[37]

Other criticisms of the threefold typology range from the postmodern critique of its necessary complicity in "comprehensive and totalizing global and world theologies,"[38] to the claim that the terms themselves—most especially 'exclusivism'—inherently contain negative connotations and thus are biased. A number of scholars willingly embrace the designation 'exclusivism' for their own position.[39] Others are willing to do so because of its wide-spread use, but regret the term's attendant connotations.[40] Still others refuse the label entirely, opting instead to be known as "particularist."[41] Unfortunately, many using the standard typology criticize the other views by suggesting—implicitly or explicitly—that one or more of the perspectives are, virtually by nature, intellectually and/or morally bankrupt. For example, a number of pluralists (and at least a few inclusivists) charge 'exclusivism' with everything from arrogance and bigotry to narrow-mindedness and "theological insanity."[42]

A final line of criticism of the standard typology revolves around a variety of claims which, in one way or another, question the definitional clarity, integrity, and/or compatibility of the three views. The issue at hand implicitly presents itself in the instances where a critic of one position characterizes it as, in reality, expressing a covert form of one of the other two positions. Thus, one can find self-proclaimed 'exclusivists'/'particularists' who have been identified as covert 'inclusivists,'[43] 'inclusivists' who have been painted as 'exclusivists' or 'pluralists,'[44] and 'pluralists' who have been purportedly unmasked as 'exclusivists' or 'inclusivists.'[45] Some apparent 'inclusivists' are said to be more pluralistic than the 'pluralists.'[46] While terminological equivocation and polemical re-labeling are often common elements of debates in many fields, the frequency and intensity with which they occur in the theology of religions discussion seems indicative of a more serious issue.

This problem has also come to the fore in a more explicit manner. Ian Markham, for instance, has offered one of the more insightful criticisms in this respect. He contends that:

> the 'theology of religions' debate has been stifled by an over-emphasis on the standard threefold paradigm....The underlying problem with the traditional classification results from the conflation of three matters:
>
> 1. The conditions for salvation.
> 2. Whether the major world religions are all worshipping the same God.
> 3. The truth about the human situation.
>
> The traditional paradigm emphasizes the first, is confused about the second, and, with regard to the third, links truth with soteriology.[47]

While Markham's critique is not as clear as it could be—a point well-stated by Gavin D'Costa in his rebuttal—he is certainly on to something here.[48] Similarly, there are others who have come to recognize that the three terms that define the standard typology—exclusivism, inclusivism, and pluralism—are actually used in at least two (if not more) quite distinct ways by scholars in the field today.[49] In his recent book, *A Christian Theology of Religions*, John Hick notes that the standard typology, which he continues to defend as the best classificatory approach, is used to make claims with regard to "both truth-claims and salvation-claims."[50]

The far-reaching implications of this problem become more apparent as one peruses the current literature for definitions of the three terms. For a number of scholars, the definitions are clearly focused upon the question of truth-claims. Here, in the words of Alvin Plantinga for instance, an 'exclusivist' would be defined as one who holds that "the tenets or some of the tenets of *one* religion—Christianity, let's say—are in fact true...[and] that any proposition, including other religious beliefs, that are incompatible with those tenets are false."[51] On the other hand, those who apply the typology from a soteriological perspective would offer definitions more in keeping with that of D'Costa, who, until more recently, defined 'exclusivism' as the view that "only those who hear the Gospel proclaimed and explicitly confess Christ are saved."[52] Others seem to blend elements of both approaches, often in ways that are not clear, and which leave one wondering just how consistently the terms are being used over the course of an argument.[53] These problems are exacerbated by the fact that one can be, say, an 'exclusivist' with regard to various truth-matters while at the same time an 'inclusivist'—or even a 'pluralist'—with regard to the soteriological question.[54]

Nowhere is the effect of this equivocation of terms seen more clearly than in the recent and rather surprising reversal of Gavin D'Costa with respect to the standard typology. From the mid-1980s to 1995, D'Costa unflinchingly used and defended the threefold typology.[55] Then, in a 1996 article entitled "The Impossibility of a Pluralist View of Religions," one finds D'Costa suddenly recanting. The article opens:

> This paper could be an act of public self-humiliation as in what follows I am going to suggest that a typology that I have promoted and defended against critics I now come to recognize as redundant....I am increasingly convinced that the logical impossibility of a pluralist view of religions means that the typology of exclusivism, inclusivism and pluralism as three approaches or paradigms regarding Christianity's view of other religions is untenable.[56]

In this article, D'Costa's driving thesis is this: "*pluralism must always logically be a form of exclusivism and...nothing called pluralism really exists.*"[57] D'Costa is not alone in this sort of assertion. Peter van Inwagen, for example, argues that "'Religious pluralism' is not the contradictory of religious exclusivism, but one more case of it."[58]

Next, D'Costa goes even further when he brings 'inclusivism' into the discussion:

> I am suggesting that both pluralism and inclusivism are sub-types of exclusivism....[I]t seems to me that it is in fact the logic of exclusivism that best explains the way in which the other two positions work: i.e., there are certain claims to truth and those other claims that do not conform to these initial claims, explicitly or implicitly, are false....I want to say there is no such thing as pluralism because all pluralists are committed to holding some form of truth criteria and by virtue of this, anything that falls foul of such criteria is excluded from counting as truth (in doctrine and in practice).[59]

More recently, in his book *The Meeting of Religions and the Trinity*, D'Costa expands upon his critique of the threefold typology.[60] Here, he argues that pluralism:

> represents a tradition-specific approach that bears all the same features of exclusivism—except that it is western liberal modernity's exclusivism....[P]luralists will be seen to be Enlightenment exclusivists....One might say, polemically, that they are hard-line exclusivists.[61]

Regarding inclusivism, D'Costa argues that it "logically collapses into exclusivism" in three ways. First, like exclusivists, inclusivists hold that their view "contains the truth regarding ontological, epistemological and ethical claims." Second, with exclusivists, inclusivists hold to the inseparability of truth and salvation. Finally, both exclusivists and inclusivists recognize the tradition-specific nature of their positions.[62] Thus, in the end, D'Costa identifies pluralists as nothing more than "anonymous exclusivists."[63] What is one to make of these claims and the change of mind it represents?

In Qualified Defense of the Standard Threefold Typology

In a response article, John Hick has challenged D'Costa's conclusions regarding the exclusivistic nature of pluralism. At one point, it seems that Hick's reply can best be characterized as bewilderment: "To say that the former of these two views, religious pluralism, is a version of the latter, religious exclusivism, would be so totally implausible that this cannot be what D'Costa means."[64] I submit that this bewilderment on Hick's part can be cleared up once it is seen that D'Costa has changed the nature of the terms on Hick in the course of the debate. In short, D'Costa's unanticipated reversal is tied intimately to the definitional equivocation problem. That this is the case becomes clear when one compares the definitions of the three terms offered by D'Costa both before and after his change of mind. From the mid-1980s to 1995, D'Costa consistently used a strongly soteriologically-oriented set of definitions. However, in the 1996 article, his definitions have been significantly modified. Here, for instance, 'exclusivism' is not defined as "only those who hear the Gospel proclaimed and explicitly confess Christ are saved"—the definition he proposed just the year before.[65] Instead, 'exclusivism' is defined as "holding that only one single revelation is true or one single religion is true and all other 'revelations' or 'religions' are false."[66] The difference between the typological definitions is clear: the first is oriented around the soteriological question; the second around the truth-claim question.

Through definitional equivocation, D'Costa has been led to miss the value of the standard threefold typology. He has failed to adequately distinguish between three very different questions that have been analyzed by various thinkers using the same terms of the threefold typology. These questions involve: (1) general philosophical truth-claims (e.g., what is the nature of human knowledge and truth-claims), (2) religious truth-claims (e.g., what is the nature of specifically religious truth-claims, and can religious truth be found in one or many religions?), and (3) soteriological issues (e.g., is salvation available in one or many religions?). I shall refer to these three applications of the three-fold typology by the following rubrics respectively: (1) alethic-philosophical, (2) alethic-religious, and (3) soteric. Which application of the typology one uses is usually determined by the questions that drive one's scholarly endeavors. Thus, one tends to find philosophers of religion using the alethic definitions, while theologians tend to be attracted to the soteric definitions. Those thinkers who work at the intersection of these two disciplines can, if not careful, find themselves using the terms in a variety of (sometimes conflicting) ways.

It is important to note here that the alethic vs. soteric terminological dichotomy has not, itself, been lost on D'Costa. My claim is not that he does not recognize the distinction, but, rather that he does not *adequately* do so. Specifically, D'Costa suggests that these two possible applications—the alethic and soteric—are, in fact, inextricably linked. In both his 1996 article and *The Meeting of Religions and the Trinity*, he claims that "[t]ruth, revelation, and salvation are tightly and explicitly connected."[67] This claim, however, is never supported by argumentation. I want to suggest that they are not so tightly woven that one cannot identify and distinguish them as distinct concerns, with different uses of the typology applying to each.

For ten years, D'Costa used the typology in a soteric sense. Now, he has moved to an alethic application of these terms (wherein he seems to blend both the philosophical and religious aspects). I would argue that this observation accounts for D'Costa's change of mind, and enables one both to appreciate the basic point he is making while, at the same time, salvaging the standard threefold typology as a useful heuristic tool for certain questions—*particularly of the soteric variety*.

D'Costa's basic thesis in the 1996 article is that, since pluralists are just as quick as exclusivists to think that they are correct and that others are wrong *vis-à-vis* their views regarding theology of religions, then pluralists simply are exclusivists. But, surely, to say this is to say no more than the rather unremarkable claim that pluralists, like other people, believe that what they think to be the case is true, and that where others disagree with them, on that count they are wrong. Here, D'Costa is narrowing his use of the threefold typology to address the alethic-philosophical issue alone. It is merely to say that pluralists, as much as anyone else, hold to the 'exclusive' view that they believe their own position to be true and those which claim otherwise to be false.[68] But no true pluralist (as opposed to a full-blooded relativist)—in the soteric and perhaps even in the alethic-religious sense of the term—would disagree. In response to D'Costa, Hick himself has admitted that in this "purely notional and trivial sense" the pluralist is an 'exclusivist.'[69]

It is important to see here that when used in this alethic-philosophical sense, the question being posed is essentially the question of the so-called 'law of non-contradiction.' Seen in this light, it would seem there are really only two live options: 'exclusivism' (i.e., affirmation of the law) and 'relativism' (i.e., rejection of the law). But to use the term 'exclusivism' in this fashion *without explicit delineation* is to equivocate upon its typical use in the theology of religions debate (where the soteric definitions have usually been assumed) to such a degree as to render it useless. D'Costa's suggestion that an inherent and necessary link exists between the alethic-religious and soteric uses of the typology is simply descriptively false. Hick is a case in point. While he believes that the truth-claims of all religions are literally false vis-à-vis the ultimate reality, he nonetheless is a soteriological universalist. This is not to say that there are not often commonalities between one's position on truth in the religions and salvation. However, contrary to D'Costa's suggestion, there is no necessary or inherent connection. A variety of thinkers within the field today can be identified as an 'exclusivist' (or 'inclusivist' or 'pluralist') with regard to one set of issues and something quite different with respect to the other.

Once the terminological equivocation is pointed out, the import of D'Costa's insight can be retained without rejecting the standard typology. One can agree with D'Costa that, speaking in alethic-philosophical terms, pluralists are as certain they are right as anyone else, and in this very qualified sense can be called 'exclusivists.' However, when speaking in soteric terms, the pluralist is no exclusivist, and the inclusivist is neither of the former. I would argue that in making these types of distinctions in the use of the standard typology, a number of the other confusions and criticisms mentioned above are resolved. Thus, the standard threefold typology can serve as a useful ideal-typical schema by which to understand certain views within the contemporary theology of religions discussion, as long as one is careful to explicitly delineate the categorical use to which the typology is being put in any specific instance. For the purposes of this study, I shall use the typology in its soteric sense unless otherwise noted.

In concluding, it is worth remembering that the threefold typology is always, at best, an ideal-typical framework and so necessarily falls short of categorizing the actual views of people as adequately and accurately as one would wish. The hazard is that those in the field will forget this fact. When this happens, rather than merely functioning as a set of tentative heuristic paradigms for theoretical orientation, open to and in need of expansion and modification as new empirical data becomes available, the threefold schema can become hardened into a systemic orthodoxy that serves to patronizingly pigeon-hole each and every participant in the discussion. Anyone with anything really new to say is immediately 'typed' by the paradigm that most nearly resembles their unique construct, and thus their carefully nuanced and often original contribution to the discussion is interpreted as merely 'another variation of paradigm X.' One detrimental effect of all this, of course, is that it prevents anyone outside of 'paradigm X' from ever having to take the new construct seriously, since, after all, they have already decided (on other grounds) that 'paradigm X' is bankrupt.

But this potential pitfall has always been recognized by perceptive proponents of the typology from the beginning. Early on, Alan Race reminded his readers that the typology will tend to foster an over-simplification of the discussion since it is "apt to miss the special and particular nuances of any one position."[70] This is hardly a problem of this typology in particular. Ideal-typical schemas are, by nature, reductionistic. The threat of over-simplification is generally recognized to be more than compensated for by the conceptual assistance an ideal-type offers to a field of discussion.

The Pluralist Paradigm

The awareness of religious diversity is virtually a given in the contemporary western world. When faced with the uncontestable fact of diversity, one is forced to make an interpretation of this fact, an assessment of some sort. Those who conclude that the various major world religions should be viewed as roughly of co-equal soteric and/or alethic value are known today as 'pluralists.' Religious pluralism should be seen against the wider backdrop of a more general 'pluralist' orientation to the diversity that presents itself to the contemporary world.[71]

Roots of Religious Pluralism

There has been a growing sense throughout the last half of the twentieth century that a pluralist interpretation of diversity in any number of areas of life is not only possible but is to be prescribed. The philosopher Eugene Garver writes, "We are all pluralists today. Ecumenism—in religion, in literary criticism, in philosophy—seems obligatory...."[72] He goes on to suggest that in the realm of philosophy, 'pluralism' is "unavoidable today because practical pluralism, the problem of how we are to live in a world of plural ultimate values, is unavoidable."[73] In defense of philosophical pluralism, Walter Watson writes of "the most significant philosophic discovery of the present century." He goes on: "This is the discovery, first, of the fact of pluralism, that the truth admits of more than one valid formulation, and, secondly, of the reason for this fact in arbitrary or conventional elements inseparable from the nature of thought itself."[74] While I will eventually argue that a 'pluralist' understanding of religious diversity is not the only viable interpretation today—and does, in fact, have its own problems—it is clear that pluralistic approaches to the various problems of contemporary diversity are attractive at a number of levels.

The general claim of religious pluralism—that both truth and/or salvation are available in a variety of the world's religions (without appeal to any other religion)—has an ancient pedigree. This basic intuition has often been a part of various Eastern religions, if in an ultimately 'inclusivist' sense (i.e., their own religion is the most effective road to salvation, and is the lens through which the 'salvation' occurring in other religions is to be understood). In the Christian West, antecedents of the contemporary pluralist paradigm can be identified in a variety of contexts. The 1893 World's Parliament of Religions held in Chicago brought together the greatest number of religious adherents from the world's religions ever assembled. In many sectors of this event, something of a proto-pluralist spirit was evident.[75] As is evident in the later work of Ernst Troeltsch, the rise of modern historical consciousness in the West served as a catalyst for a pluralistic approach to the world's religions.[76] Those Christians who gravitated to the mystical expression of the faith, wherein religious experience is privileged over doctrinal claims—often have demonstrated a quasi-pluralist attitude.[77] It appears that Christian thinkers such as William Ernest Hocking and (the later) Paul Tillich would have found the atmosphere of the contemporary pluralist paradigm to be quite hospitable to their own proposals.[78]

Defining Religious Pluralism

An understanding of religious 'pluralism' is required that is both general enough to cover the variety of pluralist models and yet specific enough to distinguish it from some of the more radical forms of inclusivism. In this light, I offer the following soterically-oriented definition: *The view that most religions function as salvific paths toward Ultimate Reality (i.e., "God" in Christian terminology) on their own terms and apart from any other religious system. Interreligious judgments are theoretically possible (based upon soteriological/praxic criteria vs. propositional/doctrinal criteria). Ultimately, however, such judgments are not possible between the world's 'great religious traditions,' since the empirical evidence suggests they are of roughly co-equal soteriological value.* Not only is it important to distinguish pluralism from 'exclusivism' and 'inclusivism' on one side, but also from 'relativism' on the other. Pluralists differ from the pure relativist in that they retain a place for some sort of inter-religious evaluation. For this reason, for instance, it is unfortunate that Hick has been branded a "relativist" by some.[79] This polemical labeling serves to cloud the fact that Hick, along with other pluralists, do offer some criteria by which to make at least minimal inter-religious assessments.

Within the pluralist paradigm are housed a number of distinct models that share a family resemblance. Several scholars have proposed typologies by which to categorize the various models within this paradigm.[80] D'Costa writes of the "philosophical pluralism" of Hick, the "pragmatic pluralism" of Paul Knitter, the "esoteric pluralism" of Huston Smith, and the "tolerant pluralism" of the Dalai Lama. Anselm Kyongsuk Min has proposed a sevenfold typology of pluralisms ranging from the "transcendentalist pluralism" of Hick to the "confessional pluralism" of Christian thinkers such as Mark Heim, J. A. DiNoia, and John Milbank (interestingly, those in the latter group are typically identified as [soteric] inclusivists or exclusivists). Vinoth Ramachandra delineates three models of pluralism: "Mystery-Centered Faith" (e.g., Stanley Samartha), "Liberating Gnosis" (e.g., Aloysius Pieris), and "Christic Theandrism" (e.g., Raimundo Panikkar). To date, there is no single predominant typology of pluralist models that is shared by those within the field.

The Pluralist Paradigm and the 'Conflicting Conceptions of the Divine' Problem

Possibly the most challenging issue that faces adherents of the pluralist paradigm involves what I shall henceforth refer to in this study as the 'conflicting conceptions of the divine' problem. The problem, in short, is this: If all the great world religions are roughly co-equal in terms of their soteriological efficacy and religious truth, how does one explain the fact that their various conceptions of ultimate Reality (i.e., God, the Divine, the Absolute, etc.) are so different—at times, even mutually contradictory—in nature? It seems safe to say that no other philosophical (as opposed to purely theological) issue has presented as persistent and challenging a conundrum to pluralists as has the conflicting conceptions of the divine problem.[81] Thus, a good case can be made that the intellectual viability of the pluralist paradigm hinges upon a convincing response to this dilemma.

Various pluralist models address this problem in different ways. Those pluralists, such as Gordon Kaufman, who have adopted a theological constructivist model, rooted in religious non-realism, find this problem to be less troubling than those who hold to a religious realism. Whereas the realist tends to be led to posit a permanent—because *ontological*—relation between the religions, their various truth-claims, and ultimate reality, the constructivist/non-realist can more easily avoid such conclusions. By adopting the conviction that religion is a fully *human* constructivist project, Kaufman is able to avoid the messy question of inter-religious criteriology, including the question of how to reconcile the conflicting conceptions of the divine on a metaphysical level. He writes:

> [I]nstead of *theological claims* about some extra-worldly or ultimate 'salvation' being made the criterion of what we should believe and practice in this world, I am proposing that what is necessary or required to build a humane order in this world should be made the criterion for assessing our theological beliefs and for determining the character of our theological tasks.

Such a criterion is fully "humanistic and this-worldly."[82]

Pragmatic/liberationist pluralists, such as Paul Knitter, tend not to spend much time on the issue. Rather, they begin with the concrete need for social liberation and justice, and, in Knitter's words, turn "a necessity into an opportunity" by structuring inter-religious encounter around this shared concern.[83] It is what one could call the philosophical-unitive pluralist—one who is a religious realist and senses the need to offer an explanation for the unity amidst the diversity of religions—who feels the force of this problem like no other. And here we are brought face to face with the thought of arguably the most recognized and influential contemporary thinker in the pluralist camp, the British philosopher of religion, John Hick.

Hick, a professed Christian and a self-proclaimed religious realist, has probably given more intellectual time and attention to the conflicting conceptions of the divine problematic than any other pluralist. He offers one of the most philosophically sophisticated and intellectually engaging responses to this problem available to date. The over-arching purpose of this book will be, first, to trace the rise and development of Hick's religious pluralism—including his response to the 'conflicting conceptions' problem, and, finally, to offer an assessment of Hick's answer to this problem. With this introductory mapping of the conceptual terrain, it is time to turn to a closer look at the thought of John Hick.

Notes

1   See e.g., S. Mark Heim, ed., *Grounds for Understanding: Ecumenical Resources for Responses to Religious Pluralism* (Grand Rapids: Eerdmans, 1998).

2   For representative examples at both ends of the theological spectrum see Gordon Kaufman, "Religious Diversity and Religious Truth," in *God, Truth and Reality: Essays in Honour of John Hick*, ed. Arvind Sharma (New York: St. Martin's, 1993), 143–64, and Harold A. Netland, *Dissonant Voices: Religious Pluralism and the Question of Truth* (Grand Rapids, MI: Eerdmans, 1991). For a liberal-evangelical dialogue on the topic see Dennis L. Okholm and Timothy R. Phillips, eds., *More than One Way? Four Views on Salvation in a Pluralistic World* (Grand Rapids: Zondervan, 1995).

3   E.g., see David Burrell, "God, Religious Pluralism, and Dialogic Encounter," in *Reconstructing Christian Theology*, ed. Rebecca S. Chopp and Mark Lewis Taylor, (Minneapolis: Fortress, 1994), 49–78; Alister McGrath, "Christianity and World Religions," in *Christian Theology: An Introduction*, 2nd ed. (Oxford: Blackwell, 1997 [1994]), 521–39; Michael Peterson, et al., "Religious Diversity," in *Philosophy of Religion: Selected Readings* (New York: Oxford, 1996), 495–526.

4   Robert Wilken, "Religious Pluralism and Early Christian Thought," *Pro Ecclesia* 1 (1992): 90.

5   John North, "The Development of Religious Pluralism," in *The Jews among Pagans and Christians in the Roman Empire*, ed. Judith Lieu, John North, and Tessa Rajak (New York: Routledge, 1992), 191.

6   On these matters see Bruce W. Winter, "In Public and in Private: Early Christians and Religious Pluralism," in *One God, One Lord: Christianity in a World of Religious Pluralism*, 2d ed., ed. Andrew D. Clarke and Bruce W. Winter, (Grand Rapids: Baker, 1992), 125–48; R. P. C. Hanson, "The Christian Attitude to Pagan Religions up to the Time of Constantine the Great," in *Aufstieg und Niedergang der Römischen Welt* (henceforth *ANRW*), ed. H. Temporini and W. Haase (New York: de Gruyter, 1980), II:23, 2, 910–73; C. A. Contreras, "Christian Views of Paganism," in *ANRW*, II:23, 2, 974–1022.

7   Kenneth Cragg, *The Christian and Other Religion* (London: Mowbrays, 1977), 7.

8   M. M. Thomas, *Risking Christ for Christ's Sake: Towards an Ecumenical Theology of Pluralism* (Geneva: WCC, 1987), 1.

9   Langdon Gilkey, "The Pluralism of Religions," in *God, Truth and Reality*, 111.

10 Gilkey, *Through the Tempest: Theological Voyages in a Pluralistic Culture*, ed. Jeff Pool (Minneapolis: Fortress, 1991), 21.

11 Richard Wenty, *The Culture of Religious Pluralism* (Boulder: Westview, 1998), 2.

12 Francis Clooney, review of Paul Knitter's *No Other Name*, etc., *Religious Studies Review* 15 (1989): 199.

13 See respectively Richard Mouw and Sander Griffioen, *Pluralisms and Horizons: An Essay in Christian Public Philosophy* (Grand Rapids: Eerdmans, 1993), 13–5 and Hick, "Religious Pluralism," in *The Encyclopedia of Religion*, 16 vols., ed. Mircea Eliade (New York: Macmillan, 1987), XII: 331.

14   Diana L. Eck, *Encountering God: A Spiritual Journey from Bozeman to Banaras* (Boston: Beacon, 1993), 191.

15   See respectively Mouw and Griffioen, *Pluralisms and Horizons*, 13–4; Hick, "Religious Pluralism," 331; Ted Peters, "Culture Wars: Should Lutherans Volunteer or be Conscripted?" *Dialog* 32 (1993): 39–45; and Keith Yandell, "Some Varieties of Religious Pluralism," in *Inter-Religious Models and Criteria*, ed. J. Kellenberger (New York: St. Martin's, 1993), 194–209.

16   Sidney E. Mead, "In Quest of America's Religion" and "The Fact of Pluralism and the Persistence of Sectarianism," in *The Nation with the Soul of a Church* (New York: Harper & Row, 1975), 1–10, 29–47.

17   Fortunately, as time goes on, this distinction is being explicitly made by more and more scholars. John Hick has tended to make this distinction explicit for years. See Hick, "Religious Pluralism," 331; idem, *A Christian Theology of Religions: The Rainbow of Faiths* (Louisville: Westminster/John Knox, 1995), 148.

18   Küng, "The World Religions in God's Plan of Salvation," in *Christian Revelation and World Religions*, ed. Joseph Neuner (London: Burns and Oates, 1967), 31, 37, 47; this essay derives from a 1964 conference.

19   Thomas, *Attitudes Towards Other Religions: Some Christian Interpretations* (New York: Harper & Row, 1969).

20   Hick, "The Christian View of Other Faiths," *Expository Times* 84 (Nov. 1972): 36–9; idem, "The Copernican Revolution in Theology," in *God and the Universe of Faiths*, 2d ed. (London: Macmillan, 1973; reprint, London: Collins-Fontana, 1977), 120–32.

21   Schineller, "Christ and Church: A Spectrum of Views," *Theological Studies* 37 (1976): 545–66.

22   Ibid., 552–53.

23   Knitter, *No Other Name?: A Critical Survey of Christian Attitudes Toward the World Religions* (Maryknoll, N.Y.: Orbis, 1985).

24   Race, *Christians and Religious Pluralism* (Maryknoll, N.Y.: Orbis, 1983).

25   Hick, "A Philosophy of Religious Pluralism," in *The World's Religious Traditions: Essays in Honour of Wilfred Cantwell Smith*, ed. Frank Whaling (Edinburgh: Clark, 1984), 147–64; Knitter, "Key Questions for a Theology of Religions," *Horizons* 17 (1990): 92. For a brief survey of the rise of this typology see D'Costa, "The Impossibility of a Pluralist View of Religions," *Religious Studies* 32 (1996): 223–24.

26   Henceforth, the term 'paradigm' will be used to designate a general approach to theology of religions, such as exclusivism, inclusivism, or pluralism. The term 'model', on the other hand, will be used to denote a specific and well-defined instance of one of these general approaches.

27   Race, "Christianity and Other Religions: Is Inclusivism Enough?," *Theology* 89 (1986): 178.

28   D'Costa, "Christian Theology and Other Faiths," 292.

29   For example, see D'Costa's "Theology of Religions," in *The Modern Theologians*, ed., David Ford (Oxford: Blackwell, 1989), II, 274.

30   Others who echo similar concerns include S. Mark Heim, *Salvations: Truth and Difference in Religion* (Maryknoll, N.Y.: Orbis, 1995), 4, 117, 175, 221, 226; J. A. DiNoia, *The Diversity of Religions: A Christian Perspective* (Washington, D.C.: Catholic University of America Press, 1992), 34–64; Schubert M. Ogden, "Problems in the Case for a Pluralistic Theology of Religions," *Journal of Religion* 68 (1988): 505; and E. Luther Copeland, "Christian Theology and World Religions," *Review and Expositor* 94 (1997): 424.

31   Griffiths, "Review Symposium: Religious Diversity," *The Thomist* 52 (1988): 319.

32   Griffiths, "Modalizing the Theology of Religions," *Journal of Religion* 73 (1993): 382.

33   Griffiths, "Encountering Buddha Theologically," *Theology Today* 47 (1990): 39–40.

34   See Griffiths, "The Properly Christian Response to Religious Plurality," *Anglican Theological Review* 79 (1997): 3–26.

35   Burrell, review of *The Diversity of Religions*, by J. A. DiNoia, *Modern Theology* 10 (1994): 107 (emphasis in text).

36   E.g., Schubert Ogden, *Is There Only One True Religion or Are There Many?* (Dallas: Southern Methodist University Press, 1992), 79–104. See also the very helpful typology of John Sanders in his *No Other Name: An Investigation into the Destiny of the Unevangelized* (Grand Rapids: Eerdmans, 1992). While making use of the standard categories, he offers an insightful analysis of sub-positions within them.

37   See respectively, Copeland, "Christian Theology and World Religions," 425–6; Martinson, *A Theology of World Religions: Interpreting God, Self, and World in Semitic, Indian, and Chinese Thought* (Minneapolis: Augsburg, 1987), 200–11; Kraft, "What Constitutes a Distinctively Christian Approach to Interfaith Dialogue?," *Dialog* 37 (1998): 282–90. For Peter's work see *God—the World's Future: Systematic Theology for a Postmodern Era* (Minneapolis: Fortress, 1992), 339–49.

38   Kenneth Surin, "A 'Politics of Speech': Religious Pluralism in the Age of the McDonald's Hamburger," in *Christian Uniqueness Reconsidered: The Myth of a Pluralistic Theology of Religions*, ed. Gavin D'Costa (Maryknoll, N.Y.: Orbis, 1990), 210.

39   E.g., Alvin Plantinga, "Pluralism: A Defense of Religious Exclusivism," in *Rationality of Belief and the Plurality of Faith: Essays in Honor of William P. Alston*, ed. Thomas D. Senor (Ithaca: Cornell University Press, 1995), 191–215; Ronald H. Nash, *Is Jesus the Only Savior?* (Grand Rapids: Zondervan, 1994).

40   Netland, *Dissonant Voices*, 34–5.

41   Geivett and Phillips, "A Particularist View: An Evidentialist Approach," in *More than One Way?*, 213–45. For a discussion of the "rhetoric" of these labels, particularly with respect to 'exclusivism,' see Okholm and Phillips' "Introduction" to *More Than One Way?*, 14–17.

42   Hick, "On Wilfred Cantwell Smith: His Place in the Study of Religion," *Method and Theory in the Study of Religion* 4 (1992): 13; Hick seems to have exclusivism in mind here. More recently, however, Hick has softened his view of exclusivism; see "The Epistemological Challenge of Religious Pluralism," *Faith and Philosophy* 14 (1997): 280–1, 286, n. 7.

43   Both Pinnock (an inclusivist) and Geivett and Phillips (exclusivists/particularists) claim that McGrath, a self-proclaimed particularist, is actually closer to inclusivism; *More than One Way?*, 188, 197.

44   E.g., see respectively Ogden, *Is There Only One True Religion or Are There Many?*, 81; Scott Cowdell, "Hans Küng and World Religions: The Emergence of a Pluralist," *Theology* 92 (1989): 85–92.

45   E.g., D'Costa, "Impossibility of a Pluralist View of Religions," 223–32.

46   Heim, "Salvations: A More Pluralistic Hypothesis," in *Salvations*, 129–57.

47   Markham, "Creating Options: Shattering the 'Exclusivist, Inclusivist, and Pluralist' Paradigm," *New Blackfriars* 74 (1993): 33–4.

48   D'Costa, "Creating Confusion: A Response to Markham," *New Blackfriars* 74 (1993): 41–7.

49   See Copeland, "Christian Theology and World Religions," 424; Paul J. Griffiths, ed., *Christianity Through non-Christian Eyes* (Maryknoll, N.Y.: Orbis, 1990), 9–10.

50   *Christian Theology of Religions*, 18; see Hick's discussion at pp. 19–27.

51   "Pluralism," 194.

52   "Christian Theology and Other Faiths," 292.

53   E.g., Netland, *Dissonant Voices*, 9–10.

54   This appears to be the case with Peter van Inwagen, "*Non Est* Hick," in *Rationality of Belief and the Plurality of Faith*, 238–39.

55   For recent defenses see "Christian Theology and Other Faiths," 292–303; "Creating Confusion."

56   "Impossibility of a Pluralist View of Religions," 223.

57   Ibid., 225 (emphasis in text).

58   van Inwagen, "Reply to Professor Hick ['The Epistemological Challenge of Religious Pluralism']," *Faith and Philosophy* 14 (1997): 300.

59   Ibid., 225–6.

60   D'Costa, *The Meeting of Religions and the Trinity* (Maryknoll, N.Y.: Orbis, 2000).

61   Ibid., 22.

62   Ibid.

63   "Impossibility of a Pluralist View of Religions," 232.

64   Hick, "The Possibility of Religious Pluralism: A Reply to Gavin D'Costa," *Religious Studies* 33 (1997): 161.

65   "Christian Theology and Other Faiths," 292.

66   "Impossibility of a Pluralist View of Religions," 223; see also *Meeting of Religions*, 20.

67   "Impossibility of a Pluralist View of Religions," 223–24; *Meeting of Religions*, 20.

68   Adrian Machiraju has reported that, upon inquiring of D'Costa (during the public reading of an earlier version of his article) whether his claim "does not reduce to the tautology that everyone naturally believes their own position to be true," he admitted that he "might not be going any further than that"; religious pluralism on-line discussion group, March 31, 1995; available at religious-pluralism-request@mailbase.ac.uk.

69   "Possibility of Religious Pluralism," 162.

70   Christians and Religious Pluralism, 139.

71   On types of pluralism one encounters in the contemporary world from a Christian perspective see Mouw and Griffioen, *Pluralisms and Horizons*, 13–9; Paul Schrotenboer, "Varieties of Pluralism," *Evangelical Review of Theology* 13 (1989): 110–24.

72   Garver, "Why Pluralism Now?," *The Monist* 73 (1990): 388.

73   Ibid., 389. On the pluralism debate in contemporary philosophy see Richard P. McKeon, *Freedom and History and Other Essays* (Chicago: University of Chicago Press, 1990); Walter Watson, *The Architectonics of Meaning: Foundations of the New Pluralism* (Albany: SUNY, 1985); Bruce Erlich, "Amphibolies: On the Critical Self-Contradiction of 'Pluralism'," *Critical* Inquiry 12 (1986): 521–49; W. J. T. Mitchell, "Pluralism as Dogmatism," *Critical Inquiry* 12 (1986): 494–502; Ellen Rooney, *Seductive Reasoning: Pluralism as the Problematic of Contemporary Literary Theory* (Ithaca, N.Y.: Cornell University Press, 1989); and the set of articles in *The Monist* 73 (1990).

74   *Architectonics of Meaning*, ix.

75   See Richard Hughes Seager, ed., *The Dawn of Religious Pluralism: Voices from the World's Parliament of Religions, 1893* (LaSalle, Ill.: Open Court, 1993).

76   Troeltsch, "The Place of Christianity among the World Religions," in *Christianity and Other Religions: Selected Readings*, John Hick and Brian Hebblethwaite, eds. (Philadelphia: For-

tress, 1980), 11–31. See also Allen C. Guelzo, "First Church of Historical Relativism: Ernst Troeltsch and the Intellectual Sources of Pluralism," in *The Challenge of Religious Pluralism: An Evangelical Analysis and Response*, David K. Clark, et al., eds. (Wheaton, Ill.: Wheaton Theology Conference, 1992), 9–25.

77   E.g., see Kevin Hogan, "The Experience of Reality: Evelyn Underhill and Religious Pluralism," *Anglican Theological Review* 74 (1992): 334–47.

78   W. E. Hocking, *Living Religions and a World Faith* (New York: Macmillan, 1940); Paul Tillich, *Christianity and the Encounter of the World Religions* (New York: Columbia University Press, 1963).

79   Cardinal Joseph Ratzinger, "Relativism: The Central Problem for Faith Today," *Origins* 26 (1996): 309–17.

80   See respectively D'Costa, "Impossibility of a Pluralist View of Religions," 226–27, 232; Min, "Towards a Dialectic of Pluralism," paper presented at the Christian Theological Research Fellowship annual meeting, Philadelphia, Pa., November 18, 1995, 32 pp.; Ramachandra, *The Recovery of Mission: Beyond the Pluralist Paradigm* (Grand Rapids: Eerdmans, 1996).

81   See Hick, *Interpretation of Religion*, 233.

82   "Christian Theology and the Modernization of the Religions," in *The Theological Imagination: Constructing the Concept of God* (Philadelphia: Westminster, 1981), 90–1.

83   From a personal conversation, Nov. 26, 1989. See Knitter, "Toward a Liberation Theology of Religions," in *Myth of Christian Uniqueness*, 3–15; Paul R. Eddy, "Paul Knitter's Theology of Religions: A Survey and Evangelical Response," *Evangelical Quarterly* 65 (1993): 225–45.

2   A Pathway to Pluralism: John Hick's Pre-Pluralist Thought[1]

The rise and development of Hick's pluralist philosophy of religions must be viewed against the background of his earlier theological and philosophical commitments. This chapter will begin with a theo-biographical sketch of Hick's pilgrimage. This will be followed by a detailed tracing of Hick's theological and philosophical development up to the eve of his move to the pluralist paradigm in the early 1970s. In both this and the following chapters, Christological soundings will be taken along the way in order to highlight the theological ramifications of Hick's developing thought.

John Harwood Hick: A Theo-Biographical Sketch[2]

John Harwood Hick was born in Scarborough, Yorkshire in 1922. He began his earliest theological imaginings as a child in the local Anglican church. Although he found the weekly services to be "a matter of infinite boredom," he recalls having "a rather strong sense of the reality of God as the personal and loving lord of the universe, and of life as having a meaning within God's purpose."[3] In hindsight, this early, profound experience of a personal loving God can be seen as a fore-shadowing of what would eventually become a central tenet of Hick's interpretation of religion: the primacy of religious experience.

During his teen years, Hick began to develop his life-long taste for things philosophical; he remembers being "thrilled by the writings of Nietzsche and greatly enjoyed reading Bertrand Russell."[4] At the age of eighteen, Hick came across a book on the principles of Theosophy, the contents of which struck him as the "first comprehensive and coherent interpretation of life" that he had ever encountered.[5] Although initially impressed by this Western version of Vedantic Hindu thought, he eventually found it to be "too tidy and impersonal,"[6] and within a year or so turned totally away from it.[7] At this point Hick's spiritual search was temporarily stymied. The view to the East through Theosophical eyes was attractive, but insufficiently so. On the other hand, the Western Christian world surrounding him "seemed utterly lifeless and uninteresting."[8]

At 19 years of age, while studying law at University College, Hull, Hick became involved with a group of students associated with InterVarsity Christian Fellowship. Discussions of things spiritual and a reading of the New Testament paved the way for a new stage in his journey: a conversion to a Christianity "of a strongly evangelical and indeed fundamentalist kind."[9] One important element of his conversion was an experience he underwent while on the top deck of a bus. As Hick relates it:

> [A]ll descriptions are inadequate. But it was as though the skies opened up and light poured down and filled me with a sense of overflowing joy in response to an immense transcendent goodness and love. I remember that I couldn't help smiling broadly—smiling back, as it were, at God—though if any of the other passengers were looking they must have thought that I was a lunatic, grinning at nothing.[10]

During this time he experienced a several-days period of intense inner turmoil as the truth of God's lordship and its implications for his entire life engulfed him. In his own words: "At first this was highly unwelcome, a disturbing and challenging demand for nothing less than a revolution in personal identity."[11] These feelings of unease, however, eventually gave way to a sense of peaceful liberation.

Because most of his new Christian friends attended, he joined the Presbyterian Church of England. This meant that the particular brand of evangelicalism within which Hick was converted was that of a "Calvinist orthodoxy of an extremely conservative kind."[12] Hick's conversion precipitated a vocational change from law to the Christian ministry. Prior to attending seminary, he decided to pursue a degree in philosophy at Edinburgh University. There, he studied under Norman Kemp Smith, a Kantian scholar in the idealist tradition. Hick also joined the Evangelical Union at this time, where he became actively involved in "Bible studies, prayer meetings, and talks" as well as in "evangelistic activities."[13] During his second year at Edinburgh, the war interrupted his studies. In 1942, Hick was faced with military service. While many of his Christian friends took up arms against Nazi Germany, Hick "felt called to be a conscientious objector on Christian grounds."[14] He joined the Friends' (Quaker) Ambulance Unit and served in this capacity for the last three years of the war. Upon his return to Edinburgh, Hick's reunion with the Evangelical Union was short-lived. In brief, Hick's philosophical training was leading him to ask "awkward questions." Questions like these, fueled by intellectual doubts concerning certain aspects of his evangelical Calvinist faith, seemed to hold little interest for his fellow believers. In fact, Hick sensed that they were perceived as "dangerous and ought not to be raised, and that they constituted a temptation to backsliding."[15] Thus, Hick eventually quit his association with the student group. This was one of several signals that served to mark Hick's movement away from the evangelical camp during the late 1940s.

Upon his graduation (with honors) from Edinburgh in 1948, Hick received the first Campbell Fraser scholarship at Oriel College, Oxford, where he began his doctoral work under H. H. Price. During his war years, Hick was afforded the opportunity to sketch out the framework for an epistemology of religion that was later developed in his 1950 Oxford doctoral thesis, "The Relationship between Faith and Belief." He would eventually published the results of this study as his first book, *Faith and Knowledge*.[16] At the heart of his theory was the conviction that religious 'faith' is best understood as "the interpretive element within cognitive religious experience."[17] Two of the primary influences upon his thought at this time were Kant's epistemology, and (in the Schleiermachian tradition) John Oman and his emphasis on the primacy of religious experience.

After the completion of his doctoral work, Hick went on to Westminster Theological College, Cambridge, to prepare for the pastoral ministry. While at Cambridge (1950–53), Hick studied under H. H. Farmer, Professor of Divinity. Through Farmer, Hick's indebtedness to Oman was reinforced; Farmer was a devoted student and friend of Oman. Hick also assisted Farmer in the preparation of his book *Revelation and Religion*. In this work, the published results of his 1950 Gifford Lectures, Farmer provides a Christian interpretation of religion. Unlike Hick's future tradition-independent 'religious' interpretation of religion, Farmer's *Revelation and Religion* offers a distinctly Christian theological interpretation of religion. Thus for Farmer, "…in the Christian revelation and faith we have, not merely one more illustration of the general class of religions, but also—and in this it stands alone—the normative concept of religion itself."[18]

During his Cambridge years, Hick remembers being "profoundly shocked by a graduate student who argued that Jesus was not God incarnate but a remarkable human being."[19] The end of Hick's days at Cambridge brought a number of changes. His life as a student ended, and he married (Joan) Hazel Bower. They moved to Northumberland and to his first and last parish appointment, at the Belford Presbyterian Church. Hick pastored this congregation from 1953 to 1956, during which time he finished the manuscript for *Faith and Knowledge*.

While at Belford Church, Hick received an unexpected invitation to join the Philosophy Department at Cornell University as an Assistant Professor of Philosophy to teach philosophy of religion. He accepted the offer, and was immediately propelled back into the academic arena. He remained there until 1959, at which time he moved to Princeton Theological Seminary and the post of Stuart Professor of Christian Philosophy. During this time, Hick continued to devote himself to three primary areas of research that would prove to be life-long interests: (1) arguments concerning the classical theistic proofs; (2) the defense of 'God talk' against attacks stemming from positivist thought; and, later, (3) the problem of evil and an acceptable Christian theodicy.

In 1960, Hick became the focal point of a controversy that served to reveal his growing discontent with traditional theology. In the course of having his ministerial credentials transferred from England to New Hampshire, he was asked if there was anything in the Westminster Confession of 1647 to which he took exception. He acknowledged that several things were, in his mind, open to question, including "the six-day creation of the world, the predestination of many to eternal hell, the verbal inspiration of the Bible, and the virgin birth of Jesus."[20] Because of his agnosticism on this last point—the historical nature of the virgin birth—Hick was embroiled in a year-long controversy that was finally resolved only at a National Assembly meeting of the United Presbyterian Church. Throughout this incident, however, he stressed that his questioning of the "theological theory" of the virgin birth in no way compromised his affirmation of the "central Christian faith in the incarnation."[21]

In 1964, Hick once again crossed the Atlantic, this time to his homeland and a position as Lecturer in Divinity at Cambridge University. During his three year stay, he saw the publication of *Evil and the God of Love*, wherein he developed his now-famous 'Irenaean'—or 'soul making'—theodicy.[22] He found his modern source for this theodicy in Schleiermacher's thought, and contrasted it with the traditional so-called 'Augustinian' theodicy with its emphasis on an original state of pristine righteousness and subsequent fall into sin. As D'Costa notes, Hick's time at Cambridge brought an end to his identification, in any real sense, with historic orthodox Christianity. It marked the beginning of "a gradual and ultimately radical shift of theological perspective."[23]

In 1967, Hick applied for and received the post of H. G. Wood Professor in the Theology Department at Birmingham University. At least four factors converged, at this time, to catalyze Hick's move to a pluralist theology of religions: (1) the influence of his previously adopted vision of soteriological universalism; (2) his decision to write a global theology of death and post mortem existence—*Death and Eternal Life*, wherein he would interact with Christian, Hindu, Buddhist, and Humanistic thought;[24] (3) the influence of Wilfred Cantwell Smith's pluralistically inclined landmark work: *The Meaning and End of Religion*;[25] and (4) his move to the multi-cultural city of Birmingham, which led to his active involvement with persons of other faiths. In regard to this last point, Hick became the president of the community relations group All Faiths for One Race (AFFOR), as well as chairperson for three other inter-religious organizations: the Birmingham Inter-Faiths Council, the Religious and Cultural Panel of the Birmingham Community Relations Committee, and a committee, provided for under the 1944 Education Act, whose purpose it was to create a new multi-faith curriculum (to replace the old exclusively Christian one) for religious education in the city's schools.[26] Thus, along with his constant theological curve to the left, these various factors combined to provide the impetus for Hick's decisive move to the pluralist paradigm.

Already in the mid-to-late 1960s, Hick was showing a rising interest in the issue of religious diversity and a recognition of the need for a solid theology of religions. In a 1966 essay written in honor of H. H. Farmer, Hick identifies the implications of an historic orthodox Christology for Christianity's relationship with other world religions as "the most disturbing theological problem that Christianity is likely to have to face corporately during the next hundred years or so."[27] The issue cropped up again in his 1968 apologetic for a liberal Christianity, *Christianity at the Centre*.[28] His move to a pluralist mode was under way. From 1970 on, he was actively developing and presenting his newly adopted hypothesis via conferences, lectures, and articles.[29] In 1970, Hick was involved in a conference, held at Birmingham University, that focused on the problem of conflicting truth-claims in the world religions. He eventually edited a book produced from the conference papers—*Truth and Dialogue in World Religions: Conflicting Truth-Claims*.[30] 1973 brought the publication of Hick's first fully developed pluralist statement: *God and the Universe of Faiths*. The better part of the last half of this book (chapters seven to twelve) serves to explicate Hick's thesis of religious pluralism, a move which, in his eyes, is so radical and far-reaching in its implications as to warrant the title of "The Copernican Revolution in Theology."[31] In sticking with this astronomical analogy, Hick relegates any theological position—from any religious tradition—that attempts to maintain the superiority or normativity of its belief system over against those of other religions to the category of "Ptolemaic theology."[32] This work also includes the essay "Incarnation and Mythology," in which Hick takes up the task of removing the single greatest barrier between Christianity and the pluralist paradigm: the historic orthodox understanding of the deity and incarnation of Jesus Christ.

From 1973 to 1976, Hick devoted the better part of his writing time to completing his monumental contribution to a global theology—*Death and Eternal Life*. The seeds for this project were already germinating as early as 1969, when he delivered the Richard Lectures at the University of Virginia on "Questions about Death."[33] In the course of his research, Hick spent the better part of a year in the East. Several universities in India served as hospitable hosts as he studied aspects of Hinduism, focusing on "indian [sic] conceptions of reincarnation."[34] He also spent time at the University of Sri Lanka, on that primarily Buddhist island. During his time in the East, Hick was able to deliver the 1975 Teape Lectures at New Dehli University, and was a visiting professor at Benares Hindu University, Visva-Bharati University, Punjab University, Goa University (India), and the University of Sri Lanka.

With the publication of his global theology of death in 1976, Hick was freed up to return full force to the theological battle-lines of his pluralist revolution. 1977 saw the publication of the highly controversial book *The Myth of God Incarnate*; Hick was the editor.[35] In this work, Hick, along with six British theologians and biblical scholars, sought to strengthen and defend the position advocated in his 1973 essay, "Incarnation and Mythology." While the book was criticized quite soundly on a number of fronts (not the least of which was the equivocal use of the term 'myth' by the seven contributors), it nonetheless served the purpose of bringing to the attention of a wide audience the fact that the historic Christian view of Jesus' incarnation was less than secure within the Christian academic world. In his own contribution to the volume, "Jesus and the World Religions," Hick presses home the problem posed by the traditional interpretation of Jesus' incarnation for a contemporary Christian approach to other religions:

> Transposed into theological terms, the problem which has come to the surface in the encounter of Christianity with the other world religions is this: If Jesus was literally God incarnate, and if it is by his death alone that men can be saved…then the only doorway to eternal life is Christian faith.[36]

In this same year, the second edition of Hick's *Christianity at the Centre* appeared. His new pluralist approach was conspicuously infused into the new

edition with the addition of several new sections. And lest anyone miscon-
strue the "deliberately ambiguous" original title—which could very easily be
read in a 'Ptolemaic' sense, the second edition was retitled *The Centre of Christianity*.[37] The year 1978 brought a conference focusing on the volatile issues
raised in *The Myth of God Incarnate*, the fruits of which were published, in
1979, under the title *Incarnation and Myth: The Debate Continued*. Here again,
Hick played a central role.

In 1979, while still at the University of Birmingham, Hick began as a part-
time Professor in the Department of Religion at Claremont Graduate School
in California. For the next three years he split his time between the two schools.
In 1980 (U.S. edition, 1982), he published an important, if occasionally redundant, collection of essays in a volume entitled *God Has Many Names*. Several
of the essays in this work represent a new approach on Hick's part toward the
intellectual problems endemic to the pluralist paradigm. Prior to this, Hick
had primarily espoused and defended his pluralist perspective from the vantage-point of a Christian *theology* of religions. Now, Hick made the conscious
attempt to develop a (tradition-independent) pluralist *philosophy* of religions.[38]

In tandem with this new perspective came a new conceptual model by which
to explicate his pluralist thesis. It has come to hold a place of high priority in
Hick's thought. In brief, the characteristic feature of this new approach comes
with Hick's conscious borrowing of the Kantian distinction between the
noumenal and the phenomenal realms, and his application of it—in a decidedly non-Kantian fashion—to the domain of religious experience.[39] In so doing, Hick developed what has proven to be one of the most philosophically
sophisticated and controversial answers to the perennial conceptual conundrum facing the pluralist paradigm: the 'conflicting conceptions of the divine'
problem. Hick's answer, in brief, is that:

> the noumenal Real is experienced and thought by different human mentalities, form-
> ing and formed by different religious traditions, as the range of [phenomenal] gods
> and absolutes which the phenomenology of religions reports. And these divine *per-
> sonae* and metaphysical *impersonae*, as I shall call them, are not illusory but are em-
> pirically, that is experientially, real as authentic manifestations of the Real.[40]

By adopting this neo-Kantian noumenal/phenomenal mechanism, Hick's pluralist model seeks to maintain a realist core—i.e., the noumenal Real—while
nonetheless anticipating radically diverse—even conceptually conflicting—
understandings of It within the various religions. This crucial feature of Hick's
thought will be fully explored below.

In 1982 Hick accepted a full-time position at Claremont Graduate School as Danforth Professor of the Philosophy of Religion. Claremont proved to be an especially hospitable environment for Hick in terms of thinking about and interacting with other religions. The school took seriously the problem of religious diversity, and actively supported "East/West interaction."[41] More specifically, two of his colleagues at Claremont, the process theologian John Cobb, Jr. and the Buddhist scholar Masao Abe, came to play important roles in his on-going attempt to refine and clarify his pluralist model.[42]

Throughout the 1980s, Hick continued to devote a good part of his time to issues involving religious diversity. In 1983 Hick began as Director of the James A. Blaisdell Programs in World Religions and Cultures at Claremont, and in this capacity has been responsible for organizing a number of conferences and lectures. He was a prime motivating force behind a "trialogue" held at Claremont in March 1985 between a number of Jewish, Christian, and Muslim theologians.[43] The early 1980s saw the publication of a number of articles by Hick in which he developed and defended the pluralist paradigm. Several of these were eventually collected and published as *Problems of Religious Pluralism*.

On March 7–8, 1986, under the auspices of the Blaisdell Lecture Series, what would prove to be a landmark conference was held at Claremont. This conference, jointly planned by Hick and the Roman Catholic pluralist Paul Knitter, hosted a variety of Christian theologians—"Protestant and Catholic, female and male, East and West, First and Third World."[44] Present among them was a group of scholars that, collectively, could be described as the vanguard of the developing pluralist paradigm, including: Tom Driver, Langdon Gilkey, John Hick, Gordon Kaufman, Paul Knitter, Raimundo Panikkar, Aloysius Pieris, Stanley Samartha, Wilfred Cantwell Smith, Marjorie Suchocki, and Seiichi Yagi. Also in attendance were a number of scholars who expressed varying degrees of dissatisfaction with the pluralist paradigm, including John Cobb, Gavin D'Costa, Schubert Ogden, and David Tracy. The literary fruits of this conference, co-edited by Hick and Knitter, were eventually published as *The Myth of Christian Uniqueness: Toward a Pluralistic Theology of Religions*. Hick's contribution was given the title "The Non-Absoluteness of Christianity."

To date, Hick's magnum opus is *An Interpretation of Religion*, published in 1989. Based upon his 1986–87 Gifford Lectures, this book was awarded the prestigious Grawemeyer Award in Religion in 1991. It is Hick's stated hope that this book:

> will make it clear that a viable justification of religious belief, showing that it is
> rational to base our beliefs upon our experience, including religious experience,

leads inevitably to the problem of religious pluralism; and that there are resources within the major world traditions themselves that can, when supported by important philosophical distinctions, point to a resolution of these problems.[45]

In this work, a number of the long-term philosophical and theological strands of Hick's thought are woven together to form a tapestry that reflects his understanding of the human religious experience. Religious phenomenology (Part I), the status of the theistic proofs and his 'Irenaean' theodicy (Part II), epistemology and the primacy of religious experience (Part III), the problem of religious diversity (Part IV), and the issue of criteria for religious evaluation—in other words, the major philosophical and religious issues to which Hick has devoted himself over the years—all find a place within this comprehensive interpretation of religion. If one is to interact with Hick's mature thought, it is to this volume that one must inevitably turn.

The publication of *Interpretation of Religion* in no way marked a decline in Hick's literary out-put on the topic of religious pluralism. In fact, since his full retirement from Claremont in 1993, Hick has maintained a rigorous writing and speaking schedule. It is interesting to note the nature of Hick's most important works since 1993. Hick's early pluralist projects, in the 1970s, were approached from a distinctly Christian vantage-point; he spoke in terms of a pluralist ('Copernican') *theology* of religions. In the 1980s, along with his refinement of the neo-Kantian mechanism, Hick made a programmatic shift to a wider, philosophical (tradition-independent) perspective; he now spoke of a pluralist *philosophy* of religions. Since 1993, the challenge of explicating and defending his pluralist enterprise from an explicitly Christian theological position has once again taken priority. This is not to say that during the 1980s Hick did nothing from a Christian *theological* approach toward the subject. Nor is it to say that, in the 1990s, Hick has simply reverted back his 1970s program. This new *theology* of religions emphasis is clearly rooted within his pluralistic (neo-Kantian) *philosophy* of religions approach, which he continues to defend. First, a new exposition of his pluralist approach to Christology appeared in 1993. Building upon his earlier notion of the incarnation as 'myth,' Hick has refined his pluralist Christology in book-length treatment entitled *The Metaphor of God Incarnate: Christology in a Pluralistic Age*.[46] Here, Hick's basic contention is that:

the idea of divine incarnation in its standard Christian form, in which both genuine humanity and genuine deity are insisted upon, has never been given a satisfactory literal sense; but that on the other hand it makes excellent metaphorical sense.[47]

In 1995, Hick produced *A Christian Theology of Religions: The Rainbow of Faiths*. This work is an up-to-date defense of his pluralist model from a distinctly Christian (as opposed to a purely philosophical, tradition-neutral) perspective, wherein he responds to a number of his most recent and challenging critics. Finally, in this same year, Hick entered into a written dialogue with several evangelical theologians on the question of a Christian approach to salvation in a religiously diverse world.[48]

Beyond his Emeritus status at Claremont, Hick is presently a Fellow of the Institute for Advanced Research in Humanities at Birmingham University. He holds membership in a number of scholarly associations, including the American Philosophical Association, the American Academy of Religion, the Society for the Study of Theology (president 1975–76), and the American Society for the Study of Religion.

The Development of Hick's Thought during the Pre-Pluralist Years

In tracing Hick's thought during his pre-pluralist years, we are concerning ourselves with the period from his evangelical conversion (the early 1940s) to his explicit adoption of a pluralist approach to religious diversity around 1970. Conveniently, the major phases of Hick's thought during this period can be roughly correlated with the three decade-long periods within this time interval. Thus, the following analysis of Hick's thought during his pre-pluralist years will be arranged under three main sections.

The 1940s: The 'Evangelical' Period

For all of its life-long influence upon Hick, particularly the double-decker bus experience, there is little to say about this period of Hick's Christian life with regard to this study. By the time Hick published his first article in 1952, he had already moved on to another stage of his thought. Hick characterizes his own theological posture at this point as "strongly evangelical and indeed fundamentalist."[49] He relates that, within this context, he came to accept:

> the entire evangelical package of theology—the verbal inspiration of the Bible; creation and fall; Jesus as God the Son incarnate, born of a virgin, conscious of his divine nature, and performing miracles of divine power; redemption by his blood from sin and guilt; his bodily resurrection and ascension and future return in glory; heaven and hell.[50]

Hick has noted that, at this stage in his thought, he held to an undeveloped form of soteriological 'exclusivism' with regard to the question of other religions and their salvific capacity. He writes:

> Certainly this [exclusivist] view, or rather this assumption, was present in my own mind for at least twenty-five years. I assumed it to be a central christian position that salvation is through Christ alone, and therefore that those who do not respond to God through Christ are not saved but, presumably, damned or lost. However, although I believed this I did not stress its negative implications....I did not dwell upon the question of what happens to those outside the faith, and had no clear beliefs about their religious status or ultimate fate....I believed by implication that the majority of human beings are eternally lost; but I did not believe this explicitly or whole-heartedly, so as to come to terms with its consequences for my other beliefs. This was of course a thoroughly illogical state of mind to be in.[51]

The 1950s: A Philosophical Turn to the 'Left'

In *Faith and Knowledge* (the published results of his 1950 doctoral thesis), Hick notes that his project, intended as a "bridging operation between philosophy and theology," is best characterized as "philosophically to the 'left' and theologically to the 'right': that is to say, it looks for enlightenment in the directions of philosophical analysis and theological neo-orthodoxy."[52] No doubt Hick's characterization of his philosophical project as "to the left" has to do, along with the analytical bent, with its strong, Kantian-influenced subjectivist element. (Actually, the question of how *far* to the 'left' it is becomes a matter of debate. W. E. Kennick writes: "It may be theologically to the 'right,' but it is misleading to say that it is philosophically to the 'left.' For although it is partially clothed in idioms of recent analytical philosophy [it 'unpacks' concepts], its basic epistemology is about as far to the 'left' as that of Josiah Royce."[53] The primary thrust of this project is the development of a religious epistemology that is able to surmount the challenges of modern secular philosophy. For Hick, the solution arose from a synthesis of his two central intellectual commitments: the primacy of *religious experience* and a *Kantian epistemology*. This synthesis gave rise to the basic religious epistemology that has served as the life-long framework for Hick's philosophy of religion. Because of its permanence in Hick's thought and its eventual influence upon his understanding of the issues surrounding religious diversity, it is vital that one has a clear grasp of Hick's religious epistemology as delineated in *Faith and Knowledge*. It is to this expository task that I will now turn.

Primary Influences upon Hick's Religious Epistemology   In tracing the primary influences upon Hick's religious epistemology, three factors are worthy of brief discussion. The first, and an influence that Hick has reacted *against* throughout his career, concerns the philosophical fall-out from the Logical Positivism movement. Though by this time it was virtually dead as a live philosophical option, through the 1950s the ghost of Logical Positivism continued to haunt the study of things religious in the Anglo-American academy. In short, the cognitive, or realist, value of religious language remained suspect in modern Western philosophy. Given that Hick's philosophical approach to religion was largely guided by the British analytic tradition, it is not surprising to find this specter appearing as a primary nemesis to his endeavors in the realm of religious epistemology.

In the light of this situation, it was left to Hick to produce a realist epistemology of religion that could surmount the challenge posed by the verificational question of the 'meaningfulness' of religious language. More recently Hick has succinctly defined what he means by a 'realist' interpretation of religion:

> the view that the objects of religious belief exist independently of what we take to be our human experience of them. For each religious tradition refers to something (using that word in its most general sense) that stands transcendingly above or undergirdingly beneath and giving meaning or value to our existence.[54]

Hick has never intended to suggest a 'naive' religious realism, but rather a 'critical' religious realism that always recognizes the subjective contribution to all awareness, including religious awareness. In contrast to this perspective are the various "non-realist" (or non-cognitivist) views of religious language which deny the existence of an independent, ontological referent to religious language. Rather, a non-realist view sees religious language as referring, ultimately, to purely human qualities (e.g., emotions, moral intuitions and ideals, etc.). Such views, Hick explains, fall under the categories of "'naturalism' and 'humanism.'"[55]

Hick's commitment to the defense of a realist interpretation of religion has remained a chief and perennial concern up to the present. Central to Hick's epistemological solution, which will be summarized in greater detail below, is an analysis of the idea of 'knowledge' itself. In *Faith and Knowledge*, he takes issue with the common definition of 'knowledge'—one which he terms the 'infalliblist theory,' and which he defines as 'ideal knowledge'—that understands "knowing (sharply distinguished from believing)" as "self-authenticating and infallible." Hick writes:

For knowledge, in the sense of a direct, self-guaranteeing acquaintance with truth (or reality) does not occur. This is conceded in principle by the inevitable admission that we sometimes erroneously *think* that we know. Indeed it is a commonplace that the state of knowing and the state of being in error are not psychologically distinguishable; to be in error is just to appear to oneself as to be knowing when in fact one does not know.[56]

Fundamental to Hick's critique of this view of knowledge (one that has since been termed a 'modernist' view, and has come under the scrutiny of 'postmodern' analysis in recent years) is an assessment of the inherent assumption within this view that humans have access to an Archimedean vantage-point, beyond their own subjective rationality, by which to objectively test knowledge claims. Regarding this supposed aerial view, Hick writes:

But such a standpoint cannot be achieved. We can 'know' only with the aid, and by the means, of the cognitive equipment with which we are endowed....In short, all our cognition is...relative to ourselves, and contains an inescapably subjective element.[57]

Human knowing is always limited by its weakest link: the individual cognizing process. Given this, the most that one can claim with regard to personal 'knowledge' is *subjective rational certainty* (Hick uses the terms "subjective certainty," "psychological certainty," and "rational certainty" interchangeably in this discussion).[58] Thus, in Hick's view, the term 'knowledge' should be reserved for:

that kind or aspect of cognition which is for us final and normative. This aspect, I submit, is the experience of absolute psychological certainty. We cannot in practice mean by knowledge more than certainty, for there is in this dimension no 'more.' Certainty is a *ne plus ultra*. To know means, from the point of view of the cognizing subject, to be certain; this is the cash value of the term as it occurs in ordinary speech.[59]

Needless to say, Hick's understanding of 'knowledge' as presented in *Faith and Knowledge* has not gone uncontested by fellow philosophers.[60]

One word of clarification is required at this point. Unlike some more recent postmodern epistemologists, in arguing for a definition of 'knowledge' as subjective rational certainty, Hick makes it clear that he is *not* abandoning the notions of *objective reality* or *objective certainty*. To the contrary, Hick's religious epistemology is in large measure a means of defending a religious realist ontology against its various foes. (Given this, it is interesting that William Alston has recently classified Hick's neo-Kantian pluralist model as a form of religious "nonrealism."[61]) Thus, Hick wants to claim that, even when construed as 'subjective certainty,' knowledge retains something of an objective character. That knowledge is 'objective' means, at least, that "it is 'the same for everyone.' That which I know is in principle knowable by others."[62] However, this hardly circumvents the inherently subjective quality of knowledge. For instance, it once seemed objectively true to most persons that the sun revolved around the earth. However, in this case, 'knowledge' (subjective rational certainty), even though apparently 'objective' (corroborated by a wide variety of human knowers), was wrong.[63] To say that 'knowledge was wrong' may sound oxymoronic to the ears. But, Hick would argue, this is only the case because an infallibilist definition of 'knowledge' (wherein 'beliefs' can be wrong, but never 'knowledge') has commonly ruled the day. Under Hick's more modest definition, there is no problem in saying: "I knew *p*, but now I know not—*p*." Hick offers this helpful summary of his discussion of subjective and objective certainty:

> [A]ll our actual moments of certainty must, just because they are *ours*, be instances of subjective, personal, or psychological certainty. The propositions of which we are thus certain may indeed also be objectively certain, i.e., they may be true. But our certainty that they *are* true remains a fallible certitude. Cognized propositions may be objectively *as well as* subjectively certain, but not *instead of* being subjectively certain.[64]

This understanding of knowledge has played a central role in Hick's religious philosophy over the years. Once it is applied to the specific question of religious epistemology, it bears interesting fruit. For instance, Hick claims that one effect of abandoning the infalliblist view of knowledge for his more "empirical" view (i.e., rational certainty) is that, in the process, we must also abandon the notion that there is any *one* way in which humans come to know. Rather, Hick's theory entails that "[t]here are just as many ways of coming to know as there are types of ground for rational certainty; and there are as many types of ground for rational certainty as there are kinds of objects of knowledge."[65] By this conclusion, Hick can contend that since God is a vastly different type of object of knowledge from any other, 'knowledge' (rational certainty) of God's existence and activity will necessarily involve a distinctly different type of ground than any other. In saying this, however, Hick acknowledges that the mode by which God will be known must fall under one of the two general cognitive avenues by which humans come to know anything: *experience* (the empirical) and *logical demonstration* (the rational). Since only tautologies are known by the latter path, knowledge of God (along with all other "matters of fact") must come via some type of experiential encounter.[66] This conclusion leads inexorably to putting a premium on religious experience, on one hand, and to necessarily devaluing the very idea of 'theistic proofs,' on the other. These important aspects of Hick's thought will be given further attention below.

A final—and perennial—component of Hick's religious epistemology that was catalyzed by discussions from within twentieth-century analytic philosophy has been the controversial notion of "eschatological verification." It was, again, the challenge to religious language rooted in the Positivists' 'Verification Principle' that led Hick to develop this concept. (The Verification Principle, in one of its more famous forms, was expressed in the maxim: 'The meaning of a statement is the method of its verification.' I.e., unless a statement can be verified in a manner comparable to the way in which scientific hypotheses are tested by publicly-accessible experiment, that statement is void of real meaning. Needless to say, all metaphysical statements were rendered meaningless by this criterion. Of course, so was the criterion itself, and thus its demise.) In brief, eschatological verification involves the idea that the basic assertions of a religious (as opposed to a naturalistic) worldview are meaningful since the believer's claim to post-mortem survival is in principle verifiable.[67]

In turning to the other two primary influences upon Hick's thought, one begins to explore the roots of the two main ideas from which his religious epistemology is synthesized: again, a Kantian epistemology and the primacy of religious experience. While at Edinburgh, Hick sat under the tutelage of Norman Kemp Smith, the Kantian Scholar. This early Kantian influence indelibly impressed upon him "both the active role of the mind in all awareness and the fact that the world as we are conscious of it (the phenomenal world) is structured by our human concepts."[68] The fingerprints of Kant are visible in Hick's religious epistemology at many turns. In the Preface to a 1974 reprint of *Faith and Knowledge*, Hick writes:

> The centre of this book is the account of faith as the interpretive elements within cognitive religious experience. If one wanted to set this in a tradition one would have to refer to Kant as the thinker whose philosophical revolution made possible theories in which the subjective contribution to knowledge is given a key role.[69]

However, Hick's appropriation of Kant was not uncritical. In the original edition of *Faith and Knowledge*, Hick criticizes the lack of place for *personal experience* of God in Kant's system:

> For the purpose of our inquiry, the main comment to be made upon this Kantian theory is that it leaves no room for any acquaintance with or experience of the

divine, such as religious persons claim....We may make a justifiable intellectual move to the belief that there is a God; but we cannot be conscious of God himself, nor therefore can we enter into any kind of personal relationship with him.[70]

Finally, regarding the notion of the primacy of religious experience, a line of influence runs from Friedrich Schleiermacher through the British thinker John Oman to Hick. Drawing upon the spirit of German Romanticism, Schleiermacher proposed a theory of religion that identified its core as an experience that he referred to as the 'sense of the Infinite' (he would eventually refer to it as the feeling of absolute dependence).[71] John Oman (1860–1939), a Scottish philosopher of religion and Christian theologian, taught for 28 years at the English Presbyterian seminary at Westminster College, Cambridge. In an article on Oman, Hick notes that the "chief influence on his developing thought was that of Friedrich Schleiermacher, whose *Reden* Oman translated into English."[72] In the introduction to *Faith and Knowledge*, Hick's admiration for, and indebtedness to, Oman is made clear when he writes:

> John Oman was probably the most original British theologian of the first half of the twentieth century, and his teaching concerning the relation between religion and environment, and the apprehension of the supernatural in and through the natural, provides (as it seems to me) an important key to the problem of religious knowledge."[73]

Hick goes on to describe his book as "an attempt to work out Oman's basic standpoint in relation to the very different world of contemporary philosophy."[74] Beyond the central place given to religious experience, other strands of Oman's thought that eventually find parallels in Hick's include: (1) the importance of an irreducible interpretive element in all human perception of both our natural and supernatural environments (here, Oman foreshadows Hick's own synthesis by bringing Schleiermacher and Kant into a dialogue of sorts);[75] (2) the importance of human *freedom* in the interpretive process and in religion as a whole;[76] (3) a lack of dependence upon the theistic proofs;[77] (4) an emphasis on God as the supremely *personal* reality; and, finally, (5) the idea that the supernatural and the redemption that it offers are variously conceived in different types of religion (this notion comes to play a strong role in Hick's thought only later in his career).

A Summary of Hick's Religious Epistemology A number of the central ideas that are developed in *Faith and Knowledge* have become enduring planks of Hick's basic religious philosophy. The following are worthy of mention:

1. *We find ourselves in a religiously ambiguous world, more or less equally capable of being interpreted either religiously or naturalistically.* Hick has recently re-stated this conviction in clear terms:

> It seems, then, that the universe maintains its inscrutable ambiguity....It permits both a religious and a naturalistic faith....Any realistic analysis of religious belief and experience...must therefore start from this situation of systematic ambiguity.[78]

This tenet is complemented by Hick's long-standing judgment that the theistic proofs are fundamentally inconclusive.[79] He is just as adamant that the typical atheistic arguments are equally nondemonstrative.[80] Viewed in the light of Hick's religious epistemology, these conclusions are not surprising. In short, the inability of any philosophical argumentation to tip the balance of reason toward either a theistic or atheistic interpretation of the world would seem to follow naturally from at least two aspects of Hick's thought. First, there is his empiricist approach to religious experience. Hick writes:

> Just as our knowledge of the physical world is ultimately based upon sense perception, so any religious knowledge must ultimately be based upon aspects of human experience which are received as revelatory. Thus, reason can never replace experience as the source of the basic religious data.[81]

A second controversial element is worthy of consideration. At first glance, it would appear that if rational argumentation for or against God's existence was successful, this could potentially spell trouble for Hick's notion of the finely-tuned religious ambiguity of the world. However, Hick has explicitly rejected this proposal in his subsequent work on the status of the theistic proofs. Of Alasdair MacIntyre's suggestion that logically compelling evidence of God's existence would effectively coerce a faith response and thus do damage to human freedom in relationship to God, Hick replies: "a verbal proof of God's existence cannot by itself break down our human freedom; it can only lead to a notional assent which has in itself little or no positive religious value or substance."[82] Hick wants to suggest that the only thing that could coerce human 'faith' in God would be an unambiguous *religious experience* of God, something a logically air-tight *conceptual argument* could never approximate. However, it seems more than coincidental that Hick's conclusions regarding the plethora of arguments for and against a theistic/religious interpretation of the world, when taken as a whole, effectively cancel each other out, leaving the very same finely-tuned religiously ambiguous universe that his religious epistemology is predicated upon. Thus, despite Hick's protestation to the contrary (which can itself be understood as a wise apologetic move to further safeguard his thesis from those who conclude otherwise regarding the world's religious ambiguity, etc.), one could argue that his apparent *a posteriori* conclusion regarding the viability of the theistic proofs actually functions as an *a priori* tenet of Hick's theory of religious knowledge. Hick himself invites this conjecture when, in the first edition of *Faith and Knowledge*, he acknowledges that the "problem to be treated here only arises for those...who have abandoned the traditional theistic proofs as being nondemonstrative."[83]

2. We now move to the linchpin of Hick's theory of religious faith: *Our knowledge of God—that is our cognitive 'faith' in God—is arrived at by a free and voluntary act of interpretation on our part, in the midst of a religiously ambiguous world.* In Hick's words, "that we 'know God by faith' means that we interpret our experience as a whole in theistic terms."[84] Hick's view of faith is predicated upon the idea that "while the object of religious knowledge is unique, its basic epistemological pattern is that of all our knowing."[85] What Hick means here is simply this: *all knowledge inherently involves interpretation.* Using Wittgenstein's notion of 'seeing as' as a springboard, Hick coined the phrase 'experiencing as' to express his view that *all* human experience of every variety is ineluctably tied to an interpretive moment. Hick introduced this term 'experiencing-as' in the mid-1960s. He incorporated it into his 1966 revised edition of *Faith and Knowledge*. While the term is new, the substance is not. It is merely shorthand for Hick's basic conviction that all experience involves an irreducibly interpretive element.[86]

Hick begins by delineating the three 'levels' of reality that humans experience: the 'natural'/'physical' realm, the 'human'/'ethical' realm, and the 'religious'/'divine' realm. He contends that, at each level, the human knower experiences reality only as he or she attributes 'significance' to the objects of knowledge via an act of 'interpretation' (where 'interpretation' is best understood as an act of 'recognition' as opposed to 'explanation'). According to Hick, at the religious level one cannot separate these two senses of interpretation.[87] Thus, for Hick, 'faith'—the interpretive moment at the religious level—is simply "a voluntary recognition of God's activity in human history, consist[ing] in seeing, apperceiving, or interpreting events in a special way."[88] It is worth noting that each 'level' presupposes the one before it; i.e., the human/ethical presupposes the natural/physical, etc. One important difference between the three levels involves the degree of cognitive freedom within one's experience.

At the natural / physical level, cognitive freedom with regard to one's experience of the objects of knowledge is at a minimum. E.g., in a boxing match, one typically experiences the opponent's fist as a brutal impingement upon one's noetic equipment. At the other end of the spectrum, one experiences the object of knowledge in the religious realm (God) only to the degree that one *voluntarily* does so. In sum, religious faith is the uncoerced exercise of cognitive freedom whereby the human mind chooses to interpret its 'total experience' of the inherently ambiguous universe in a religious mode. In explicating this understanding of faith in *Faith and Knowledge*, Hick contrasts it both with the propositional (e.g., 'Thomistic') and voluntarist (e.g., William James's view) views of faith.

3. *God's purpose in creating the world in such a fashion is to enable us as finite creatures to operate in a state of cognitive freedom toward him, which itself is the pre-condition for a personal relationship between God and humanity.*[89] The world's state of finely-tuned religious ambiguity and the fact that 'faith' functions as an interpretive moment in the midst of this ambiguity are no accidents; they are indispensable parts of the divine plan. By creating us at an 'epistemic distance' from himself, we are free to choose whether or not we will respond to God's offer of personal relationship. Hick explains the "ultimate and determining reason" behind this state of affairs: "the infinite nature of the Deity requires him to veil himself from us if we are to exist as autonomous persons in his presence."[90] (Incidentally, Hick notes at this point a second and more immediate reason for this state of affairs: namely the inherent limitations of human apprehension of God's presence given our cognitive equipment and its primary orientation to the material world.) Interestingly, Oman had a similar view on this matter. In *Natural and Supernatural* he writes: "The peculiarity of the Supernatural environment is that we cannot enter it except we choose it as our own."[91] Thus, in Hick's view, for an unambiguous awareness of God's existence to be part of the common human experience (i.e., in the same manner that physical objects are perceived) would be to coerce cognitive 'faith' (*fides*) in God. Such coercion of faith could only come at the expense of the human being's freedom as a personal agent. Hick expounds:

> Only when we ourselves *voluntarily* recognize God, desiring to enter into a relationship with him, can our knowledge of him be compatible with our freedom, and so with our existence as personal beings. If God were to reveal himself to us in the coercive way in which the physical world is disclosed to us, he would thereby annihilate us as free and responsible persons.[92]

In short, "If man is to be personal, God must be *deus absconditus*."[93]

4. *God's self-revelation to humanity is 'non-propositional' in nature. God reveals himself by acting in history through events capable of being freely interpreted either revelationally or non-revelationally.*[94] This *'heilsgeschichtliche'* view of revelation comports nicely with—and is even demanded by—his understanding of the dynamics of religious experience and faith.[95] In Hick's theory, religious experience—and the 'faith' which catalyzes it—does not involve any kind of supernatural, other-worldly experience of divine intervention into the natural world. Rather, religious experience entails experiencing the natural realm—via the interpretive act of faith—in a religiously significant manner. Thus, miracles, answered prayer, and special divine revelations, which presuppose an *unambiguous* divine intervention within the natural realm, find no real room within Hick's religious philosophy. It should be noted that Hick does not rule out apparently fantastic events *a priori*; in fact, he has long been a serious student of parapsychological phenomena (he has held membership in the Society for Psychical Research for many years). However, on Hick's view, just because of the possibility of purely human parapsychological phenomena, fully naturalistic explanations of purported divine acts cannot be ruled out. For Hick, then, a 'miracle' is never simply an unambiguous intrusion of the divine into the ordinary state of human affairs. Rather, since *every* human experience involves an unavoidable element of interpretation (i.e., all human experience is "experience-as"), a miracle is "any event that is experienced as a miracle; and this particular mode of experiencing-as is accordingly an essential element in the miraculous." Thus, an atheist, for example, may experience a "startling happening," even one that involves "a suspension of the natural law." But unless this event is experienced by the atheist as "religiously significant" (i.e., as an event through which he or she becomes "vividly and immediately conscious of God acting towards" him or her), then this event does not constitute for that person a 'miracle.'[96]

In Hick's view, then, revelation (experience) of God is thus always *mediated* through the natural world. As Hick explains:

> Sometimes two different orders or levels of significance are experienced within the same situation; this is what happens when the religious mind experiences events as occurring within human history and also as mediating the presence and activity of God. A religious significance is found superimposed upon the natural significance of the situation in the believer's experience.[97]

By adopting a non-propositional view of revelation, Hick has moved significantly from his earlier evangelical understanding of God's mode of communication to humanity. Under a non-propositional view, any theological propositions or doctrines—including the Scriptures—are at best fallible human attempts to understand and communicate the significance of God's self-revelation in and through particular historical events.[98] Once again, Hick's central concern in adopting a *heilsgeschichtliche* (non-propositional) view of revelation is the preservation of human freedom for the purpose of freely entering into a relationship with the personal God: "God is self-revealingly active within the world that he has made. But his actions are not overwhelmingly manifest and unmistakable; for then men would have no cognitive freedom in relation to their maker."[99]

To return to a common theme, Hick consistently emphasizes that his religious epistemology is in no way an attempt to demonstrate the existence of God. To attempt such would be to fly in the face of the theory itself. Rather, his theory is meant simply to describe, from an epistemological vantage-point, that "the kind of cognition of God which religious people profess to experience is the kind that they might reasonably be expected to enjoy if there is indeed a God to be known such as theism asserts."[100] When it comes to the question of establishing the reality of this God, Hick refuses to grant any academic specialty such license. As his theory of knowledge—applied to the religious realm—suggests, the question of God's existence and activity in human affairs "is a question for each individual exercising his cognitive powers in relation to the environment in which he finds himself, and responding in his own personal freedom and responsibility to its claims and calls."[101] What this all means for Hick, in practical terms, is that the religious believer who has a subjective certainty about the existence and activity of God—rooted in personal religious experience—*is fully within her epistemic rights (i.e., is acting rationally) when she trusts that this experience is a real one.* (As Hick himself has noted, this view is not unlike the so-called 'Reformed' approach to religious epistemology, with its claim that belief in God is 'properly basic'; more on the points that unite and divide Hick and the Reformed epistemologists in the next chapter.) Hick states this conclusion baldly when he writes:

> It seems that a sufficiently vivid religious experience would entitle a man to claim to know that God is real. Indeed if his sense of the divine presence is sufficiently powerful he can hardly fail to make this claim. He is sure that God exists, and in his own experience of the presence of God he has a good, and compelling, reason to be sure of it.[102]

The conclusions that Hick arrives at in the area of religious epistemology are crucial for understanding the subsequent development of his thought, both philosophically and theologically. In fact, one could argue that nearly every major development in his thought throughout the last four decades was, in one sense or another, implicitly contained within this early religious philosophy.[103] For the purposes of this study, it is particularly important to note that this early religious epistemology eventually led Hick, in a seemingly inescapable manner, face to face with a pluralist interpretation of religious diversity.

Hick's 'Conservative' Theology: A Christological Sounding

While Hick acknowledges that at this stage of his pilgrimage his religious thought is "philosophically to the 'left'," he recognizes that his theological slant—which he attributes to an appropriation of "theological neo-orthodoxy"—has remained essentially tipped toward the "right."[104] Although he had definitely departed from an evangelical position with his adoption of a non-propositional view of revelation and the attendant implications for the Scriptures, he nonetheless maintained a generally conservative theology until the mid-1960s. The tension between his religious philosophy and his Christian theology arose from the fact that the intellectual foundations for a more conservative theology had been severely undercut by his religious epistemology. Thus, in tracing Hick's Christian theological movement from this point on, one is largely tracing the workings of the logical implications of his religious epistemology upon his theology.

One way to begin to trace Hick's theological development in his pre-pluralist years involves the distinction drawn by Hick between "dogma"/"facts of faith" and "doctrine."[105] By Hick's definition, the former have to do with "the basic assertions of faith which are characteristic of that religion and which constitute for its adherents data for theological reasoning," while the latter consist of "propositions officially accepted as interpreting its dogmas and as relating them together in a coherent system of thought."[106] Hick goes on to explicate this critical distinction:

> The formulation of dogmas is thus a descriptive and empirical process, the aim of which is to express the basic data apprehended by faith. The construction of doctrine, on the other hand, is speculative in method, being philosophical thinking undertaken within the dogmatic boundaries of a particular religion.
>
> The dogmas of a religion should be fixed and unchangeable; for they define the religion in question by pointing to the area of primary religious experiences from which it has arisen. Doctrines, on the other hand, can and do change.... [T]he re-

jection of orthodox dogma constitutes heresy, while the rejection of orthodox doctrine amounts only to heterodoxy.[107]

The practical import of this distinction is most clearly visible in Hick's Christological musings at this time. Hick views every Christological theory as a *doctrinal* attempt to express what must be the "fixed and unchangeable" *dogma* that "in Jesus Christ God became incarnate."[108] Hick expands upon the centrality of this Christological dogma for the Christian faith:

> There is, I think, no room for debate as to the content of this basic claim of Christian faith concerning Christ. This claim is succinctly expressed in an early creedal formula (quoted by Harnack): "*Jesus Christus, Deus et homo.*" The conviction out of which the entire theology of the Incarnation has arisen is that Christ is in some sense both God and man.[109]

In light of the primacy of the dogma of the incarnation for Christianity, it is clear that the speculative theological endeavor of providing a doctrinal explication of this fundamental 'fact of faith' has some inherent constraints upon it. In Hick's words:

> the task of any Christology which intends to serve the historic faith of the ecumenical creeds is to illumine for modern man the conception of the deity of Christ—or, more cumbrously, of the substantival as distinguished from the adjectival divinity of Christ.[110]

That is, to say that Jesus Christ was God incarnate means not merely that God's Spirit, power, and/or love were operative in Jesus to a higher or fuller *degree* than in other humans, but rather that—in regard to his deity—Jesus was ontologically "continuous with the life of the Godhead."[111] Here, Hick is clearly marking anything like an adoptionist or 'degree' Christology as outside the bounds of acceptable Christian doctrine. In a 1958 article, Hick analyses D. M. Baillie's "paradox of grace" Christology by these dogmatic and doctrinal criteria. In the end, Baillie's "adoptionist"-like Christology fails since it "does not perform the central Christological task of giving meaning to the dogma of the deity of Christ."[112] And thus, it also fails in "the task of restating the faith of the creeds for the modern world."[113]

Hick nonetheless recognized at this time the problematic nature of the "static," substantival expression of the incarnation traditionally associated with Chalcedon and the *homoousion* formula. Thus, in 1959 he published an article in which he attempted to restate the dogma of the incarnation in a non-sub-stantival—and yet dogmatically faithful—manner, using the dynamic category of *agape*.[114] Hick's strategy is as follows. He begins by noting that the static category of *homoousion* was entirely appropriate for early Christian formula-tions of Christological doctrine given the fact that Greek (Neoplatonic) thought largely supplied *the* philosophical vocabulary of the day. He goes on to argue, however, that, since we are no longer living in the fourth century, and since no one philosophical language rules the day in our century:

> we are thus free, and indeed obliged, to return to the biblical starting point of Christology, to take our bearings there independently of the Nicene and Chalcedonian formulations, and then to try as Christians of our day to express intelligibly to our-selves and our contemporaries the central conviction which makes us Christians.[115]

In his own attempt at this biblical retrieval project, Hicks notes that bibli-cal categories tend to be "dynamic—categories of action rather than of be-ing."[116] More specifically, he concludes that one can best summarize God's attitude and actions toward humanity in history by "the assertion that God is *Agape*."[117] Using this observation as a springboard, Hick proposes an *agape* Christology as a more appropriate and understandable way to express the doc-trine of the incarnation in our contemporary world. Hick explains:

> The incarnation was, so to speak, a temporal cross-section of God's *Agape*....We want to say of Jesus that he was "wholly God" in the sense that his *agape* was genuinely the *Agape* of God at work on earth, but not that he was "the whole of God" in the sense that the divine *Agape* was expressed without remainder in each or even in the sum of his actions....Jesus' *agape* is not a representation of God's *agape*; it *is* that *Agape* operating in a finite mode; it is the eternal divine *Agape* made flesh, inhistorised.[118]

The term 'inhistorised' was coined by Hick's theological mentor, H. H. Farmer. In speaking of divine 'inhistorisation'—rather than 'divine incarnation'—Hick wants to emphasize that "God in Christ has not merely acted *upon* or *into* human history, like a meteor falling from above, but has acted *within* and *through* man's history by becoming an actual part of the ongoing stream of human life and influencing the course of our history from the inside."[119]

And so, by making use of the biblical notion of *agape*, Hick proposes what he believes to be a more contemporarily relevant way of stating what has al-ways been at the center of the Christian faith—the dogma of the incarnation of Jesus Christ. Hick is clear in this article that his project is about a new doctrinal statement of the dogma—the basic assertion—of Christ's incarnation. It is *not* a philosophical explication of this dogma. He writes:

> The assertion that Jesus' agaping was continuous with the divine Agaping is no more self-explanatory than the assertion that Christ was of one substance with the Father. Neither of these formulations, strictly speaking, explains anything. Each is concerned merely to point to a fact of faith; and each is concerned to point to the same fact of faith.[120]

The 1960s: Setting the Stage for the Pluralist Move

Hick's controversy with the Presbyterian church in the early 1960s had been precipitated by his response to the question of whether there was anything in the Westminster Confession with which he did not agree. Hick confessed that he had intellectual doubts about "the six-day creation of the world, the pre-destination of many to eternal hell, the verbal inspiration of the Bible, and the virgin birth of Jesus."[121] In early 1960, Hick closes an article on his notion of eschatological verification with a tantalizing comment wherein he notes that it is his "personal opinion that the logic of the New Testament as a whole, though admittedly not always in its explicit content, leads to a belief in ultimate universal salvation."[122] Such statements at the turn of the decade serve as early markers of the progressive liberalization of what Hick had previously recognized as his generally 'conservative' Christian theology (I shall use the often polemical terms 'liberal' and 'conservative' here, since Hick himself has consistently described his movement in these terms).

Throughout the early 1960s, this theological tendency toward the left was nurtured as he wrestled with the difficult intellectual issues surrounding the problem of evil and suffering. In constructing the theodicy that would comprise his *Evil and the God of Love*, Hick was moved to reject a literal understanding of several planks of the historic Christian faith, including the notions of: the original created righteousness of the world and humanity, the angelic and human falls, a transmittable "original sin," and eternal hell.[123] Rather, he came to view these ideas as "Christian myths," a category whose contents would grow through the years as Hick continued to widen its borders to include more and more (formerly literal) doctrines. At this point in time, Hick understood 'Christian myth' as:

> the great persisting imaginative pictures by means of which the corporate mind of the church has expressed to itself the significance of the historical events upon

which its faith is based, above all the life, death and resurrection of Jesus who was the Christ.[124]

It is interesting to note that, through this period, Hick continued to classify the "resurrection of Jesus" (though undefined in nature) as one of the foundational "historical events" upon which Christianity was built.[125] Eschatologically, Hick rejected any notion of a "bad eschaton"—including the annihilationist option—in favor of the ultimate universal salvation of all humanity.[126]

The Roots of Hick's Religious Pluralism The first stark indications that the problem of religious diversity was beginning to impress itself upon Hick's thought appear in the mid-1960s. Already by 1962, in connection with a conference on the existence of God, Hick had momentarily broached the problem of conflicting religious experiences among the various religions. As noted above, given Hick's theory of religious experience, this issue was bound to surface for Hick as soon as he applied his theory outside the narrow confines of his own Christian theological world. Hick's relevant comments appear within a paper on the existence of God and the nature of religious experience.[127] In the midst of delineating the differences between sensory and religious experience, Hick notes the problem that "religious awareness of different individuals varies greatly in degree of coherence."[128] While his main explanation for this problem is that religious experiences can vary greatly in degree—and thus coherence, he parenthetically adds: "(It also seems, however, to be due in part to real differences in the nature of what, within different religions, is claimed to be apprehended in religious experience; and there is an important problem here which I shall not even attempt to consider in the present paper.)"[129] By 1966, Hick was describing the confrontation with other religious traditions and truth-claims as the "most disturbing theological problem that Christianity is likely to have to face corporately during the next hundred years or so."[130]

As Gavin D'Costa has noted, Hick's move to Birmingham University in 1967 effectively marks the end of his identification, in any real sense, with traditional orthodox Christianity.[131] As indicated previously, at least four strands of influence combined at this time to create the bridge of ideas and experiences that would prove to be Hick's path to a pluralistic perspective. One factor was Hick's conviction of the ultimate universal salvation of all humanity. While Hick's universalism was no doubt solidified in conjunction with the development of his 'Irenaean' theodicy, one can trace this proclivity as far back as 1960.[132] Hick was eventually to set the issue within the context of the religious diversity prob-lematic: "How then to reconcile the notion of there being one, and only one, true religion with a belief in God's universal saving activity?"[133]

A second factor involved his decision to begin working on what would be-come his monumental contribution to a "global theology"—the book *Death and Eternal Life*. Hick's six-year preparation for this book included research trips to India and Sri Lanka, where he was struck by "the immense spiritual depth and power" of both Hinduism and Buddhism.[134] The book, an eschatological theology woven from the combined thought of Hinduism, Bud-dhism, Christianity, and Humanism, would eventually be finished after his decisive move to a pluralist theology of religions.

A third source of influence at this time was the thought of Canadian-born Wilfred Cantwell Smith, former Professor of World Religions at Harvard Uni-versity and Director of Harvard's Center for the Study of World Religions.[135] Smith's ground-breaking interpretation of religion is set forth in his book, *The Meaning and End of Religion*. In brief, Smith's thesis suggests that every so-called 'religion' is simply the combination of two components: a complex historical "cumulative tradition" and the personal "faith" of those within that tradition. According to Smith, the standard approaches to the study of 'reli-gion' have failed by neglecting either of two important elements of human religious life: the "mundane" historical realities of religion or "the transcen-dent."[136] He proposes a new theory that does justice to both aspects, and, along the way, deconstructs the very notion of (a) 'religion' as such. Smith summa-rizes his proposal and its implications for the study of 'religion' as follows:

> I ask whether these studies may not proceed more satisfactorily in the future if, putting aside the concept of 'religion' or 'the religions'…we elect to work rather with two separate concepts.
>
> I propose to call these 'cumulative tradition', on the one hand, and 'faith', on the other. The link between the two is the living person.
>
> By 'faith' I mean personal faith…, an inner religious experience or involvement of a particular person; the impingement on him of the transcendent, putative or real. By 'cumulative tradition' I mean the entire mass of overt objective data that constitute the historical deposit, as it were, of the past religious life of the commu-nity in question.…
>
> It is my suggestion that by the use of these two notions it is possible to concep-tualize and to describe anything that has ever happened in the religious life of mankind.…[137]

This thesis has important implications for the question of religious 'truth.' In Smith's eyes, the locus of religious truth is to be found not in the realm of 'cumulative tradition,' but rather in that of personal 'faith.' In short, Smith proffers a "personalist" view of religious truth that, while not denying the importance of "propositional" truth, nonetheless radically subordinates the latter to the former. In Smith's view, a personalist view of truth rests on the conviction that it is "not statements that are true or false but the use of them by individuals."[138] In his 1967 book *Questions of Religious Truth*, Smith further explicated his views on religious truth. In one instance he does so via application of his theory to the concrete case of the Christian tradition:

> Christianity, I would suggest, is not true absolutely, impersonally, statically; rather it can *become* true, if and as you or I appropriate it to ourselves and interiorize it, insofar as we live it out from day to day.[139]

With such a view of religious truth in place, Smith is prepared to declare the problem of so-called '*conflicting* religious truth-claims' a misnomer. In a manner not unlike the more recent turn to a 'cultural-linguistic' understanding of doctrinal claims as espoused by George Lindbeck and the 'postliberal'/Yale school,[140] Smith concludes that religious views that are embedded in two different traditions can be identified as 'different,' without having to juxtapose them in such a way that interprets them as in 'conflict.' For example:

> when a Hindu and a Christian, let us say, make different statements, neither of them, nor a Western secularist listening in, is in a position hastily to determine whether they agree or disagree. Each statement is made within a total world view; the meaning of each term of each, as well as of each whole, derives from the total complex of which it is a more or less coherent part; the function of religious statements within each system is itself particular....[W]hat appears is not conflict but difference....The perception of conflict in the present situation, of a pluralism just beginning to become self-conscious, is an unwarranted prior judgement as to what the outcome will eventually be, and an unkind prior decision as to what our mood be now.[141]

Although Hick never did adopt all the particulars of Smith's pluralist model, it appears to have been a significant catalyst for his own shift in that direction.

A fourth and final influence toward a pluralist stance, and one often mentioned by Hick himself, relates to his involvement in an assortment of interreligious experiences in the multi-cultural city of Birmingham, experiences that brought him into relationships with a wide variety of religious persons.

In the process, Hick found himself face to face with persons who, though outside of the Christian tradition, seemed to be as much in touch with the Divine as any Christian he knew. In Hick's words:

> And occasionally attending worship in mosque and synagogue, temple and gurdwara, it was evident to me that essentially the same kind of thing is taking place in them as in a Christian church—namely, human beings opening their minds to a higher divine Reality, known as personal and good and as demanding righteousness and love between man and man.[142]

Hick's subsequent visits to India and Sri Lanka confirmed these experiences. In this light, Hick has commented that "it was not so much new thoughts as new experiences that drew me, as a philosopher, into the issues of religious pluralism, and as a Christian into inter-faith dialogue."[143] Thus, these four streams of influence converged in the mid-to-late 1960s to produce a significant current in Hick's thought toward a pluralist perspective of the religions.

Hick's Growing Awareness of the Problem of Religious Diversity   On October 31, 1967, Hick delivered his Inaugural Lecture at Birmingham University.[144] Here, Hick explored what he took to be theology's primary challenge in the contemporary world. This challenge involved the realm of religious language—that "old-established firm of God-Talk, Ltd."—and centered on the question of "whether distinctively religious utterances are instances of the cognitive [realist] or the noncognitive [non-realist] uses of language."[145] In the paper, Hick once again offers an apologetic for a realist/cognitivist interpretation of religious language, as opposed to the various non-realist, naturalistic interpretations offered by those still caught in the vortex of Logical Positivism, as well as by the provocative 'death of God' theologians. Specifically, Hick suggests the risk of defending a realist "transcendental theism"—defined as "belief in a transcendent personal God, together with the major corollaries of this belief"— over against a non-realist vision of religion is worth taking. The risk, of course, is that such a realist interpretation of religion "makes assertions which are logically capable of being either true or false. Thus in claiming to be true it inevitably runs the risk of being false."[146]

Hick ends his lecture with a brief discussion of the "four great matters of debate" that present the most troubling challenges to a transcendental theism: (1) the short-comings of the theistic proofs and the related fact that the world can be rationally understood in purely naturalistic terms; (2) the "ancient and grisly" problem of evil; (3) the question of whether the theological claims regarding the Judeo-Christian concept of God are logically coherent and sufficiently verifiable; and, finally, (4) the problem of "the conflicting truth-claims of the different world religions."[147] It is the last of the four challenges to Hick's 'transcendental theism' that concerns us here, and Hick's understanding of the problem, at this point in time, is worth reproducing:

> The problem can be stated very simply. If I had been born in India I would probably be a Hindu; if in Egypt, probably a Moslem; if in Ceylon, probably a Buddhist; but I was born in England and am, predictably, a Christian. However, these different religions each profess to be true....But in the end it is far from evident that they can all be true. Are we then to say that one is true and all the others false—whether equally false or false in varying degrees? Or are we to say that each is true subjectively, for its own adherents—with the implication that probably none is objectively true? There is here an agonizing dilemma for anyone committed to a particular faith.[148]

It is very important to note, at this point, the context within which Hick raises the problem of conflicting religious truth-claims. He poses the problem as one of four great intellectual challenges in the contemporary world to a Christian-theistic worldview. The other three challenges are all issues that Hick had already spent much time and ink responding to in defense of Christian theism. In the course of answering the first three challenges throughout the 1950s and 1960s, Hick found himself modifying his Christian theology, in a 'liberal' direction, in order to save its intellectual respectability. The fourth difficulty—the problems posed by an awareness of religious diversity and conflicting truth-claims—now presented itself as the newest apologetic challenge for the Christian faith. It is within this light that Hick's response must be read. In hindsight (and as will be articulated in chapter four), one can see that Hick's apologetic attempt to save a realist understanding of Christian theism from the intellectual problems raised by religious diversity came, eventually, at the high cost of denying the very ultimate reality of the notion of a transcendent personal God that he had originally determined to defend. And for this very reason, that it *was* an apologetic attempt should never be lost sight of. Any religious apologetic is only as good as it is successful in vindicating its intended religious object. If, in the course of its development, it rejects the very object it was designed to defend, this should give one pause to reconsider its nature and deployment.

The concerns expressed in the 1967 lecture can be correlated with the central burden of Hick's next book. 1968 brought the publication of *Christianity at the Centre*, an apologetic for a 'liberal' Christianity. Here, Hick's primary purpose was to argue for a "middle way between a conservative cleaving to the traditional structure of belief" on one hand, and a "radical rejection of all traditional content including the transcendent" on the other.[149] Hick's liberal theological leaning is everywhere present in this volume. He begins by noting that the development of "modern science" has forced modern Christianity to reassess many of its traditional beliefs, including: the origin of the universe as a divine act of creation, miracles, an historical fall, the virgin birth, the atonement, and the idea that Jesus' corpse came back to life after his death.[150] Nonetheless, he stands in equal resistance to the "radical response" of "Christian humanism or humanistic Christianity," epitomized at that time in the 'God is dead' slogan.[151] Once again, he comes to the defense of a realist understanding of God. At this point he even retains a place for the literal incarnation of Jesus and a real resurrection (that may or may not have involved his former body).[152] Although Hick devotes very little space to the question of a proper Christian response to religious diversity, one does find this tantalizing paragraph at the end of an unrelated chapter:

> Although there is not enough space in this small book to devote a chapter to the very important question of the relation between Christianity and the other world religions, I shall end this chapter by trying to glance briefly beyond the future hoped-for reunion of Christendom to the possibility of a growing together of the different religions of the world. The Christian basis for this possibility rests upon the idea of the Logos, the divine self-expression in relation to the creation, which or who has always been at work in the religious life of mankind and was incarnate in personal form in Jesus of Nazareth. The divine Logos has become manifest in this personal way to peoples whose deepest presuppositions and ways of thinking lead them to respond to the personal nature of the Divine, but in other ways to other peoples, especially in the East, whose character leads them to a more mystical experience of impersonal depths of divine being. But as the different regional cultures and temperaments interpenetrate one another in a world which is rapidly becoming a communicational unity, and contribute to a common though rich and many-sided human culture, it may be that a common attitude and approach to the Divine will also become possible.[153]

With this suggestion we see Hick poised at the so-called Rubicon that stands between a strong normative-inclusivism and the pluralist paradigm. In retaining a literal incarnational agape/Logos Christology, Hick still stood on the inclusivist bank. He as much as acknowledges this himself when he notes that such a Christology gives rise to "a religion claiming universal validity. For if in Christ's actions God himself was at work on earth, those actions *decisively* reveal God to us."[154]

Hick's 'Liberal' Theology: A Christological Sounding

Throughout the 1960s and with the liberal turn in his theology, various aspects of Hick's Christology underwent significant development. For example, the traditional notion that Christ's death on the cross provides atonement and redemption is now classified as "myth."[155] Thus, the historic Christian understanding of the atonement as cosmically redemptive in an objective sense is exchanged for the view that the function of Jesus' death was primarily to manifest God's self-giving love. (Hick qualifies his view at this point by stressing that Christ's death "was more than a dramatic revelation of the depth of God's love. Indeed it could only be this because it was more than this." However, when it comes to explaining just what this "more" is, Hick offers little in the way of concrete explanation beyond a detailed discussion of the "human forces" that brought about Jesus' death.[156]

In spite of his theological turn to the left, Hick continued to regard "the divinity of Christ," as expressed in his *agape* Christology, as central to his theology.[157] In his 1966 essay, "Christology at the Crossroads," Hick once again presents his agape incarnational Christology. The majority of the article is given to arguing against a "neo-Arian"—or "degree"—and for a "neo-Chalcedonian" Christology. Yet, in the midst of an attempt to champion the historic understanding of the incarnation, the article ends on a Christologically foreboding note:

> But...if we make this Chalcedonian claim today we shall have to face the problem which it now brings with it in ever-increasing force: what does this claim imply concerning the other religions of the world? And do the facts of history permit us to believe what it implies?[158]

At the heart of the problem raised by the Chalcedonian claim "lies the question of the uniqueness of Christ." It is in this sense, Hick writes, that "Christology stands...at the crossroads."[159] Thus here, on the eve of Hick's move to a pluralist theology of religions, we find him championing a robust incarnational Christology as essential to a legitimate exposition of the Christian faith. But, as Hick clearly understands, such a view of Christ implies "a religion claiming universal validity," one wherein Jesus' very actions "decisively reveal God to us."[160] This view is difficult to square with a pluralist vision of human religious life. Thus, not surprisingly, Hick's literal understanding of the incarnation would not long survive the pluralist atmosphere within which he was about to immerse himself.

Notes

1   The broad outline and a significant amount of the content of this chapter owes much to my previously published essay: "John Hick's Theological Pilgrimage," in *The Challenge of Religious Pluralism: An Evangelical Analysis and Response*, 26–38.

2   Sources for this chapter include: Hick, "A Spiritual Journey," in *God Has Many Names* (Philadelphia: Westminster, 1980), 13–28; Hick, "Three Controversies," in *Problems of Religious Pluralism* (New York: St. Martin's, 1985), 1–15; Hick, "A Personal Note," in *Disputed Questions in Theology and the Philosophy of Religion* (New Haven: Yale University Press, 1993) 139–45; Hick "A Pluralist View," in *More than One Way?*, 29–32, as well as brief comments from personal correspondence with Professor Hick. Also: Paul Badham, "The Philosophical Theology of John Hick," in Hick, *A John Hick Reader*, ed. Paul Badham (Philadelphia: Trinity, 1990), 1–14; John Begley, "Philosophy of the World Religions: The Views of John Hick," *Australian Catholic Record* 72 (1995): 306–15; Gavin D'Costa, *John Hick's Theology of Religions: A Critical Evaluation* (Lanham, Md.: University Press of America, 1987), 5–16; Lowell D. Streiker, "John Hick," in *Modern Theologians: Christian and Jews*, ed. Thomas E. Bird (Notre Dame: University of Notre Dame, 1967), 152–68.

3   *God Has Many Names*, 14.

4   "A Pluralist View," 29.

5   *God Has Many Names*, 14.

6   Ibid.

7   Personal correspondence, May 16, 1990.

8   *God Has Many Names*, 14.

9   Ibid.

10   Michael Goulder and John Hick, *Why Believe In God?* (London: SCM, 1983), 40–1.

11   "A Pluralist View," 30.

12   "A Personal Note," 139.

13   *God Has Many Names*, 15.

14   "A Pluralist View," 30.

15   Ibid., 31.

16   *Faith and Knowledge: A Modern Introduction to the Problem of Religious Knowledge* (Ithaca, N.Y.: Cornell University Press) was published in 1957. In 1966, Hick produced a revised edition of *Faith and Knowledge* (Ithaca: Cornell University Press, 1966; reprint, London: Collins–Fontana, 1974). All citations from *Faith and Knowledge* will be from the original 1957 edition unless otherwise noted.

17   *Faith and Knowledge* (1974), viii.

18   *Revelation and Religion: Studies in the Theological Interpretation of Religious Types* (London: Nisbet, 1954), 41.

19   "A Pluralist View," 32.

20   Hick, *Problems of Religious Pluralism*, 2.

21   Ibid., 3; see also *Philosophy of Religion*, 1st ed., 77; on the controversy see "Assembly Will Rule in New Jersey Case," *Presbyterion Life* 15 (April 15, 1962): 30–31.

22   *Evil and the God of Love* (London: Macmillan, 1966; reprint, London: Collins–Fontana, 1968).

23   D'Costa, *Hick's Theology of Religions*, 12.

24   *Death and Eternal Life* (San Francisco: Harper and Row, Publishers, 1976).

25   Smith, *The Meaning and End of Religion: A New Approach to the Religious Traditions of Mankind* (New York: Mentor/New American Library, 1964 [1962]).

26   "Personal Note," 140.

27   "Christology at the Crossroads," in *Prospect for Theology: Essays in Honour of H. H. Farmer*, ed. F. G. Healey (London: Nisbet, 1966), 139.

28   Hick, *Christianity at the Centre* (London: SCM, 1968), 80–81.

29   "The Reconstruction of Christian Belief for Today and Tomorrow," *Theology* 73 (1970), 339–45, 399–405; *Arguments for the Existence of God* (London: Macmillan, 1970), 117–20; "Philosophy, Religions, and Human Unity," in *Philosophy: Theory and Practice*, ed. T. Mahadevan, Proceedings of the International Seminar on World Philosophy, Madras, December 7–17, 1970 (Madras: University of Madras, 1974), 462–77.

30   (Philadelphia: Westminster, 1974).

31   "The Copernican Revolution in Theology," in *God and the Universe of Faiths*, 120–32.

32   Ibid., 125.

33   *Death and Eternal Life*, 14.

34   Ibid., 16.

35   *Myth of God Incarnate* (Philadelphia: Westminster, 1977).

36   Ibid., 180.

37   *The Centre of Christianity*, 2nd ed. (London: SCM, 1977; New York: Harper & Row, 1978 [1968]), 8.

38   E.g., Hick, "Toward a Philosophy of Religious Pluralism," in *God Has Many Names*, 88–115.

39   See the essays comprising chapters 3, 5, and 6 in *God Has Many Names*; and, especially, "The Pluralistic Hypothesis," in *Interpretation of Religion*, 233–51.

40   *Interpretation of Religion*, 242.

41   *Interpretation of Religion*, xiv.

42   *God Has Many Names*, 9.

43   The published results of this trialogue are found in John Hick and Edmund Meltzer, eds., *Three Faiths—One God: A Jewish, Christian, Muslim Encounter* (Albany, NY: State University of New York Press, 1989).

44   Hick and Knitter, eds., *The Myth of Christian Uniqueness: Toward a Pluralistic Theology of Religions* (Maryknoll, N.Y.: Orbis, 1987), viii.

45   *Interpretation of Religion*, xv.

46   (Louisville, KY: Westminster/John Knox, 1993).

47   Ibid., 12.

48   See Hick's "A Pluralist View" and his responses to the other thinkers in *More than One Way?*, 29–59, 81–91, 124–28, 181–86, 246–50.

49   *God Has Many Names*, 14.

50   Ibid., 15.

51   Ibid., 121–22.

52   *Faith and Knowledge*, v.

53   Review of *Faith and Knowledge*, *Philosophical Review* 67 (1958): 407.

54   *Interpretation of Religion*, 172. See also Hick, "Religious Realism and Non–Realism," in *Disputed Questions in Theology and the Philosophy of Religion*, 3–16; Hick, "Transcendence and Truth," in *Religion without Transcendence?*, ed. D. Z. Phillips (New York: Macmillan, 1997), 41–59.

55   Ibid., 175.

56   *Faith and Knowledge*, 4, 6.

57   Ibid., 6.

58   Ibid., 13–15.

59   Ibid., 7.

60   See e.g., Kennick's review of *Faith and Knowledge*, 407–09.

61   Alston, "Realism and the Christian Faith," *International Journal for Philosophy of Religion* 38 (1995): 37–60.

62   *Faith and Knowledge*, 15.

63   Ibid., 18.

64   Ibid., 17.

65   Ibid., 21.

66   See ibid., 21–22.

67   See *Faith and Knowledge*, 134–63; also Hick, "Theology and Verification," *Theology Today* 17 (1960): 12–31.

68   Personal correspondence, August 26, 1990.

69   *Faith and Knowledge* (1974), viii.

70   *Faith and Knowledge*, 75.

71   *On Religion: Speeches to Its Cultured Despisers*, John Oman, trans. (New York: Harper, 1958), 39.

72   Hick, "Oman, John Wood," in *The Encyclopedia of Philosophy*, ed. Paul Edwards (New York: Macmillan, 1967), v–vi:537. On Oman see Stephen Bevans, *John Oman and His Doctrine of God* (Cambridge: Cambridge University Press, 1992); F. G. Healey, *Religion and Reality: The Theology of John Oman* (Edinburgh: Oliver & Boyd, 1965); F. R. Tennant, "John Wood Oman, 1860–1939," *Proceedings of the British Academy* 25 (1939): 333–38.

73   *Faith and Knowledge*, xix.

74   Ibid. See also Hick's introduction to the Association Press edition of Oman's *Grace and Personality* (New York: Association, 1961 [1919]), 5–10.

75   Oman, *The Natural and the Supernatural* (Cambridge: Cambridge University Press, 1931), 58, 175.

76   See ibid., 298–311.

77   Ibid., 72–3.

78   Hick, *Interpretation of Religion*, 124; see *Faith and Knowledge* (1974), 147, 157–62. For critical reflections on the specifics of Hick's claim see Terence Penelhum, "Reflections on the Ambiguity of the World," in *God, Truth and Reality*, 165–75.

79   *Faith and Knowledge*, xvi–vii; *Philosophy of Religion*, 1st ed., 30; Hick, ed., *The Existence of God* (London/New York: Macmillan, 1964), 18–19; *Interpretation of Religion*, 73–110, 122–24.

80   *Philosophy of Religion*, 1st ed., 47; *Interpretation of Religion*, 111–24.

81   *Philosophy of Religion*, 1st ed., 76.

82   *Existence of God*, 18; see also Hick, "Faith and Coercion," *Philosophy* 42 (1967): 273. For MacIntyre's argument, proffered in his earlier days as a Christian apologist, see his *Metaphysical Beliefs* (New York: Allenson, 1957), 197.

83   Ibid., xvi–vii.

84   *Faith and Knowledge* (1974), 121.

85   *Ibid.*, 111.

86   See "Religious Faith as Experiencing–as," in *Talk of God*, ed. G. N. A. Vesey (London: Macmillan, 1969), 20–35 (reprinted in *God and the Universe of Faiths*, 37–52); Hick, "Seeing–as and Religious Experience," in *Problems of Religious Pluralism*, 16–27.

87   *Faith and Knowledge*, 116; for the wider discussion see 109–33.

88   Ibid., 167–80.

89   Ibid., 177–91.

90   Ibid., 178.

91   *Natural and Supernatural*, 309; see the discussion at 306–11.

92   *Faith and Knowledge*, 179.

93   Ibid.; see also *Philosophy of Religion*, 1st ed., 70–3.

94   *Philosophy of Religion*, 1st ed., 70–7.

95   Ibid., 70; *God and the Universe of Faiths*, 50.

96   God and the Universe of Faiths, 51.

97   *Philosophy of Religion*, 1st ed., 72; also *Faith and Knowledge*, 109–10.

98   *Philosophy of Religion*, 1st ed., 70; *Faith and Knowledge*, 198f.

99   *God and the Universe of Faiths*, 50.

100   *Faith and Knowledge*, 190.

101   Ibid., 191.

102   Ibid., 210. More recently, see *Interpretation of Religion*, 210–30.

103   I originally made this claim in a 1992 essay, "John Hick's Theological Pilgrimage," 29. That same year, L. Philip Barnes published an article that came to the same conclusion; see Barnes, "Continuity and Development in John Hick's Theology," *Studies in Religion/ Sciences Religieuses* 21 (1992): 395–402. These observations on the continuity within Hick's thought render questionable Gerard Loughlin's claim that Hick has tried to create an artificial and unjustifiable sense of continuity between the quite disparate stages of his intellectual life; "Prefacing Pluralism: John Hick and the Mastery of Religion," *Modern Theology* 7 (1990): 29–55. Loughlin does not seem to be adequately aware of the underlying continuity, provided by the religious epistemology, that ties together the various stages of Hick's thought. In a response to Loughlin, Hick shows quite clearly that he is cognizant of both the discontinuities and continuities within his intellectual development. Among the continuities Hick notes are: "...the belief that religious experience is the living heart of religion; that this realm of experience authorizes us to believe in the reality of the Transcendent; that the religious meaning of life presupposes our present life is only a part of our total existence; that human awareness is always interpretive in character..."; Hick, "A Response to Gerard Loughlin," *Modern Theology* 7 (1990): 66.

104   *Faith and Knowledge*, v.

105   Ibid., 198.

106   Ibid.

107 Ibid., 198–99.
108 Ibid.
109 Ibid., 200.
110 "The Christology of D. M. Baillie," *Scottish Journal of Theology* 11 (1958): 4.
111 Ibid.
112 Ibid., 8, 11.
113 Ibid., 11.
114 "A Non–Substance Christology?," *Colgate–Rochester Divinity School Bulletin* (1959): 41–54; edited and reprinted as "Christology at the Crossroads."
115 "A Non–Substance Christology," 42.
116 Ibid.
117 Ibid., 43.
118 Ibid., 50.
119 Ibid., 44.
120 Ibid., 53–54.
121 Hick, *Problems of Religious Pluralism*, 2.
122 "Theology and Verification," 31.
123 *Evil and the God of Love*, 263, 283.
124 Ibid., 281.
125 Ibid.
126 Ibid., 377–81.
127 This paper, along with other contributions to the conference, was published as "Chairman's Retrospect: Sceptics and Believers," in *Faith and the Philosophers*, ed. J. Hick (New York: St. Martins, 1964).
128 Ibid., 245.
129 Ibid., 246–47.
130 "Christology at the Crossroads," 139.
131 D'Costa, *Hick's Theology of Religions*, 17.
132 See "Theology and Verification," 31; *Evil and the God of Love*, 377–81; *God Has Many Names*, 17.
133 *God Has Many Names*, 17.
134 Ibid., 18.
135 In his tracing of Hick's thought, D'Costa mentions only three of the four influences under discussion here; see *Hick's Theology of Religions*, 12–13. Specifically, he does not include the work of Smith, which I would want to highlight as well.
136 *Meaning and End of Religion*, 141.
137 Ibid. For Smith's pluralistic approach religion see Smith, *Towards a World Theology: Faith and the Comparative History of Religion* (Maryknoll, NY: Orbis, 1981; Edward J. Hughes, *Wilfred Cantwell Smith: A Theology for the World* (London: SCM, 1986); Kenneth Cragg, "Wilfred Cantwell Smith," in *Troubled by Truth: Life–Studies in Inter–Faith Concern* (Edinburgh: Pentland, 1992), ch. 13.
138 Smith, "A Human View of Truth," *Studies in Religion* 1 (1971): 6.
139 *Questions of Religious Truth* (New York: Scribner's Sons, 1967): 68.
140 For the classic statement from this school of thought see Lindbeck, *The Nature of Doctrine: Religion and Theology in a Postliberal Age* (Philadelphia: Westminster, 1984).

141   Smith, "Conflicting Truth–Claims: A Rejoinder," in *Truth and Dialogue in World Religions*, 158, 160.
142   *God Has Many Names*, 17–18.
143   "Personal Note," 141.
144   Published as "Theology's Central Problem," *Expository Times* 80 (1969): 228–32.
145   Ibid., 228.
146   "Theology's Central Problem," 231.
147   Ibid.
148   Ibid., 231–32.
149   *Christianity at the Centre*, 16.
150   Ibid., 9.
151   Ibid., 10–11.
152   On the incarnation see ibid., pp. 31–38; on the resurrection see pp. 47–49.
153   Ibid., 80–81.
154   Ibid., 38 (emphasis added).
155   *Evil and the God of Love*, 283–4; here Hick speaks of "the great creation–fall–redemption myth."
156   *Christianity at the Centre*, 42; see 43–46.
157   Ibid., 16; see especially pp. 31–40.
158   "Christology at the Crossroads," 166.
159   Ibid., 139.
160   *Christianity at the Centre*, 38.

3   The Pluralist Move: Hick's Early Model of Religious Pluralism

This chapter shall serve to chronicle Hick's earliest foray into the pluralist paradigm. Important sources of influence upon Hick's thought shall be summarized, and the contours of his early model shall be sketched. Finally, the theological ramifications of his pluralist move shall be explored by reviewing the Christological development it served to catalyze.

By 1970, John Hick had made a decisive, if embryonic, move to a pluralist paradigm with regard to his theology of religions. This shift is evident in several publications and conference papers that appeared in this year.[1] By 1973, with the publication of *God and the Universe of Faiths*, Hick offered a detailed explication of his early (pre-neo-Kantian) model of religious pluralism. At this point, a description of his early model, with an emphasis on its primary impetus and central pillars, is in order.

The Pluralist Catalyst: Hick's Religious Epistemology

As early as 1958, in a review of *Faith and Knowledge*, William Christian recognized the logical implications of Hick's religious epistemology: "The evidence also permits an atheistic interpretation, the author says—and also Spinoza's interpretation, *Therevada Buddhism's interpretation and others, I suppose.*"[2] These implications, which pointed toward the pluralist paradigm, eluded Hick for more than a decade. Finally, in a 1970 book-length treatment of the arguments for God's existence, Hick explicitly extended the logic of his religious epistemology beyond the borders of his own Christian tradition. In doing so, Hick sees himself as simply applying what he would eventually refer to as "the intellectual Golden Rule," which calls us to grant "to others a premise on which we rely ourselves."[3] In the course of defending a "rational theistic belief without proofs," one rooted in the experienced-based epistemology explicated in *Faith and Knowledge*, Hick exposes a problem that "qualifies and threatens to erode" his approach: namely, "the immense variety of the forms of religious experience, giving rise as they do to apparently incompatible beliefs."[4] Hick goes on to frame the issue in its clearest terms:

> since one could restate the argument [for the rationality of Christian theism]…from the point of view of many different religions, with their different forms of religious experience and belief, the question arises whether the argument does not prove too much. In establishing the rationality of the Judaic-Christian theist's belief in the reality of God, must it not also and equally establish the rationality of the Buddhist's belief, arising out of *his* own coercive religious experience, and likewise of Hindu belief and of Islamic belief, and so on? We need, I think, have no hesitation in accepting this implication.[5]

Hick is hardly alone in seeing the troubling implications of religious diversity for an *experience-oriented* religious epistemology. The grandfather of this tradition, Schleiermacher himself, while he would always (inconsistently?) hold to the "exclusive superiority of Christianity," nonetheless recognized the implications that his theory held for the wider religious life of humanity. For it was hardly Christianity alone that offered a 'sense of the Infinite.' Once Schleiermacher had concluded that "the true nature of religion is neither this idea [i.e., monotheism] nor any other, but immediate consciousness of the Deity as He is found in ourselves and in the world," the rudimentary pluralist implications could not be far behind.[6] He is clear that his thesis "presupposed the plurality of religion," and he is quick to correct those who think otherwise:

> Would you then understand [religion] as it really exists and displays itself, would you comprehend it as an endlessly progressive work of the Spirit that reveals Himself in all human history, you must abandon the vain and foolish wish that there should only be one religion; you must lay aside all repugnance to its multiplicity….[7]

Schleiermacher explains the reason for his insistence upon the need for religious diversity:

> Why have I assumed that religion can only be given fully in a great multitude of forms of the utmost definiteness? Only on grounds that naturally follow from what has been said of the nature of religion. The whole of religion is nothing but the sum of all relations of man to God, apprehended in all the possible ways in which any man can be immediately conscious in his life. In this sense there is but one religion…[y]et all men will not by any means apprehend [it] in the same way, but quite differently.[8]

While the differences are very significant, the general 'family resemblance' of Schleiermacher's statement here to Hick's pluralist assumptions is plain. As noted above, Schleiermacher went on practically to undercut the force of his argument by asserting the superior religious intuition of Christianity. However, this does not vitiate the fact that his experience-oriented theory of religion led him to become, in Richard Crouter's words, "a pioneer in the development of the historical and theological understanding of the relation between world religions."[9]

In our century, especially in the last few decades, and often in critique of an 'Enlightenment,' 'Modernist' mentality, a growing number of philosophers of religion have begun to explore various religious epistemologies that share strong similarities with Hick's. Among these is the interesting and controversial 'Reformed' epistemology. (I will be focusing here on the interesting similarities between Reformed epistemology and Hick's own experience-oriented religious epistemology. However, there are equally important differences between these two perspectives. While I will be suggesting that both of these religious epistemologies can be heuristically described as 'experience oriented,' I do not intend to imply that each ground their theories on experience in the same way, or even construe experience in the same way.) Several of North America's leading philosophers of religion, including Alvin Plantinga, William Alston, and Nicholas Wolterstorff, have contributed to its rise in recent years.[10] Reformed epistemology holds that belief in God's existence can be a "properly basic" belief. As such, it is rational to believe in God without having to justify this belief through an appeal to a more basic 'foundation' of knowledge.

The Reformed perspective on religious epistemology has important similarities with Hick's view, as noted by Hick himself.[11] In commenting upon Plantinga's claim that the experience of 'seeing a tree' is generally a good ground for the properly basic belief that one is seeing a tree, Hick has stated that "[i]f religious experience is recognized as the parallel justifying ground of religious beliefs, then Plantinga's argument and [mine] virtually coincide."[12] It should be noted that Plantinga himself does not tend to use the term 'religious experience' in the course of his argument. Hick admits this, but goes on to assert that the types of situations that Plantinga offers as grounds for his notion of the 'proper basicality' of belief in God's existence are, in fact, "occasions of religious experience."[13] Caroline Franks Davis comes to a similar conclusion: though Plantinga's argument is not generally considered an argument from religious experience, it actually is one, for belief in God turns out to be properly basic only because it is generated by experiences—religious experiences—which there is no good reason to think delusive."[14] Hick has also drawn parallels between his claim and Richard Swinburne's 'principle of credulity,' which states that "what one seems to perceive is probably so. How things seem to be is good grounds for a belief about how things are."[15]

Recently, Alston has produced a work on religious epistemology that, as Hick has pointed out, shares some similarities with Hick's perspective, particularly the claims that the structure of experience is similar regardless of the nature of the object, and that one of the primary grounds for religious belief is its rooting in religious experience (he prefers the phrase "perception of God" over "experience of God").[16] In fact, Alston acknowledges that his ideas regarding human perception of God were "strongly influenced by John Hick's treatment in *Faith and Knowledge*."[17] With Hick, those who hold to a Reformed (or other experience-oriented) religious epistemology usually acknowledge that the *fact* of religious diversity—coupled with the above-mentioned principle—quickly becomes a formidable *problem* of religious diversity. Alston, for instance, expresses the problem in terms not unlike Hick's:

> The existence of a plurality of religious communities, each with its own belief system that is incompatible in various respects with each of the others, poses a serious and well advertised problem for the claims of each community. After all, it looks as if Moslems, Hindus, and Buddhists have grounds of the same general sort (revelation, religious experience, miracles, authority, etc.) as my fellow Christians and I have for the truth of our respective systems of doctrine.... [W]hy should I suppose that we are right and they are wrong?[18]

The fact of religious diversity raises both theological and epistemological questions for any religious epistemology. However, as William Hasker has noted, it seems to be the case that religious diversity poses "the most serious" problem to be faced by an experience-oriented religious epistemology, such as Hick's.[19] The heart of the problem is this: If religious experience provides a reliable and solid grounding—for Hick, the *only* reliable and solid grounding—for human religious beliefs, then one would prima facie expect that all human religious experience would be roughly similar in nature.[20] Clearly, however, such is not the case. Instead, one finds a bewildering array of religious ultimates, traditions, and doctrines. At the heart of the problem of conflicting interreligious beliefs (henceforth referred to as the 'conflicting truth claims' problem) is the 'conflicting conceptions of the divine' problem: some religions are based upon experiences of the divine that correlate to a personal theistic God (e.g., Judaism, Christianity, Islam), while others experience an impersonal, nontheistic Absolute or Force (e.g., Advaita Vedanta Hinduism, Therevada Buddhism, Taoism). Thus it is this problem of conflicting interreligious claims (not to mention conflicting intrareligious claims) that calls into question the assertion that religious experience provides a reliable basis for veridical religious knowledge.

One can sense the import of the conflicting claims problem more readily by comparing it with another realm of epistemology. One could argue that human *sensory* experience is, in many ways, roughly similar across history and cultures. In fact, when someone—or even a group of people—claim to have experienced something in the physical realm that is beyond the normal range of experience for the rest of humanity, their claims are usually viewed with suspicion, if not out right disbelief (i.e., 'hallucinations,' etc.). It is the generally shared commonality and (at least theoretical) public verifiability of our sense perception that upholds its claim to deliver reliable knowledge. In turning to the question of human religious experience, it is just such a generally shared commonality that is lacking. Rather, conflicting claims abound. Faced with the fact of religious diversity and its conflicting claims, those, like Hick, who hold to a religious epistemology that is primarily rooted in religious experience seem forced to conclude with Hasker that "these conflicting claims furnish at least a prima facie defeater of the claims of reliability" for religious experience.[21] Thus, Hick has rightly perceived the magnitude of the problem. It remains to trace his search for a solution.

In *Arguments for the Existence of God*, Hick follows his statement of the religious diversity problematic by mapping out the various conclusions that one could draw from it. He proposes that one is first faced with two possible options: either the various human claims of religious experience are illusory or they are not. That is, the first response that one could give to the challenge of the conflicting claims problem is that *no* purported 'religious experience' is delivering reliable information about actual (spiritual) states of affairs. Such a view would hold that so-called religious experience can be entirely explained by—and thus reduced to—purely human elements (sociological, psychological, physiological, etc.). This naturalistic option challenges Hick's perennial concern to defend a realist interpretation of human religious experience. In Hick's words, the question being raised here is that of the "ultimate public verifiability and falsifiability of religious faiths."[22] He concludes that, for the

Christian theist, along with religious realists generally, the choice is clear. The eventual and ultimate verifiability of religious faith (i.e., eschatological verification) must be affirmed. Assisted by the realist hope of an eschatological experience that will verify one's religious belief, it becomes "as rational for the religious man to treat his experience of God as veridical as it is for him and others to treat their experience of the physical world as veridical."[23] Thus, Hick's notion of eschatological verification survives the transition into the pluralist universe, and continues to provide a defense against the threat of naturalistic interpretations of religion. However, this is not the end of the story. Like his religious epistemology which produced the problem, this philosophically-based apologetic for religious realism can also be applied to a wide variety of religious persons within the various religious traditions. It is time to face the religious diversity problematic head on.

This leads the Christian theist (i.e., religious realist) to a "second fork in the road," and another dilemma. In Hick's words: "Along one path we affirm the ultimate compatibility of the plurality of religious faiths, whilst along the other path we deny this."[24] Here Hick chooses the former path—thus making the crucial shift to the pluralist paradigm—and so reaches this conclusion in the final paragraph of the book:

> the different forms of religious experience, giving rise to the different religions of the world, are properly to be understood as experiences of different aspects of one immensely complex and rich divine reality. If this is so, the beliefs of the different religions will be related to a larger truth as the experiences which gave rise to those beliefs are related to a larger reality....[W]e are led to postulate a divine reality of which the different religions of the world represent different partial experiences and partial knowledge. This latter possibility remains, however, to be adequately developed and examined.[25]

Hick lost no time in doing just that. The remainder of this chapter will be devoted to delineating the original supporting argumentation for his pluralist move. However, before we proceed to this next step, two final observations deserve attention.

First, it is important to note that this general thesis, offered in a few brief paragraphs at the end of *Arguments for the Existence of God*, has continued to function as the ever-present, though not always explicit, cornerstone for Hick's religious pluralism throughout the last three decades. It is driven by Hick's original religious epistemology, and moves decisively, via the two-stage argu-

ment, from the recognition of the *fact* of diverse religious experience to a pluralist *interpretation* of that diversity. Hick has offered a variety of supporting
arguments for this foundational thesis over the years. Remarkably few of them
have remained untouched over time. Throughout the last three decades Hick
has modified many of his original arguments, and completely jettisoned others. However, despite the often radical modifications to his supporting structure, this basic foundation of, and original impetus for, Hick's religious
pluralism has remained essentially unchanged.

Eighteen years later, in a new Preface to the 1988 reissue of *Faith and Knowledge*, Hick notes that his original epistemology "remains foundational" for his
more recent books. He clearly states that his "subsequent writings in the philosophy of religion," the bulk of which have been apologetic works for the
pluralist paradigm, "have proceeded in a natural trajectory from the epistemology of *Faith and Knowledge*."[26] In his 1989 *An Interpretation of Religion*,
Hick justifies the "need for such a [pluralist] hypothesis" by offering essentially
the same two-stage argument that he did in the 1970 volume.[27] Even more
recently, in both article and essay form, Hick has continued to present this
foundational thesis with little modification.[28] His understanding of the problem, though nuanced, remains essentially unchanged:

> Clearly this basic principle [i.e., that religious experience can properly ground re-
> ligious belief] has to be applied, not only to Christian but also to other forms of
> theistic experience; and indeed not only to theistic but also to non-theistic forms
> of religious experience. Perhaps some (Christian) theologians feel that they can
> properly exclude from attention information concerning the wider religious life of
> humanity....But a philosopher of religion has to take account, in principle, of reli-
> gion in all its forms throughout the world....Within the philosophy of religion,
> then, we find that by solving one major problem—namely, how to justify belief in
> God—we have brought to light another equally major problem, that posed by the
> fact of religious plurality.[29]

His solution offers the same basic two-step response: he continues to defend the religious realism option in the face of the naturalistic challenge;[30] and
he continues to champion the pluralist paradigm, as opposed to an exclusivistic
or inclusivistic vision of religious truth, as the most attractive solution to the
conflicting claims problem. Indeed, on this last count, his most recent statements evince little change, beyond further sophistication and nuance, from
his original proposal:

we postulate the transcendent divine Reality which lies…beyond our networks of human concepts; which is the ground of all existence and the source of all salvific power; which is conceptualized in a variety of ways…; which is accordingly humanly experienced in correspondingly different ways; and which is responded to in correspondingly different forms of religious life.[31]

Over the years, critics of Hick's pluralist hypothesis have suggested a variety of phenomena as the driving core of Hick's thought. The above analysis suggests that the answer to this question is clear. It is in this thought complex, called into existence by the implications that arise from the juxtaposition of the fact of religious diversity with his *experience-oriented religious epistemology*, that we find the originating impetus and unchanging conceptual core of Hick's religious pluralism.[32]

A second observation is also worth noting. It is simply this: While Hick's religious epistemology, and others like it, do appear to contain an inherent pluralist tendency, there are other logical options. In two recent articles, Hick presents his case by contrasting it with the views of several other philosophers of religion who have entertained similar approaches to religious epistemology.[33] Specifically, he has in mind the work of such thinkers as Terence Penelhum, William Wainwright, and especially Alston and Plantinga.[34] Hick notes that each of them would tend to share with him a "basic principle" of religious epistemology which states that "as our experience of the physical world properly gives rise to our belief in its existence, so experience of God's presence can properly give rise to belief in the reality of God."[35] (It should be noted that, in making this claim, Hick does not ignore the important differences between sense and religious experience, differences that raise questions for any easy parallel between these two modes of knowing. In conjunction with such considerations, Hick suggests that, especially when dealing with religious experience, one must talk of "*degrees* of 'well-groundedness' or of 'justifiedness,' depending on the strength or weakness and the coherence-and-persistence or fleetingness, of the experience that grounds the belief.")[36] With Hick, as noted above, they also recognize the problem that religious diversity poses for them. However, unlike Hick, they are not convinced that this problem leads logically and inexorably to an adoption of a pluralist interpretation of these facts.[37] Hasker, for example, delineates four different conclusions that, faced with Hick's problem, one could come to. Three of these avoid pluralist implications.[38] (One might cite, for example, James Beilby's proposal—building on the work of Plantinga—that we recognize a distinction between 'rationality' and 'warrant,' wherein "rationality alone is a necessary but not sufficient condition for warrant." Thus, while anyone may be able to justifiably claim that their religious experience is a legitimate basis for counting their religious belief as 'rational,' this would not necessarily mean that this same belief is 'warranted.' Rather, in seeking warrant one would be searching for "that elusive quality or quantity which adjudicates between competing properly basic beliefs.")[39] Hick, of course, has his specific reasons for choosing the pluralist path, and it is to an analysis of these reasons and arguments that we now turn. But it is important to recognize that Hick's choice was not inevitable, even given the logical tendency toward a pluralist drift implicit within his religious epistemology.[40]

Supporting Arguments of Hick's Early Pluralist Model: Theological Support

It is clear that the driving impetus behind Hick's pluralism has always been of a philosophical type, namely his experience-based religious epistemology. The arguments that Hick has used to support this model over the years are various and often evolving. One can categorize the most important supporting arguments for his early model under two rubrics: theological and phenomenological. It is to an examination of these that we now turn.

The 'God of Universal Love' Argument

As noted above, Hick's line of thought toward pluralism culminated with a final dilemma. The religious realist, confronted with the fact of religious diversity, was forced to choose between two options: "Along one path we affirm the ultimate compatibility of the plurality of religious faiths, whilst along the other path we deny this."[41] Upon explicating the latter option, a form of exclusivism, Hick rejects it—and for what he judges to be a decidedly 'Christian' consideration. At this point, Hick introduces an interesting and specifically Christian *theological* reason for choosing the pluralist option, one that would become a primary weapon in his apologetic arsenal for over a decade. Hick makes the argument that the Christian God—the God whose very nature is agape-love—could never support an exclusivistic response toward the other religions. In Hick's words:

> There is however a specifically Christian reason for abandoning [an exclusivist] stance. This is that belief in the redeeming love of God for all his human creatures makes it incredible that the divine activity in relation to mankind should have

been confined to those within the reach of the influence of the Christian revelation....Thus the doctrine that there is no salvation outside historic Christianity would in effect deny the universal love and redeeming activity of God.[42]

The ubiquity of this argument (henceforth referred to as the 'God of universal love' argument) in Hick's early pluralist apologetic is noteworthy.[43] In fact, almost immediately one finds Hick presenting the 'God of universal love' argument as the primary defense of the pluralist paradigm. For example, in another 1970 article on this same topic, Hick never explicitly refers to his religious epistemology as the basis for a pluralist view. Rather, he presents as his "starting point" the claim that if "God is the God of the whole world, *we must presume* that the whole religious life of mankind is part of a continuous and universal human relationship to him."[44]

In his famous essay, "The Copernican Revolution in Theology," Hick sets up the 'God of universal love' argument as the primary logical *and moral* impetus behind the call to a pluralist perspective:

> We say as Christians that God is the God of universal love....But we also say, traditionally, that the only way to salvation is the Christian way....Can we then accept the conclusion that the God of love who seeks to save all mankind has nevertheless ordained that men must be saved in such a way that only a small minority can in fact receive this salvation? It is the weight of *this moral contradiction* that has driven Christian thinkers in modern times to explore other ways of understanding the human religious situation.[45]

The rhetorical power of this argument is hard to miss. By calling the traditional Christian view that salvation comes through Jesus Christ/Christianity alone into question, Hick presents the pluralist option as the obvious path toward both theological integrity and the moral high ground. Similar moral charges, such as 'intolerance,' 'imperialism,' and other terms that conjure images of self-absorbed, narrow-minded parochialism, have become commonplace among the various pluralist critiques of the more traditional perspectives on religious diversity. The pressing questions of whether and when such charges can be made to stick—and, ironically, whether the various models of pluralism can, themselves, avoid similar charges—will be addressed in another context.[46] At this time, it is simply to be emphasized that Hick's early pluralist apologetic is strongly driven by the theological and moral implications that he draws from the 'God of universal love' argument.

It is, in fact, under the aegis of this argument that Hick announces his 'Copernican Revolution' to the pluralist paradigm.[47] With the help of this astronomical heuristic, Hick tags any traditional exclusivist—or what he referred to at this time as "ecclesiocentric"—approach to religious diversity with the label "Ptolemaic theology." The ecclesiocentric approach is epitomized for Hick in the slogan *extra ecclesiam nulla salus* (i.e., "outside the church, or outside Christianity, there is no salvation").[48] Those who attempted to modify traditional ecclesiocentrism by adopting one of the many forms of inclusivism (Hick notes at least eight different models in his 'Copernican' essay) are viewed as simply doing (ultimately fruitless) epicyclic patch jobs upon the floundering Ptolemaic craft.[49] Rather, the Copernican Revolution in theology, for which Hick functions as a religious ambassador, calls for

> a shift from the dogma that Christianity [or any other religious tradition] is at the centre [of the 'universe of faiths'] to the realization that it is *God* who is at the centre, and that all religions of mankind, including our own, serve and revolve around him.[50]

Hick was to make liberal use of this Copernican analogy in a variety of writings up until 1984, roughly the same time when he generally stopped using the 'God of universal love' analogy.[51]

Supporting Arguments of Hick's Early Pluralist Model: Phenomenological Support

Hick For and Against W. C. Smith's Thesis

Hick notes that Wilfred Cantwell Smith's theory of religion, as presented in the 1962 *The Meaning and End of Religion*, proved to be a "valuable clue" to his own understanding of the world's religious situation.[52] In the early years, Hick's standard phenomenological argument for pluralism included an explicit appeal to Smith's theory.[53] Smith's thesis was especially helpful for Hick in pointing toward a new (pluralist) paradigm for thinking about the relationship between the 'religions,' one that emphasized an essential unity in spite of the obvious attendant diversity. In connection with the aforementioned 1970 conference on conflicting religious truth claims, Hick produced an essay entitled "The Outcome: Dialogue into Truth." Here, one can recognize the significance of Smith's theory for Hick's own budding pluralism. With an appeal to Smith,

Hick offers a critique of the modern Western "invention" of 'religion'—rooted in the "illicit reification, the turning of good adjectives into bad substantives," to which the Western mind is prone—with its conceptualization of the world's 'religions' as "mutually exclusive entities" that "see themselves and each other as rival ideological communities."[54] Instead, Hick aligned himself with Smith in proposing that the religious life of humanity be viewed as "a dynamic continuum within which certain major disturbances have from time to time set up new fields of force."[55] These major disturbances within the unified human religious continuum are those "creative moments" in human history that mark the:

> intersections of divine grace, divine initiative, divine truth, with human faith, human response, human enlightenment. They have made their impact upon the stream of human life so as to affect the development of cultures; and Christianity, Islam, Hinduism, Buddhism are among the resulting historical-cultural phenomena.[56]

From Smith's theory of religion, Hick draws the logical pluralist conclusion:

> This means that it is not appropriate to speak of a religion as being true or false, any more than it is to speak of a civilization as being true or false. For the religions, in the sense of distinguishable religio-cultural streams within man's history, are expressions of the diversities of human types and temperaments and thought forms.[57]

A decade later, in a moment of self-reflection, Hick would summarize the import of Smith's thesis for his pluralist vision:

> [According to Smith we] ought to think of the religious life of mankind as a continuum within which the faith-life of individuals is conditioned by one or other of the different streams of cumulative tradition. From this point of view it is not appropriate to ask, Which is the true religion? For a true relationship to God may occur in the lives of people in each of the great religious traditions. With the problem in its older insoluble form having thus been dismantled, it was possible to develop...the idea of a "Copernican Revolution" in our theology of religions.[58]

One should not read too much into the lack of extensive mention of Smith in Hick's more recent phenomenological argument. For example, although Hick has dropped explicit appeal to Smith at the point at which in his 'history of religion' argument (see below) one had come to expect it, he continues to make it clear that his proposal has been "deeply influenced" by Smith's work.[59] At an appropriate point in *An Interpretation of Religion*, Hick includes an endnote that directs the reader to Smith's work in regard to "the unity of human religious history."[60]

It is important to note that, for all of his appreciation of Smith's thesis over the years, Hick was unable to adopt it wholesale. For Hick, the most significant problem with the theory involved Smith's understanding of religious truth and the implications it held for the question of conflicting inter religious truth-claims and attendant issues of religious criteriology. First, Hick remained, at this point, too much the analytical philosopher to adopt a strong personalist definition of truth. In the midst of sincere gratitude for Smith's general approach, Hick warns of "an unnecessary and confusing divorce between personalistic and propositional truth."[61] Hick was willing to endorse the idea of *supplementing* a purely propositional view of truth with a personalist/pragmatic element. However, to radically diminish the importance of—let alone replace—the former was, to Hick, entirely unjustified. It is worth noting Hick's corrective remarks to Smith in this regard: "I hope that Cantwell Smith is not saying that the truth of a 'religion' or of faith consists simply in the fact that it 'works', producing good fruits in human life, even if its basic associated beliefs should be false."[62] Interestingly, Hick's pluralist model would eventually come to hinge upon a position not unlike the one that he here chides Smith for entertaining.

Hick recognized that his decision to reject Smith's view, in order to retain a significant role for the notion of propositional religious truth, left the conflicting religious truth claims problematic fully intact. Upon appealing to the radically conflictive conceptions of ultimate reality represented by the theistic traditions' notion of a personal God and the nontheistic traditions' concept of an impersonal Absolute, Hick concludes as follows:

> But how can it be true both that there is and that there is not a personal God…? This is the problem of the conflicting, or at least apparently conflicting truth claims of different religions; and this problem is not dissolved by Wilfred Cantwell Smith's otherwise extremely illuminating and valuable new way of seeing religion and religions.[63]

Hick's concrete illustration here is also worth noting, given the role that the 'conflicting conceptions of the divine' problematic—particularly in the form of the personal vs. impersonal ultimate reality question—was to play in the future development of his thought. Ironically, Hick's pluralist model would eventually be built around a philosophical mechanism devoted to demonstrating just how it can be true that there both is and is not a personal God.

A final problem of Smith's theory for Hick is that it left no real means of assessing morally intolerable forms of religion, or out right superstition, as religiously inappropriate. He noted that, given a personalist view of truth, "Nazism was a true faith, as is warlock worship, and faith in witchcraft and in astrology."[64] This resistance to a complete religious relativism has remained a hallmark of Hick's approach to religious diversity up to today.

And so, along with Hick's great appreciation for Smith's thought over the years, there have always remained enough differences between the two to keep him from simply affirming Smith's model in its entirety.[65]

The History of Religion: Its Nature and Development

Hick garnered another line of supporting argument for his pluralist shift from an analysis of the nature and history of religion. In short, he argues that the pluralist interpretation of religions "makes sense of the history of religions."[66] According to Hick's analysis, amidst the complex, multifarious "facts" and theories generated by the modern study of religious phenomena, two "broad interpretive concepts" have arisen that are safely beyond the bounds of controversy. First, there is the observation that humans beings are, generally speaking, incurably religious animals. The second indisputable observation involves the rise of what Hick (following Karl Jaspers and others) would eventually come to call the golden "axial age" of religion.[67] This near-millennium of religious history ran roughly from 800 to 200 BCE, and marked a radical shift in human religious experience.[68]

According to this schema, pre-axial religion (which Hick also refers to throughout the years as 'natural,' 'primitive,' or 'archaic' religion) was primarily concerned with "the preservation of cosmic and social order."[69] In terms of development, the earliest stages of pre-axial religion focused upon *mana*-empowered sacred objects, multiple spirits requiring appeasement, and a vision of the divine as "a plurality of quasi-animal forces."[70] In locations such as Mesopotamia and the Indus valley, the eventual merger of tribes into larger groups brought a new stage of pre-axial religious life. Here, hierarchies of gods emerged, with an emphasis on various national deities within complex polytheistic systems. Throughout this period, a cyclical view of time and history reigned. Hick summarizes his understanding of pre-axial religion thus:

> So far, the whole development can be described as the growth of natural religion. That is to say, primal spirit worship expressing man's fears of the unknown forces of nature, and later the worship of regional deities…represent the extent of man's religious life prior to any special intrusions of divine revelation or illumination.[71]

Such religions, including the 'primal' religions that continue to exist in various forms today, and the now-deceased priestly religions of the ancient world, served to stabilize the life of the community, presenting it with a common worldview around which its people could coalesce. This type of religion was especially suited for a people whose corporate identity overshadowed the sense of the 'individual.' As human life evolved, however, "the conditions gradually formed for the emergence of individuality."[72] Humanity was ready for a new type of religious experience suited to their new level of consciousness.

With the first millennium B.C.E., the coming of the axial age produced a startling number of religious leaders. It was during this period that the bulk of what we know today as the 'world religions' had their beginnings. In China Confucianism and Taoism were born. In India Buddhism and Jainism came to light, while the Upanishads and probably the Bhagavad Gita—the post-Vedic Hindu scriptures—were produced. In Persia Zoroastrianism flourished. Greece played host to a wide variety of 'lovers of wisdom,' including Pythagoras, Socrates, Plato, and Aristotle. Israel saw the rise of its great Hebrew prophets. Even Christianity and Islam, while actually arising after the axial age, both trace their origins back to the Semitic religious tradition. The distinctive hallmark and unifying characteristic of the various religious traditions that arose during this time can be described in terms of a common soteriological orientation—a "radical transformation of the human situation"—that one does not generally find in the pre-axial religions.[73] Hick would eventually come to define this common soteriological structure as "the transformation of human existence from self-centeredness to Reality-centeredness."[74] And so, Hick summarizes the crucial difference between pre- and post-axial religion:

> Whereas in the various forms of pre-axial religion there has always been a realistic awareness of suffering, insecurity and mortality, in the great post-axial traditions these are now thought of in terms implying a contrast with something fundamentally different—whether that different state lies in the future (as also perhaps in the remote past) or in the unrealized depths of the present moment.... [In any case,] the ultimate, the divine, the Real, is that which makes possible a transformation of our present existence.[75]

The import of this interpretation of the history and development of religion for Hick's pluralist enterprise is clear. It provides a reading of the phenomenological data that would support the pluralist thesis that one and the same divine Reality is at work in the major (post-axial) world religions, a divine Reality that, although differently conceived and experienced in the various traditions (due to their cultural variations), reveals Its singular presence in all of them by effecting the same soteriological transformation in each case.

(It is clear that for Karl Jaspers the phenomena connected to the axial period provide an empirical basis for the unity of humanity. In Jaspers' words, the mystery of the axial age appears to be "the manifestation of some profound common element, the one primal source of humanity." In the course of considering the question of what "caused" the phenomena of the axial period, Jaspers eliminates a variety of possible responses, only to conclude that "[n]o one can adequately comprehend what occurred here and became the axis of world history!...It might seem as though I were out to prove direct intervention on the part of the deity, without saying so openly." However, Jaspers finally refuses to provide even this answer, choosing instead to withhold judgment and live with the mystery at present.)[76] The rise of the multiple religious traditions which characterize the axial age, united—in spite of all their diversity—by a generally similar salvific vision, is presented by Hick as being far too similar a series of phenomena to be unrelated. Hick's apparent sense of the persuasive force of this argument is noteworthy. It has appeared in many of his pluralist apologetic works from 1970 to the present. It is thus one of the few early supporting arguments that have survived virtually unchanged in substance over time. Given its importance to Hick's pluralist paradigm, several related matters deserve discussion at this point.

Excursus: The Future of Religion

Given Hick's scenario of religious history, the amazing rate of globalization, and the attendant possibility of a potential future cultural unity (relatively speaking), the question naturally arises as to how this religious development will eventually culminate. This question has been a matter of conjecture for Hick for years. Already by 1968, he entertained the hope that "a common attitude and approach to the Divine will also be possible."[77] Early on in his pluralist musings, Hick's optimism ran high with regard to the possibility of an eventual convergence of the world's religious traditions. In 1970, Hick writes:

> However, now that, in the 'one world' of today, the religious traditions are consciously interacting with each other in mutual observation and in inter-faith dialogue, it is possible that their future developments may be on gradually converging courses....The future I am thinking of is accordingly one in which what we now call different religions will constitute the past history of different emphases and variations within something that it need not be too misleading to call *a single world religion*....I do not mean that all religious men will think alike, or worship in the same way, or experience the divine identically....Thus we may expect the different world faiths to con-

tinue as religious cultural phenomena, though phenomena that are increasingly interpenetrating one another. The relation between them will then be somewhat like that now obtaining between the *different denominations* of Christianity.[78]

In this same essay, Hick writes of "the historical inevitability of the plurality of religions in the past, and its non-inevitability in the future."[79] Hick's vision is not unlike that of the protopluralist, William Ernest Hocking, who, in the 1950s, predicted that the forces at work in the modern world would eventually "promote the silent *rapprochement* of the great faiths, without canceling the differences in historic rootage." Hocking continues:

> The time is ripe for that radical reconception…whereby the concept of the Christ is extended to include that unbound Spirit who stands and has stood at the door of every man, and who, in various guises, still appears to him who opens.…This reconception would involve putting away an inherently noble but limiting type of Only-Way Christianity.…Retaining the symbols of their historic pieties, the great faiths will grow in their awareness of a unity more significant than the remaining differences.[80]

Hick has long maintained an optimistic hope of a future 'growing together' of the religions.[81] However, since the early 1980s, his hopes for such a convergence appear to have dimmed. Since then, at the place in his now familiar argument where one had come to expect the expression of this hope—that is, following his explication of the axial-age phenomenon—it begins to be noticeably absent.[82] In his 1989 *An Interpretation of Religion*, Hick ends with a short Epilogue entitled "The Future." Hick begins with his observation of the "marked growth in the pluralistic outlook"—a perspective that Hick believes will "in due course" come to be held by "most educated Christians."[83] However, he goes on to note the "powerful opposite trend" at work in our world, one which manifests itself in the "us against them" attitude that characterizes "religious fundamentalism and political nationalism."[84] Within the Christian church these two forces have been identified by Hick as the "two Christianities": a traditional, "conservative" Christianity and an "experimental," liberal Christianity.[85] When it comes time to prognosticate upon the future religious landscape one can detect a dampening of Hick's former vision of future harmony:

> But if a world ecumenism does increasingly develop during the coming decades and generations this will not entail an eventual single world religion. The religious life of humanity will no doubt continue to be lived within the existing traditions, though with less and less emphasis upon their mutually exclusive claims.[86]

Excursus: Hick and the Status of 'African Primal Religion'—A Fly in the Axial Ointment?

Another point of related interest involves the placement of African primal religion within Hick's pre- vs. post-axial schema. One would expect to see it placed firmly, by Hick, among the other forms of pre-axial 'archaic' religion. In fact, prior to 1980, Hick's listings of the 'great world faiths' of the axial age—including Hinduism, Buddhism, Islam, and the Judeo-Christian complex[87]—never include African primal religion, which, rather, clearly fits his description of pre-axial religious life. By 1980, however, Hick states that, alongside the post-axial traditions, "there also flows the 'primal' religious life of Africa as, arguably, another major world faith."[88] By the mid-1980s, even this hesitancy was removed in Hick's mind. He now writes of "the great religious traditions of the world—Christianity, Buddhism, Islam, Hinduism, Taoism, African primal religion—as representing different awarenesses of and different responses to a divine Reality."[89] In his most recent book, *A Christian Theology of Religions*, Hick has even introduced a new term in connection with "African primal and native American religion": "extra-axial religion."[90]

It seems that African primal religion is now to be categorized as something other than merely pre-axial (i.e., "extra-axial"?) and is, along with the other post-axial religious traditions, now described as an "awareness" of the Real (i.e., as a form of revealed religion as opposed to what Hick has called purely 'natural' religion?). This juxtaposition of African primal religion with the post-axial faiths is hardly an incidental adjustment. It serves to raise the question of the very viability of the purported distinction between pre- and post-axial religion—a distinction that has long functioned as a central element of Hick's pluralist apologetic. To the degree that Hick's clear schema of religious development, dependent as it is on the axial divide, is muddied in this way, it would appear that its former apologetic value is correspondingly diminished. It may be that Hick's noble desire to grant a major living religious tradition—namely African primal religion, and, one would suppose, the many variant religious movements it has spawned (e.g., the Afro-Caribbean religions)—equal recognition and status alongside the great 'post-axial' faiths has ultimately served to weaken a long-standing pillar within his defense of the pluralist paradigm.

The 'Genetic Relativity' of Religion

A third and final matter related to the overall phenomenological evidence offered by Hick in support of pluralism is the concept of what Hick has referred to as the "genetic and environmental relativity" of religion.[91] This principle is rooted in the observation that one's membership within one of the world's religions is generally a factor of *parentage* and *birth place*. A boy born in Iran will most likely become a Muslim; a girl raised in a Hindu family in India will most likely adhere to Hinduism. Hick suggests that any theory of religious diversity that cannot make sense of this apparent arbitrariness of one's "religious ethnicity"—and in the process provide a way of avoiding "genetic confessionalism"—is inadequate.[92] Hick's argument here hinges upon attaching moral implications to this phenomenological observation—namely a notion of divine fairness. The 'genetic relativity' of religions really poses a problem only if it is assumed (1) that there is only one true and saving religion, (2) that those outside of that true religion, through no choosing of their own, are salvifically doomed, and (3) that there is one loving divine Reality who wants to be in relation with all humans, and so would never have set things up in such an arbitrary fashion. It is important to note that there are other resources for alleviating this potential problem beyond the pluralist paradigm. Various forms of inclusivism, for instance, have been proposed as solutions to this very problem.[93]

The 'Conflicting Truth Claims' Problematic: Hick's Early Response to the Perennial Pluralist Bane

As noted earlier in this study, every pluralist model must, in some way, speak to what is no doubt the most pressing conceptual problem for this paradigm: the 'conflicting truth claims' problem. It is to Hick's credit that he has always taken very seriously this challenge to his pluralist enterprise. Even prior to his pluralist move, Hick was well aware that the most daunting challenge to overcome would be the attempt to reconcile the apparently contradictory views of the divine as personal and impersonal.[94] It will become clear that most of the modifications to his model over the years have been catalyzed by one form or another of this problem.

Hick's original approach to this problem was sketched out in an essay connected with the 1970 Birmingham conference devoted to this topic. He began by suggesting a tripartite schema for categorizing conflicting interreligious truth claims. First, there are "different modes of experience of the divine reality."[95] This first category involves the central interreligious truth claim conflict: the 'conflicting conceptions of the divine' problem. Here, the major conflictual faultline in the field of human religious experience manifests itself in the dichotomy between those who conceptualize the divine as personal vs. those who conceive of the divine as nonpersonal.

A second type of truth claim conflict involves "difference in philosophical and theological theory or doctrine."[96] Here, within his method of reconciliation, one can again witness the fundamentally contingent and mutable nature of doctrine for Hick:

> [such doctrinal conflicts] are part of the still developing history of human thought, and it may be that sooner or later they will be transcended. For they belong to the historical, culturally conditioned aspect of religion, within which any degree of change is possible.[97]

In another 1970 article, Hick expounds on just how protean religious doctrine and theology really are:

> Thus not only do we stand in a tradition of change but as it faces the future this tradition is open-ended. We cannot say in advance that Christianity, as man's faith-response to Jesus of Nazareth, may not continue to change as the human situation changes, nor can we set any limits to the extent of the change it can undergo without ceasing to be Christianity. So long as the person of Jesus of Nazareth is remembered, and gives rise to a continuing faith-response, the men and women in whom the faith response occurs will be the Church, and the ways in which they conceptualize their faith will be Christian theologies.[98]

Third and finally, Hick addresses the type of truth claim conflict that for him, at this point in time, constituted "the largest difficulty in the way of religious agreement"—namely the unique, revelatory (often historical) experiences and other phenomena that inform a given religious tradition (e.g., holy founder, scripture, etc.).[99] As a Christian, Hick recognized that the dogma of the incarnation, along with its attendant implications for the soteriological uniqueness of Jesus Christ, presented the greatest challenge with regard to reconciling Christian revelatory claims with those of other religions.

Given this schema, it is plain to see that Hick takes seriously the problem of conflicting interreligious truth claims.[100] His initial response to this problem was two-pronged, involving both theological-conceptual and experiential facets. First, on the conceptual level, Hick suggests that this basic doctrinal clash can be thought of as "complementary rather than as rival truths," and can be accounted for by the fact that:

> if, as every profound form of theism has affirmed, God is infinite, and accordingly exceeds the scope of our finite human categories, He may be both personal lord and impersonal ground of being....[101]

In support of this proposal, Hick cites the work of the Hindu philosopher Sri Aurobindo, specifically his "logic of the Infinite," wherein "different phenomenological characteristics are not mutually exclusive."[102] Specifically, Hick cites Jehangir Chubb's articulation of Aurobindo's thought. Chubb, describing the essence of such logic, writes:

> The finite lives by exclusion. The infinite, however, suffers from no such limitation. Its acceptance of a predicate is unconditional and does not involve a denial of any predicate except the contradictory of the predicate affirmed. Thus there is no contradiction in saying that God is both personal and impersonal."[103]

Hick went on to borrow another Hindu-inspired concept to further illuminate the path toward reconciling apparently contradictory notions of the divine. He suggests that "the Hindu distinction between Nirguna Brahman and Saguna Brahman is important and should be adopted into western religious thought."[104] In brief, Hick calls for the conceptual distinction between "Nirguna God" (literally "God without attributes"—God as the self-existent, utterly transcendent reality that is beyond all human categories including the personal) and "Saguna God" ("God with attributes"—God as in relation to creation, and thus experienced in personalistic categories). By dislocating the Nirguna/Saguna dichotomy from its specifically Hindu context, and by emphasizing God's infinite nature, Hick argues that "the one ultimate reality is both Nirguna and nonpersonal, and Saguna and personal, in a duality which is in principle acceptable to human understanding."[105]

Second, Hick goes on to support such a distinction by suggesting that—when it comes to actual religious experience—all of the major religious traditions exhibit some type of parallel conceptual dichotomization of the divine. As examples he offers the personal God Iswara and the nonpersonal absolute Brahman, both found in Hinduism, and, within Christianity, he notes that the typically personal conception of God has been sometimes characterized otherwise by Christian mystics (e.g., Meister Eckhart).[106] In this way, Hick hoped to point the way toward the reconciliation of conflicting conceptions of the divine on a higher level of reality.

Theological Implications of Hick's Pluralist Move: A Christological Sounding

Interestingly, it appears that Hick's initial hope was to somehow retain a place within the pluralist paradigm for both a literal incarnation and the (at least relative) uniqueness of Jesus. It is not surprising that he was reticent to relinquish what he had, for many years, fought so tirelessly for: the traditional incarnational core that lay at the heart of his agape Christology. It was just this essence of the 'orthodox' dogma of the incarnation that he had held as a non-negotiable throughout the 1950s and 1960s. And so, in 1970 one finds Hick attempting to reconcile a literal incarnation with the pluralist paradigm:

> It is therefore not, I would suggest, necessary to "water-down" the traditional understanding of Christ—as, on the whole, those working in this field have tended to do—in order to relate it realistically to the wider religious life of mankind. Could it not be that Christ is indeed the incarnation of God as personal love; but that this fact does not preclude an equally valid awareness of other aspects of the divine in other religions?[107]

However, in that same year, Hick expressed his unease with any simple solution rooted in the traditional notion of the incarnation:

> We cannot, I think, yet claim to be able to see a way through the obstacle that the traditional doctrine of the incarnation presents to a future global theology. This is the point at which fresh dialogue and fresh exploration are most needed and yet most difficult....[W]e must trust that continuing dialogue will prove to be dialogue into truth, and that in a fuller grasp of truth our present conflicting doctrines will ultimately be transcended.[108]

Despite Hick's original inclination, Jesus' status as the literal incarnation of God's love did not long survive the new pluralist atmosphere. In a 1972 article, Hick broached the possibility of reinterpreting the traditional notion of the incarnation as "a mythological use of language."[109] One year later, the first of many book-length treatments of his pluralist theology was published—*God and the Universe of Faiths*. In a chapter entitled "Incarnation and Mythology," Hick develops his 'incarnation as myth' thesis. While he acknowledges Bultmann's previous work in this regard, Hick opts to define myth in a "slightly different way":

> a myth is a story which is told but which is not literally true, or an idea or image which is applied to something or someone but which does not literally apply, but *which invites a particular attitude* in its hearers. Thus the truth of myth is a kind of practical truth consisting in the appropriateness of the attitude to its object, which may be an event, a person, a situation, or a set of ideas.[110]

Thus, understood mythically, the Christian claim that Jesus is God (or, with Hick, God's agape) incarnate

> cannot apply *literally* to Jesus. But as a poetic image—which is powerfully evocative even though it conveys no literal meaning—it expresses the religious significance of Jesus in a way that has proved effective for nearly two millennia. It thus fulfills its function, which is to evoke an appropriate response of faith in Jesus.... The myth is thus an appropriate and valid expression of the experience [of one's having encountered God through Jesus].[111]

The question arises at this point as to why one should think that the orthodox language of the incarnation is properly understood as mythical rather than literal. In the 1973 essay "Incarnation and Mythology," Hick supplies at least three lines of evidence in response, lines of evidence that remain to this day at the core of his critique of a literal incarnation. First, drawing upon contemporary New Testament and historical Jesus studies, Hick argues that "almost certainly Jesus himself did not teach that he was God incarnate."[112] Second, Hick proposes that one can trace the genesis and development of the notion of the incarnation in the early church up through the fourth century, along with the very human concerns that motivated it. Finally, Hick contends that the mythological nature of incarnational language is betrayed in the fact that every attempt to explain it on a philosophical level reveals it to be nothing short of logically incoherent and thus literally meaningless.[113] It is from this stance that Hick has challenged orthodoxy that if they have a "viable understanding of the incarnation" to "lay it on the table" for theological and philosophical examination.[114] Thus, taken together, these three considerations provided the supporting arguments for Hick's pluralistically driven rejection of a literal incarnation.

Hick continued to declare and develop his 'incarnation as myth' thesis throughout the 1970s and into the early 1980s.[115] Over a period of three years during the mid-1970s, Hick met with six other scholars to discuss the path toward a reconstruction of the traditional understanding of the incarnation. The results of this collaborative venture, edited by Hick, were published in 1977 as the controversial work *The Myth of God Incarnate*.[116] In this volume, Hick offers his own perspective in an essay entitled "Jesus and the World Religions." Here, Hick clearly expresses the problem posed by the incarnation:

> Transposed into theological terms, the problem which has come to the surface in the encounter of Christianity with the other world religions is this: If Jesus was

literally God incarnate, and if it is by his death alone that men can be saved, and by their response to him alone that they can appropriate that salvation, then the only doorway to eternal life is Christian faith.[117]

The very suggestion that Christian faith might be the "only doorway to eternal life" is, of course, anathema to the pluralist paradigm—ergo, the incarnation must be relativized. By 1977, Hick's pluralist Christology was rounded out when he finally dropped the last sentimental vestiges of what had become merely the hollow shell of traditional "substantival" incarnation language, and adopted the very "adjectival"/"degree" Christology that he had rejected for so many years. In a 1977 letter to the editors of the journal *Theology*, Hick writes: "Incarnation then becomes a matter of degree: God is incarnate in all men in so far as they are Spirit-filled, or Christ-like, or truly saintly."[118]

Notes

1   *Arguments for the Existence of God*, 117–20; "The Reconstruction of Christian Belief for Today and Tomorrow: Part 2"; "The Outcome: Dialogue into Truth," presented at the Conference on Philosophy of Religion, April 1970, Birmingham University (published in *Truth and Dialogue in World Religions*, 140–55); "Philosophy, Religions, and Human Unity," presented at the International Seminar on World Philosophy, December 1970, University of Madras. The two publications, published in 1970, were no doubt originally written prior to the turn of the decade.

2   Christian, review of *Faith and Knowledge, Religion in Life* 27 (1958): 627 (emphasis added).

3   *Interpretation of Religion*, 235; also "On Conflicting Religious Truth-Claims," *Religious Studies* 19 (1983): 488.

4   *Arguments for the Existence of God*, 117.

5   Ibid.

6   Schleiermacher, *On Religion*, 101.

7   Ibid., 212–14.

8   Ibid., 217.

9   Introduction to *On Religion*, trans. Richard Crouter (New York: Cambridge University Press, 1988), 49. See Elias K. Bongmba, "Two Steps Forward, One Step Backward: Schleiermacher on Religion," *Journal of Theology for Southern Africa* 97 (1997): 81–96.

10   On Reformed epistemology see the related essays by Plantinga, Alston, Wolterstorff, et al. in *Faith and Rationality: Reason and Belief in God*, ed. Alvin Plantinga and Nicholas Wolterstorff (Notre Dame: University of Notre Dame, 1983) and *Rationality, Religious Belief and Moral Commitment*, ed. Robert Audi and William Wainwright (Ithaca: Cornell University Press, 1986). For critiques of the Reformed view see Mark S. McLeod, *Rationality and Theistic Belief* (Ithaca: Cornell University Press, 1993); Linda Zagzebski, ed., *Rational Faith: Catholic Responses to Reformed Epistemology* (Notre Dame: University of Notre Dame Press, 1993).

11   E.g., see Hick, "Epistemological Challenge of Religious Pluralism," 277. This article represents Hick's response to criticisms of his religious pluralism from several Reformed epistemologists. It is followed by brief responses from Alston, Plantinga, George Mavrodes, and Peter van Inwagen.

12   *Interpretation of Religion*, 229, n. 2.

13   "Religious Pluralism and the Rationality of Religious Belief," 244.

14   *The Evidential Force of Religious Experience* (Oxford: Clarendon, 1989), 87.

15   *Interpretation of Religion*, 214; see Swinburne, *The Existence of God* (New York: Oxford University Press, 1979), 254.

16   Hick, "A Concluding Comment," *Faith and Philosophy* 5 (1988): 455; "Religious Pluralism and the Rationality of Religious Belief," 243.

17   *Perceiving God: The Epistemology of Religious Experience* (Ithaca: Cornell University Press, 1991), xi. Alston is equally quick to point out where his views differ from Hick's; see *Perceiving God*, 27–28; "John Hick: *Faith and Knowledge*," in *God, Truth and Reality*, 24–30; idem., "Realism and the Christian Faith."

18   Alston, "Religious Diversity and Perceptual Knowledge of God," *Faith and Philosophy* 5 (1988): 433.

19   Hasker, "Proper Function, Reliabilism, and Religious Knowledge: A Critique of Plantinga's Epistemology," in *Christian Perspectives on Religious Knowledge*, ed. C. Stephen Evans and Merold Westphal (Grand Rapids: Eerdmans, 1993), 82, cf. 83–5.

20   As Hick notes: "If there were only one religious tradition, so that all religious experience and belief had the same intentional object, an epistemology of religion could come to rest at this point" (*Interpretation of Religion*, 233).

21   Ibid., 83.

22   *Arguments for the Existence of God*, 118.

23   *God and the Universe of Faiths*, 51–52; for Hick's extended argument on this point see *Arguments for the Existence of God*, 101–116.

24   *Arguments for the Existence of God*, 119.

25   Ibid., 119–20.

26   *Faith and Knowledge* (New York: Macmillan, 1988), vii, ix.

27   *Interpretation of Religion*, 233–36.

28   See "Religious Pluralism and the Rationality of Religious Belief"; "Religious Experience: Its Nature and Validity," in *Disputed Questions in Theology*, 17–32; "On Religious Experience," in *Faith, Scepticism & Personal Identity: A Festschrift for Terence Penelhum*, ed. J. J. MacIntosh and H. A. Meynell (Calgary: University of Calgary Press, 1994), 17–29.

29   "Religious Pluralism and the Rationality of Religious Belief," 245–46.

30   E.g., see *Interpretation of Religion*, 172–230.

31   "Religious Pluralism and the Rationality of Religious Belief," 248.

32   As others have noted; see e.g., L. Philip Barnes, "Continuity and Development in John Hick's Theology," 395–402; Paul Badham, "John Hick and Human Response to Transcendent Reality," *Dialogue and Alliance* 5 (Summer 1991): 44.

33   "Epistemological Challenge of Religious Pluralism" and "Religious Pluralism and the Rationality of Religious Belief."

34   Hick notes the following works: Penelhum, *God and Skepticism* (Boston: Reidell, 1983); Wainwright, "Mysticism and Sense Perception," *Religious Studies* 9 (1973): 257–78; Alston, "Reli-

gious Diversity and Perceptual Knowledge of God"; Plantinga, "Reason and Belief in God."

35   "Religious Pluralism and the Rationality of Religious Belief," 245.

36   Ibid., 244 (emphasis in text).

37   See, for example, the criticisms of Hick's thesis in a series of brief response articles by several leading Reformed epistemologists in *Faith and Philosophy* 14 (1997): 287–302.

38   "Proper Function, Reliabilism, and Religious Knowledge," 83–86.

39   Beilby, "Rationality, Warrant, and Religious Diversity," *Philosophia Christi* 17 (1994): 10.

40   For a comparison between Alston and Hick at this point, see Philip Quinn, "Towards Thinner Theologies: Hick and Alston on Religious Diversity," *International Journal for Philosophy of Religion* 38 (1995): 145–64.

41   *Arguments for the Existence of God*, 118–19.

42   Ibid., 119. Hick's prior adoption of soteriological universalism no doubt fueled this conviction.

43   See e.g., *Arguments for the Existence of God*, 119; "Reconstruction of Christian Belief," 400; "Philosophy, Religions, and Human Unity," 463; "The Copernican Revolution in Theology," in *God and the Universe of Faiths*, 122–23; "Learning from Other Faiths: The Christian View of Other Faiths," *Expository Times* 84 (Nov. 1972): 36; "Jesus and World Religions," in *The Myth of God Incarnate*, ed. John Hick (Westminster, 1977), 180; *Center of Christianity*, 79; "Is There Only One Way to God?," *Theology* 85 (1982): 6; *The Second Christianity*, 3rd ed. (London: SCM, 1983 [1968, 1978]), 92; "The Theology of Religious Pluralism," *Theology* 86 (1983): 338.

44   "Reconstruction of Christian Belief," 400 (emphasis added).

45   "The Copernican Revolution in Theology," in *God and the Universe of Faiths*, 122–23 (emphasis added).

46   Such questions will be explored below in the fifth chapter.

47   "Copernican Revolution in Theology," see especially 122–31.

48   Ibid., 121.

49   Ibid., 123–30.

50   Ibid., 131.

51   For instances of Hick's use of this analogy see "Learning from Other Faiths," 36–39; "Copernican Revolution in Theology"; *Philosophy of Religion*, 2d ed. (1973), 129; "Whatever Path Men Choose is Mine," *Modern Churchman* 18 (1974): 12–13; "Religious Pluralism and Absolute Claims," in *Religious Pluralism*, ed. Leroy Rouner (Notre Dame: University of Notre Dame Press, 1984), 199–201.

52   *God Has Many Names*, 18.

53   See e.g., "Reconstruction of Christian Belief," 400–01; "The Outcome"; "Philosophy, Religions, and Human Unity," 465; "New Map of the Universe of Faiths," in *God and the Universe of Faiths*, 133; *Philosophy of Religion*, 2d ed., 123–24. Smith's theory has been discussed in summary form in chapter two above.

54   "The Outcome," 141.

55   Ibid.

56   Ibid.

57   Ibid., 142.

58   *God Has Many Names*, 18.

59   *Interpretation of Religion*, xiii–iv. In a 1984 essay that he contributed to a Festschrift vol-

ume for Smith, Hick is able to explicate his own views quite easily within the context of Smith's general theory; see "A Philosophy of Religious Pluralism," reprinted in Hick's *Problems of Religious Pluralism*, 28–45.

60   *Interpretation of Religion*, 17, n. 13.

61   "The Outcome," 147.

62   Ibid.

63   Ibid., 148–49.

64   Ibid., 148.

65   Hick's ongoing appreciation of Smith's theory was no doubt a factor in his being asked to write the Foreword to the 1978 reissue of Smith's *The Meaning and End of Religion*, as well as the Preface to Edward Hughes's *Wilfred Cantwell Smith: A Theology for the World*.

66   "Whatever Path Men Choose is Mine," 13.

67   *Interpretation of Religion*, 21–22.

68   On the 'axial age' notion see Karl Jaspers (who coined the term, *Aschenzeit*), *The Origin and Goal of History*, Michael Bullock, trans. (London: Routledge & Kegan Paul, 1953 [1949]), esp. ch. 1; Lewis Mumford, *The Transformation of Man* (London: Allen & Unwin, 1957), ch. 4; John B. Cobb, *The Structure of Christian Existence* (Philadelphia: Westminster, 1967), ch. 5; Robert Bellah, *Beyond Belief: Essays on Religion in a Post-Traditional World* (New York: Harper & Row, 1970), 22–32.

69   *Interpretation of Religion*, 22.

70   "The Outcome," 149.

71   *Philosophy of Religion*, 2nd ed., 125.

72   Ibid., 29.

73   Hick, "Religious Pluralism and Salvation," *Faith and Philosophy* 5 (1988): 365.

74   *Interpretation of Religion*, 36.

75   Ibid., 33.

76   *Origin and Goal of History*, 12, 18.

77   *Christianity and the Centre*, 81.

78   "The Outcome," 151–52 (emphases added).

79   Ibid., 149.

80   *The Coming World Civilization* (New York: Harper, 1956), 168–70. Thus, at least at this point, I see more similarity between Hocking and Hick's hopeful visions of the future of religion than does D'Costa (*Hick's Theology of Religions*, 22).

81   See e.g., *Philosophy of Religion*, 2nd ed., 127; *Death and Eternal Life*, 33; *Christianity at the Centre*, 78; *A Christian Theology of Religions*, 123–24.

82   E.g., *God Has Many Names*, 48, 114.

83   *Interpretation of Religion*, 377.

84   Ibid.

85   See *The Second Christianity*, 73–74; *Christian Theology of Religions*, 133–34.

86   Ibid., 378–79.

87   E.g., *God Has Many Names*, 47–48.

88   Ibid., 48. This fact was originally brought to my attention by D'Costa, *Hick's Theology of Religions*, 61.

89   *The Second Christianity*, 8; see also Hick, "Religious Diversity as Challenge and Promise," in *The Experience of Religious Diversity*, John Hick and Hasan Askari, eds. (Aldershot,

UK: Avebury/Gower, 1985), 3; idem., "The Non-Absoluteness of Christianity," in *The Myth of Christian Uniqueness: Toward a Pluralistic Theology of Religions*, John Hick and Paul Knitter, eds. (Maryknoll, N.Y.: Orbis, 1987), 17.

90   *Christian Theology of Religions*, 108–10. It is not absolutely clear from this passage whether Hick is equating both African primal and native American religion as "extra-axial," or merely the latter of the two.

91   Hick, "On Grading Religions," in *Problems of Religious Pluralism*, 73; see 71–3 for discussion. See also "Reconstruction of Christian Belief," 399; "Philosophy, Religions, and Human Unity," 462; "Learning from Other Faiths," 39; "Religious Pluralism and Absolute Claims," 194; *Interpretation of Religion*, 301.

92   "Religious Pluralism and Absolute Claims," 194; "On Grading Religions," 73.

93   D'Costa's thoughts on Hick's notion of 'genetic confessionalism' are relevant here; see *Hick's Theology of Religions*, 139–41.

94   *Christianity at the Centre*, 80–81.

95   "The Outcome," 152.

96   Ibid., 153.

97   Ibid.

98   "Reconstruction of Christian Belief," 340. In this light, see Hick's argument that the doctrine of reincarnation, in its popular form, "is not incompatible with the essentials of Christian faith"; "Christianity and Reincarnation," in *Sri Aurobindo: A Garland of Tributes*, Arabinda Basu, ed. (Pondicherry: Sri Aurobindo Research Academy, 1973), 65.

99   "The Outcome," 154.

100   It has previously been noted that this was a crucial point at which Hick took issue with W. C. Smith's idea of personalistic truth. Thus, in the second edition of his *Philosophy of Religion* (19–23), Hick introduces the work of William A. Christian on interreligious doctrinal conflicts, and sides with him (i.e., against Smith) that such conflicts are *real*. See, however, his continued use of Smith toward a solution (123–24).

101   "The Outcome," 152.

102   Ibid., 153. (297).

103   Chubb, "Presuppositions of Religious Dialogue," *Religious Studies* 8 (1972): 296–7.

104   "New Map of the Universe of Faiths," in *God and the Universe of Faiths*, 144.

105   Ibid.

106   Ibid., 144–45.

107   "Reconstruction of Christian Belief," 404.

108   "The Outcome," 155.

109   "Christian View of Other Faiths," 39.

110   "Incarnation and Mythology," in *God and the Universe of Faiths*, 166–67 (emphasis added, particularly because *this* idea becomes the central feature of Hick's notion of myth from this time to the present).

111   Ibid., 172 (emphasis in text).

112   Ibid., 169.

113   Ibid., 169–70.

114   "Is there a Doctrine of the Incarnation?," in *Incarnation and Myth: The Debate Continued*, ed. Michael Goulder (Grand Rapids: Eerdmans, 1979), 50.

115   See e.g., "Whatever Path Men Choose is Mine," 15; "Jesus and the World Religions";

"Incarnation and Atonement: Evil and Incarnation," in *Incarnation and Myth*, 77–84; "Is There a Doctrine of the Incarnation?"; "A Response to Brian Hebblethwaite," in *Incarnation and Myth*, 192–94; *The Center of Christianity*, 26–32; "Christology in an Age of Religious Pluralism," *Journal of Theology for Southern Africa* 35 (1981): 4–9; "Pluralism and the Reality of the Transcendent," 48.

116   Critical responses to *Myth of God Incarnate* were swift. See e.g., Michael Green, ed., *The Truth of God Incarnate* (Grand Rapids: Eerdmans, 1977); George Carey, *God Incarnate* (Downers Grove, Ill.: InterVarsity, 1977); Herbert McCabe, "The Myth of God Incarnate," *New Blackfriars* 58 (1977) 350–7; Norman Anderson, *The Mystery of the Incarnation* (London: Hodder & Stoughton, 1978); Alasdair Heron, "Article Review: Doing Away with the Incarnation?," *Scottish Journal of Theology* 31 (1978): 51–71.

117   "Jesus and the World Religions," 180.

118   "Letter to the Editors: Incarnation," *Theology* 80 (1977): 205.

4 The Development of Hick's Model of Religious Pluralism

This chapter will trace the development of Hick's pluralism from his early model to the present. His well-known 'neo-Kantian' proposal and his more recent soteriological turn will serve as important benchmarks along the way. With the assistance of a final Christological sounding, the theological implications of Hick's mature model will be noted.

Since his pluralist move more than twenty five years ago, John Hick has continued to develop his model both in sophistication and precision, often in response to a variety of critiques. The bulk of the criticism of Hick's pluralism focused upon two areas. First, there were philosophical critiques of the model itself. Here, the general contention was that Hick's model, in one way or another, was unable to do what it needed to.[1] The most challenging criticisms in this regard centered on the 'conflicting truth-claims' problematic. Second, there were various theological critiques, most of which focused upon Hick's Christology and the 'incarnation as myth' thesis.[2] The primary concern here will be the first type of criticism, the philosophical, since it is primarily this type that has served as a catalyst for change in Hick's model.

Interestingly, one of the principal critiques related to the conflicting conceptions of the divine problem was in a sense already anticipated by Hick himself in *God and the Universe of Faiths*. When constructing his own critique of the inclusivist paradigm, Hick made it clear that Christianity was not the only religion in danger of such ultimately fruitless "Ptolemaic epicycles." In fact, he states that "the most striking example of this today in the religious realm is provided by contemporary philosophical Hinduism."[3] Here, the non-personal Brahmanic Absolute, beyond all human thought and categories, represents the true vision of ultimate reality. Thus, the personalistic images associated with the world's deities are merely partial conceptions of the Absolute, made available for those unable to arise above anthropomorphic thought—the non-personal is fundamentally privileged above the personal. And so, Ptolemaic Vedantism is as real a threat as its Christian counter-part.[4] Interestingly, Hick does not mention the Nirguna/Saguna dichotomy here—which is another way of naming this type of 'anonymous Hinduism,' but, apparently, decides to save it for explicating the personal vs. non-personal problematic, having detached it from its Hindu context.

In spite of his attempts to rinse the fundamentally non-personalistic Brahmanic stains from the Nirguna/Saguna conceptual cloth, it was not long before Hick's religious Copernicanism was charged with covert Vedantic Hinduism. Philip Almond, for instance, refers to Hick's attempt to avoid this problem as "an epi-cyclic addition to what remains fundamentally a Vedantin solution."[5] Hick's pluralist model, at the same time, became the target for charges of covert theism.[6] One can identify two primary reasons that served to support this latter accusation. First, in spite of his attempts to provide parity for the conceptions of a personal *God* and a non-personal *Absolute* within his model, Hick nonetheless continued to grant the word "God" most favored terminological status when describing the ultimate Reality at the center of all things. (Reflecting upon this stage of Hick's project, Harold Coward has noted that, despite his best efforts, in continuing to use the term 'God' for the ultimate Reality, Hick yet remained on the "bridge of theism.")[7] Hick was to wrestle with this terminological problem for the next decade. Second, as noted earlier, one of Hick's primary motivations for his Copernican Revolution was the implications that flow from the idea of a God of universal love. However, once ultimate reality is deemed to be just as faithfully conceptualized as *non-personal*, the 'God of universal love' upon which Hick's pluralist move ostensively depends is revealed as parochially Christian—or, at best, parochially theistic. Thus the paradox: to be consistent, Hick must remove from the center of the universe the very conception of the loving God that led him to re-map the universe of faiths to begin with. In essence then, the charge of covert theism is tied to the observation that Hick assumes as primary impetus for his Copernican revolution the very thing—the (ontological) centrality and universality of the personal God of love—that it must explicitly preclude if it is to be successful.[8]

John Hick's Neo-Kantian Proposal

At a 1976 conference on mysticism, held in Calgary, Alberta, John Hick unveiled a new development in his model. It would quickly become his primary solution to the conflicting conceptions of the divine problem, as well as the defining hallmark of his mature pluralist model. This new development, referred to hereafter as Hick's 'neo-Kantian' proposal, takes its cue (not surprisingly) from an aspect of Kant's epistemology as developed in *The Critique of Pure Reason*: namely the noumenon/phenomenon distinction. In brief, Hick argues that both personalistic and non-personalistic conceptions of ultimate reality are:

> divine phenomena constituting forms in which the unknown divine noumenon impinges upon human consciousness. The status of these divine phenomena…is thus comparable with that of the phenomenal world in Kant's critical philosophy.[9]

It is interesting to note that in his 1970 Birmingham conference paper—one which Hick clearly appreciated—J. J. Chubb had made a brief suggestion in a similar vein:

> In the first place it is difficult to determine or indicate what is being indicated by our affirmations. The same difficulty is met with in Kant's concept of the thing-in-itself. A great gulf is fixed between reality and concepts which make it impossible to indicate what we are speaking of when we say that 'it' is beyond thought and speech and cannot in any way be described.[10]

By the early 1980s, Hick's neo-Kantian proposal was being developed in earnest.[11] The Nirguna/Saguna dichotomy took on a new function as merely an explicitly Hindu *analogy* to the noumenal-phenomenal mechanism.[12] Hick made it a point to emphasize that his new model was "a significantly different hypothesis" from this Advaitic Hindu dichotomy in regard to which it has only a "partial resemblance" at best.[13] In fact, he saw his new proposal as the critical path that avoided both a covert (non-personal) Vedantism and a covert (personal) theism.[14]

Hick's most comprehensive exposition of his neo-Kantian proposal is found in *An Interpretation of Religion*. Here, his response functions as the central apologetic pillar of his pluralist hypothesis, an hypothesis that he now presents in the following succinct form:

> the great world faiths embody different perceptions and conceptions of, and correspondingly different responses to, the Real from within the major variant ways of being human; and that within each of them the transformation of human existence from self-centeredness to Reality-centeredness is taking place.[15]

More recently, Hick has clarified and defended his pluralist hypothesis in his 1995 book *A Christian Theology of Religion* (which represents an expanded version of Hick's Auburn Lectures delivered in April 1994 at Union Theological Seminary, New York).[16] Hick's neo-Kantian thesis is constructed from the two primary strands of thought that have informed his religious worldview throughout the last four decades: the primacy of religious experience and a Kantian epistemology. In its simplest terms, his proposal is an attempt to combine a realist understanding of religious experience that is, at the same time, seriously qualified by a critical subjectivizing element. It is a legitimate question to ask just how compatible, ultimately, these two strands of thought are. In one sense, Hick's philosophical career can be read as an on-going attempt to reconcile the various implications of these two foundations of his thought, namely: (1) his strong Kantian-like epistemology and the various effects it has had upon his religious worldview, and (2) his realist/cognitivist view of religion. As Sumner Twiss has correctly noted, these ostensively tensive strands of Hick's thought serve to complexify any attempt to understand and critique Hick's project.[17]

Hick begins with the "highly generalized" Kantian insight that the human mind actively interprets sensory information in terms of its inherent mental concepts.[18] More specifically, Hick focuses on the noumenal-phenomenal distinction that allowed Kant to distinguish between an entity as it is in itself and as it appears in the act of human perception. By taking this Kantian epistemological principle and applying it—in a decidedly unKantian fashion—to human religious experience, Hick arrives at a synthesis that forms the foundation for his response to the conflicting conceptions problem. In fact, given Hick's proposal, conflicting images of the divine are not merely understandable, but are even to be expected. In Hick's words:

> I want to say that the noumenal Real is experienced and thought by different human mentalities...as the range of gods and absolutes which the phenomenology of religions reports. And these divine [phenomenal manifestations] are not illusory but are empirically, that is experientially, real as authentic manifestations of the Real.[19]

In this manner, Hick's model seeks to maintain a realist core—i.e., the noumenal Real, while nonetheless anticipating radically diverse understandings of It within the various religions. According to Hick, the key to preserving parity between the variety of religious conceptions of the divine is the fundamental insistence that absolutely *nothing* can be said or known about the divine in and of itself. Clearly then—if Hick is right—on the one hand, the divine in itself is neither personal nor non-personal; on the other, *both* personal and non-personal conceptions can represent authentic manifestations of the divine as perceived in the various religions. In this manner, he offers a religious realist—as opposed to a naturalistic—interpretation of religion, while at the same time allowing the subjectivist component to create the space for radically divergent human understandings of the divine Reality.

As the above summary of Hick's pluralist hypothesis reveals, he has finally settled on a terminology in regard to the divine Reality that seems best fitted to allow for either personal or non-personal phenomenal manifestations in an equally unbiased manner. In the earlier years of his pluralist shift, Hick had used the term "God," if in a qualified sense. Thus, in the original presentation of his Copernican revolution, Hick calls for:

> a shift from the dogma that Christianity is at the centre to the realization that it is *God* who is at the centre, and that all the religions of mankind, including our own, serve and revolve around him.[20]

Soon, Hick began to experiment with a variety of terms, in search of a more religiously neutral title, including "the transcendent," "the Eternal One," "the Ultimate," and "divine Reality." However, as late as 1980, Hick is still found using the term "God" in a general (i.e., 'philosophical') presentation of his thesis:

> How are we to name the postulated transcendent reality...? One is initially inclined to reject the word 'God' as too theistic....The fact is, however, that we have no fully tradition-neutral or tradition-transcending term....As a Christian I shall accordingly use the word 'God,' but shall not use it in a straightforwardly theistic sense.[21]

Finally, by 1983, Hick had settled on what was to remain his term of preference: "the Real" (interestingly, a term used by William Hocking in 1940 to denote the divine).[22] It should, however, be noted that, to this day, whenever Hick finds himself discussing his pluralistic hypothesis and its implications *in an intra-Christian context*, he is very willing to appeal to "God" in order to make his case.[23]

In *An Interpretation of Religion*, Hick fleshes out his basic proposal in two critical sections.[24] The first represents an attempt to locate the rudimentary essence of his model, in terms of a distinction between the divine in itself and as humanly experienced, within the various religious traditions. The second explicitly develops the neo-Kantian proposal itself. Both of these aspects will now be explored.

The Divine in Itself vs. the Divine as Humanly Experienced

Hick claims that his neo-Kantian proposal is essentially a complex philosophical articulation of a more general religious observation—namely that an inherent epistemological rift exists between the divine Reality as it exists in itself and as it is humanly experienced. He supports this claim by offering evidence of this awareness in such diverse religious traditions as Hinduism, Mahayana and Pure Land Buddhism, Taoism, Kabbalist Judaism, and Islam, both in its traditional and Sufist forms. Within Christianity, he detects this insight in the traditional distinction between God *a se* and God *pro nobis*, as well as in Eckhart's mysticism, and the progressive ventures of such modern theologians as Paul Tillich, Ninian Smart, and Gordon Kaufman.[25]

Hick identifies the root of this "basic [inter-religious] assumption" as the conviction that divine reality:

> is unlimited and therefore may not be equated without remainder with anything that can be humanly experienced and defined. Unlimitedness, or infinity, is a negative concept, the denial of limitation.[26]

Such a notion, Hick suggests, is logically entailed by the claim to divine ultimacy. For if the divine is limitable in some external mode, this would render it, by definition, non-ultimate. Part and parcel with the concept of unlimitedness is "the equally natural and reasonable assumption that the Ultimate, in its unlimitedness, exceeds all positive characterizations in human thought and language."[27]

Hick garners support for this notion of divine ineffability—based on infinity—from a gamut of Christian theologians including Gregory of Nyssa, Augustine, Aquinas, Eckhart, and St. John of the Cross, as well as from Hindu and Islamic traditions. He derails the criticism that making such an appeal to the ineffable—or more recently the "transcategorial"—is itself an application of a human concept to the Infinite by drawing the distinction between formal and substantive properties.[28] While he allows that "purely formal and logically generated properties such as 'being a referent of a term'" can legitimately be predicated of the divine, it nonetheless "makes perfectly good sense to say that our *substantial* concepts do not apply to the Ultimate."[29] In this manner, Hick baptizes his radical neo-Kantian subjectivism in the pure waters of the classical Christian tradition. It is worth noting that, although Hick has denied that his model owes anything significant to the notion of divine infinity, the fact that he nonetheless continues to devote a significant amount of space to it in the explication of his pluralist hypothesis suggests that he is still gaining currency from this connection.[30]

Kant and Hick's Neo-Kantian Proposal

It is only with an examination of Hick's modified Kantian epistemology that the full force of his proposal's radical subjectivism (i.e., constructivism) is revealed. Hick spends a significant amount of time delineating the exact nature of his hypothesis' relation to Kant's own epistemology. Here, both detailed explication and qualification are critical to his thesis. A distinct, oscillating pattern emerges as Hick alternately links—and then distances—himself from Kant. One can identify four important strands of continuity. First, there is the use of Kant's noumenal-phenomenal distinction, which, when transposed from the realm of sensory to religious experience, allows Hick to 'postulate' a single divine noumenon as the common source of the various, often conflicting, human experiences of the divine. Precursors to Hick in the using these Kantian categories to unpack religious experience include Rudolf Otto and Robert Oakes.[31]

Second, there is the employment of Kantian-like "category-analogues."[32] Here, Hick suggests that the conceptions of the Real as personal (i.e., 'God') vs. non-personal (i.e., 'the Absolute') function analogously to Kant's categories of the understanding. Fleshing out this neo-Kantian parallel, Hick claims that similar to the role played by *time* in Kant's system the range of human cultures serve as the particularizing factor by which the two larger categories are schematized, thus resulting in the range of human conceptions of the divine. Hick explains:

> the divine Reality is not directly known *an sich*. But when human beings relate themselves to it in the mode of I-Thou encounter they experience it as personal. Indeed in the context of that relationship it *is* personal, not It but He or She. When human beings relate themselves to the Real in the mode of non-personal awareness they experience it as non-personal, and in the context of this relationship it *is* non-personal. ·
>
> Each of these two basic categories, God and the Absolute, is schematised or made concrete within actual religious experience as a range of gods or absolutes. There are, respectively, the *personae* and *impersonae* in terms of which the Real is humanly known. And the particularizing factor (corresponding, in its function, to time in the schematisation of the Kantian categories) is the range of human cultures, actualizing different though overlapping aspects of our immensely complex human potentiality for awareness of the transcendent. It is in relation to different ways of being human, developed within civilizations and cultures of the earth, that the Real, apprehended through the concept of God, is experienced specifically as the God of Israel, or as the Holy Trinity, or as Shiva, or as Allah, or as Vishnu....And it is in relation to yet other forms of life that the Real, apprehended through the concept of the Absolute, is experienced as Brahman, or as Nirvana, or as Being, or as Sunyata...[33]

One might suppose that, practically speaking, Hick's 'religious' theory of religion actually offers a *new and truer religion*, one that reveals the actual and ultimate noumenal Real that lies behind the other religions' mere phenomenal penultimates. However, Hick is quick to dispel such speculations. An important implication of Hick's understanding of the noumenal Real is that, while it can be formally referred to as a postulate of the pluralist hypothesis, it can never, Itself, be the object of religious devotion: "the Real *an sich* cannot be the object of a religious cult. We worship one or other of its personae, or we seek union with one or other of its impersonae."[34] Thus, religiously speaking, no one—not even the Hickian pluralist—can penetrate beyond the phenomenal realm to reach the 'real' noumenal Reality.

Third, like Kant, Hick maintains that his use of the noumenal category is a *negative* one. That is, he does not mean to make any positive claims regarding the unknowable divine noumenon—a charge with which he is often faced. Rather, he wants to refer to it only as a necessary postulate—one required by his broader religious philosophy—by way of formal categories. Thus, as in his reading of Kant, Hick emphatically declares that the noumenal exists independently of our experience of it, and, accordingly, he stresses that "the phenomenal world is that same noumenal world as it appears to our human consciousness."[35]

Finally, Hick strengthens his association with Kant by offering corroborating evidence for the general Kantian model derived from several modern disciplines. Specifically, he states that the basic Kantian epistemological program has been "massively confirmed as an empirical thesis by modern work in cognitive and social psychology and in the sociology of knowledge."[36]

There are, however, specific junctures at which Hick wants to distance himself from Kant. This explicit distancing actually serves as a preemptive apologetic for his proposal. It provides the context within which he can respond to two critical types of attack on his model: first, to those that criticize him for particular aspects of his model that conflict with Kant's ideas, and, second, to those that criticize him on the basis of problems endemic to Kant's philosophy. As noted above, he makes it abundantly clear throughout his discussion that the general distinction upon which his model rests—i.e., between the Real in itself and as humanly experienced—in no way *depends* upon Kant's philosophical insights. Rather, Kant is merely the one to have developed this general observation in the most philosophically detailed manner. Hick claims that Aquinas' similar dictum, that "Things known are in the knower according to the mode of the knower," could just as easily form the departure point for a pluralist hypothesis. Likewise, the Muslim thinker al-Junaid's maxim, "The colour of the water is the same as that of its container," contains the same truth.[37] Hick goes on to broaden his appeal by pointing out that every human being can arrive at the same basic insight via reflection on their own empirical experience. We all know that the *same* object can appear quite *differently* depending on a particular human observer's spatial location, the condition of their sensory organs, and their own unique recognition and interpretive abilities.

On this basis, Hick does not hesitate to acknowledge those features of his model that are quite distinct from—even conflictive with—Kant's own philosophy. He notes two specific instances. First, his decidedly unKantian shift of the noumenal-phenomenal distinction from the realm of sensory epistemology to the realm of religious epistemology, and the fundamental contrast between their respective understandings of religious experience that such a move evinces. As far as Hick is concerned, this presents no problem whatsoever. Simply because Kant did not choose to relate his insights regarding sensory experience to the realm of religious epistemology, this should not "bar others" from making such a move.[38] In fact, Hick's general apologetic response to those who bring Kantian-related criticisms against his model is that they do not apply given his transposition of Kant's ideas to the realm of religious epistemology. Based on this distinction, Hick feels that he can safely refuse to enter into the sticky nest of problems associated with modern Kantian interpretation.[39]

The second acknowledged divergence from Kant involves the nature of Hick's category-analogues. Specifically, while Kant's forms and categories are *a priori*, and are thus universal and necessary in nature,[40] Hick's analogues are both culture-relative and contingent.[41] And so, Hick's neo-Kantian proposal represents a complex attempt to allow for a pluralist interpretation of religions, while still safeguarding his realist core belief that religious experience, ultimately, is a non-illusory experience of transcendent Reality.

Related Modifications of Hick's Pluralist Model

In the early-to-mid 1980s, Hick modified a number of other elements of his original model. Several of the developments, like the neo-Kantian proposal, came as adjustments to aspects of the early model that had drawn the most fire. They were generally designed in tandem with the development of his neo-Kantian proposal, and served to further protect his hypothesis from charges of covert *anything* (i.e., theism, pantheism, etc.).

*From a 'Theology' to a 'Philosophy' of Religions: Hick's 'Religious
Interpretation of Religion'*

In the early 1980s, Hick, for the most part, ceased describing his pluralist shift
in terms of the Copernican analogy. It appears that 1983 is roughly the critical
year in which some of the last *consistent* uses of the Copernican-Ptolemaic
analogy in general presentations of his pluralistic hypothesis can be found.[42]
Around this time, Hick began to excise from his pluralist apologetic the formerly ubiquitous appeal to a grounding in the 'God of universal love.'[43] This
move indicates the determined initiation on Hick's part of a program designed
to distance the general presentation of his pluralist hypothesis—and, specifically,
its noumenal Real—from the Christian God of universal love or any other theistic bias. The Christian "God" is merely one of the Real's many possible phenomenal manifestations. The question of just what would replace the prominent
and crucial 'God of universal love' argument in Hick's re-vamped pluralist apologetic is an important one, and is a matter to which we shall return below.

The primary impetus for these modifications is transparent. They mark
the conscious shift on Hick's part from addressing the problem of religious
diversity as a Christian theologian to facing it as a (presumably tradition-neutral) philosopher of religion.[44] Such a shift in Hick's self-consciousness is seen
in the fact that, beginning in the early 1980s, he begins, more and more, to
intentionally connect the term "philosophy" to his pluralist project.[45] His published Gifford Lectures, *An Interpretation of Religion*, represents the crowning
attempt of Hick to present his pluralist hypothesis from and within a purely
philosophical perspective. Here Hick sees himself as offering not a (Christian)
'theology of religions,' but rather a tradition-neutral, philosophically-driven
field theory of religion.

The potential for confusion between these two different projects—both for
others and even for Hick himself—arises from a distinctive quality of Hick's
philosophy of religions. Unlike most attempts to provide a philosophical, descriptive interpretation of the religious life of humankind, Hick offers what he
calls a distinctly "religious" philosophy of religion. In the opening paragraph
of *An Interpretation of Religion*, Hick explains his project:

> There are many general interpretations of religion. These have usually been either
> naturalistic, treating religion as a purely human phenomenon or, if religious, have
> been developed within the confines of a particular confessional conviction which
> construes all other traditions in its own terms. The one type of theory that has

seldom been attempted is a religious but not confessional interpretation of religion in its plurality of forms; and it is this that I shall be trying to offer here.[46]

Here, the pluralist hypothesis has explicitly been rendered subservient to a larger project. Hick's wider concern is to offer a theory of religion rooted in a *generally 'religious'* perspective, one that avoids methodological naturalism on one hand, and any *particular* confessional orientation on the other.

The attempt to render a generally religious interpretation of religion is not, of course, new. One can see antecedents to Hick's approach as far back as Friedrich Max Müller (1823-1900), the generally recognized 'father of comparative religion.' It is interesting to note that Müller, like Hick, was influenced by Kant's thought. Also, one cannot help recognizing parallels with Hick's thought (especially in light of his 'soteriological turn'; see below) in Müller's definition of religion: "...the perception of the infinite under such manifestations as are able to influence the moral character of man."[47]

Scholarly assessment of Hick's particular verion of a 'religious theory of religion' is still in the early stages. However, already there have been serious questions raised about its methodological appropriateness. In their book, *Religion Defined and Explained*, Peter Clarke and Peter Byrne reach the heart of the issue in a chapter devoted to analyzing Hick's theory:

> If Hick can produce a religious but non-theological theory of religion, he must be able to register a commitment to a transcendent, non-human source of religion while being agnostic, and sceptical to a degree, about all specific, historically located affirmations of the existence of transcendent beings and states. Some will wonder how he can have this commitment alongside his agnosticism. This query relates to how, if at all, his own references to the transcendent can remain free of the factors which make those found in the faiths unusable in a critical theory of religion. It also relates to the kind of content Hick can give to his reference to a religious source of religion while distancing himself from what the faiths say about this object. It would not seem to be possible to have a religious but non-theological interpretation of religion unless these questions can be answered.[48]

Pressing Hick's 'religious theory of religion'—and the pluralist hypothesis it houses—for answers to these sorts of fundamental questions in order to determine its viability *on its own terms* will be the focus of the sixth and final chapter of this study.

In light of such matters, the perspectival/methodological dilemma of 'John Hick the Christian theologian' vs. 'John Hick the philosopher of religion' surfaces. First, a number of criticisms raised against Hick over the years have not taken this distinction as seriously as it needs to be.[49] Beyond this, I would suggest that Hick himself has contributed to this confusion at times by, unconsciously I presume, shifting back and forth between these two perspectives in an incautious manner—often within a single text. As Chester Gillis rightly notes, there have been numerous instances when:

> Hick blurs the lines between philosophy of religion and theology. For while it is certainly proper for philosophy of religion to analyze the concepts and claims of a particular theological tradition such as Christianity, it is generally not the role of philosophy of religion to offer alternative constructive positions which are designed to reshape the tradition from within. Occasionally Hick engages in such internal reconstructions and thus takes upon himself the task of the theologian whose charge it is to speak for and from within the tradition and not simply about the tradition.[50]

In Hick's most recent full-scale defense of his pluralist model, *Christian Theology of Religions*, it is clear that he is quite conscious of this distinction.[51] Thus, 'Phil' the philosopher deals with the more philosophical challenges to Hick's model in chapters two and three, while 'Grace' the theologian poses the more theological criticisms in chapters four and five. However, even in this venue, it is questionable whether Hick himself is able to actually keep his 'philosopher' vs. 'Christian theologian' roles as distinct as he theoretically should.

A related problem is the fact that Hick's corpus as a whole contains both of these perspectives in a rather confusing mix. Certainly it would be unfair to charge him with self-inconsistency and perspectival confusion simply by setting his earlier works at odds with those that followed his neo-Kantian awakening. After all, as Hick has so often reminded us, anyone can change their mind![52] However, it is clear that even in his more recent works, Hick has not yet entirely purged this methodological conflation. For example, although Hick has drastically edited and/or rewritten other parts of his *Philosophy of Religion* over the course of its four editions, often to render it consistent with his neo-Kantian perspective, he has left his original chapter on "Revelation and Faith" virtually untouched. It is very difficult—one could say impossible—to square this older *heilsgeschichte* view with his more recent neo-Kantian understanding of religious revelation and doctrine. The former is clearly rooted in the theism of his Christian theological persona, and yet it appears in a 1990 work that purports to be a 'philosophy of religion,' which, for the post-1980 Hick, *must* mean a tradition-neutral approach.[53] In any case, it is important to realize that these two differing perspectives present themselves throughout Hick's corpus.

The Soteriological Turn: Religion as 'Salvation/Liberation'

Beginning in the early 1980s, one can also notice a growing emphasis on the notion of "salvation/liberation" in Hick's pluralist writings.[54] In this regard, it is interesting to compare the expression of his pluralist hypothesis at the beginning of this decade with a similar statement at the end of this period. In 1981, Hick offered this synopsis of his thesis:

> the different streams of religious experience represent diverse awarenesses of the same transcendent reality, which is perceived in characteristically different ways by different human mentalities, formed by and forming different cultural histories."[55]

By 1989, he had modified his standard summary as follows:

> the great world faiths embody different perceptions and conceptions of, and correspondingly different responses to, the Real from within the major variant ways of being human; *and that within each of them the transformation of human existence from self-centeredness to Reality-centeredness is taking place.*[56]

The addition of this closing portion is significant. It represents Hick's most basic definition of human salvation/liberation in the post-axial traditions. As such, Hick clearly intends for the category of salvation/liberation to identify a unifying phenomenon across the diverse landscape of post-axial religious life. His claim is that a purely inductive study of the post-axial traditions delivers this common soteriological structure. In *An Interpretation of Religion*, after spending an entire chapter canvassing the Hindu, Buddhist, Christian, Jewish, and Muslim traditions, Hick reaches his conclusion:

> Each of the great post-axial streams of religious experience and belief has been shown to exhibit a soteriological structure: a recognition of our human moral weakness and failure or of the pervasive insecurity and liability-to-suffering of all life; the proclamation of a limitlessly better possibility arising from another reality, transcendent to our present selves; and the teaching of a way, whether by our 'own power' spiritual discipline or the 'other power' of divine grace, to its realization. They are thus centrally concerned with salvation or liberation....We can express this abstractly by saying that post-axial religion embodies a cosmic optimism.[57]

The need for, and benefit of, such a unifying category is readily apparent in light of the ramifications of Hick's neo-Kantian proposal for knowledge of the divine. The noumenon/phenomena distinction leads to the conclusion that, in the face of the wide diversity of concrete and 'knowable' religious phenomena, any conceptual grasp of the supposed (i.e., 'postulated') unifying noumenon is, by definition, ruled out from the start. Thus, Hick's theory requires a 'knowable' reality within the phenomenal religious realm which can function as an indicator of, and thus as an anchor to, the postulated Real. In one of his first essays devoted to fleshing out his neo-Kantian hypothesis, Hick appears to have already recognized this dilemma:

> Thus in expounding this situation [i.e., his neo-Kantian thesis] we have to try to keep two themes in balance: the agnostic theme that we only know God partially and imperfectly, and the positive theme that we really do know God as practically and savingly related to ourselves.[58]

Once Hick recognized that "the great business of religion is salvation," and that salvation/liberation can be defined broadly enough to encompass the soteriological goals of each of the various post-axial religious traditions, he was well on the way to establishing it as the one unifying factor among the otherwise radically diverse great world religions.[59] Hick's common soteriological structure argument has been taken by many of his critics as evidence that he is working with a questionable 'common core' definition/theory of religion. However, Hick has explicitly stated that he rejects a "common essence" definition/theory of religion in favor of a "family resemblance" view, wherein there are "no characteristics that every member must have."[60]

Avoiding Relativism: Hick's Soteriological Religious Criterion

Hick has always refused to allow his pluralist inclinations to lead him into the abyss of sheer religious relativism. He has consistently maintained the importance of being able to make some type of judgment about particular religious phenomena. But the question of how to do so in a *non-arbitrary* fashion has always posed a challenge to those within the pluralist paradigm. Human reason, of course, could offer one obvious tool for religious assessment. However, there is a problem here. On Hick's theory of religion, it is first and foremost *religious experience* that requires assessment. And this is a realm where reason does not much help:

> It does not appear, first, that we can speak of the rationality or irrationality of an experience. It is not experiences, but people and their beliefs and reasonings, that are rational or irrational. The distinctive experiences of Gautama, Jesus, Muhammad, and the Hindu saints, which lie at the originating basis of Buddhism, Christianity, Islam, and Hinduism, were not rational constructs; they were, puta-

tively, encounters with reality. Each of these root experiences was overwhelmingly powerful, and could only be accepted as authentic by the person whose experience it was. The test of the veridical character of such an experience must thus be the test of a larger religious totality which has been built around it. *And such a test can only be pragmatic....* [A]nd so it does not seem that the tool of reason can enable us to test and assess the different basic religious experiences and their associated visions of reality.[61]

By 1981, Hick had realized that the common religious experience of salvation/liberation that served as a practical unifying reality among the great post-axial faiths could also function as the *pragmatic* criterion that was required for the assessment of human religious phenomena in general. In his article, "On Grading Religions," Hick writes:

Let us begin by noting the broad common pattern in virtue of which it makes sense to attempt a comparative study of religions. For unless they had something in common it would be impossible to compare them, still less to grade them on a common scale. They do however in fact, I suggest, exhibit a common structure, which is soteriological in the broad sense that it offers a transition from a radically unsatisfactory state to a limitlessly better one.... [For each of the post-axial world religions,] salvation/liberation consists in a new and limitlessly better quality of existence which comes about in the transition from self-centeredness to Reality-centeredness.... [R]eligious phenomena—patterns of behavior, experiences, beliefs, myths, theologies, cultic acts, liturgies, scriptures, and so forth—can in principle be assessed and graded; and the basic criterion is the extent to which they promote or hinder the great religious aim of salvation/liberation.[62]

Since its debut, this double use of the salvation/liberation motif has remained a hallmark of Hick's theory of religion.[63] Hick's provocative suggestion that salvation/liberation is the "basic criterion" of all religious phenomena forces the question of how the various religions stack up against each other. Hick's theory and response run as follows. He begins with the claim that "the function of post-axial religion is to create contexts within which the transformation from self-centeredness to Reality-centeredness can take place."[64] Thus, Hick recognizes the production of "saintliness"—that is, "ego-transcending Reality-centeredness"—as the purpose of the great world religions.[65] Given this, it follows that "the basic criterion must be soteriological."[66] But how can one make a concrete judgment about the presence or absence of 'saintliness' in any given instance? To answer this question, Hick isolates a common, yet concrete, ethical criterion within the major world religions. In brief, Hick claims that "all the great traditions teach the moral ideal of generous goodwill, love, compassion epitomized in the Golden Rule." Hick refers to this common ethical ideal as "*agape/karuna*."[67] (*Agape*, of course, is the Greek term most commonly used in the New Testament to indicate self-sacrificial love. *Karuna*, a term used in the Buddhist Pali texts, can be translated as 'compassion.') It is this criterion that Hick offers as the concrete measuring rod for any and all religious phenomena.

Practically speaking, just how effective is Hick's criterion? When it comes to particular religious phenomena, Hick is willing to apply it and find a variety of religious instances—including doctrines, practices, and even 'minor' religious movements as a whole—to come up soteriologically short. For example, the Augustinian-Calvinist Christian doctrine of double predestination "cannot express the unqualified love, limitless compassion or generous forgiveness which constitutes the common ethical ideal."[68] Likewise, the unjust caste-system and the practice of widow burning (*suttee*) associated with the Hindu tradition stand condemned by the agape/karuna principle.[69] Finally, Hick is even prepared to make totalizing judgments upon what he considers to be several minor religious (and/or ideological) movements. For years, his standard examples of indisputable contexts of soterioloical failure have included such notorious traditions as "Satanism" and "Nazism," as well as the People's Temple associated with the infamous Jonestown mass suicide.[70] Recently, three other movements have been added to Hick's list of religious phenomena that "are not authentic human responses" to the Real: the Branch Davidian group of the 1993 Waco massacre, the Order of the Solar Temple associated with the mass suicides of recent years, and the Aum Shin Rikyo cult, which was responsible for the 1995 Tokyo nerve gas incident.[71] With this willingness on Hick's part to speak a strong soteriological "No!" to a wide variety of religious phenomena comes the evidence he needs to prove that his soteriological criterion effectively distinguishes his religious 'pluralism' from mere religious 'relativism.'

One might wonder at this point if Hick has not jeopardized his pluralist enterprise. It appears that he has safeguarded the parity of the great world religions in the conceptual realm (via his neo-Kantian proposal) only to return to an 'exclusivistic' ranking of them in the soteriological realm. Has Hick betrayed the pluralist paradigm by conjuring up the specter of the "truest religion" once again—this time, not in regard to doctrinal matters, but rather as a factor of pragmatic soteriological effectiveness? Hick does not allow his reader to entertain such fears for long. For when it comes to the question of applying this criterion, things become "comparatively easy," and yet "extremely difficult."

Hick explains:

> It is easy in the sense that we can readily list actions and patterns of behavior which are good and evil respectively under this criterion....But when we seek to go beyond the identification of particular phenomena as good or evil to make judgments concerning the religious traditions as totalities, we encounter large complicating factors which must give pause to any project for the moral grading of the great world faiths.[72]

In fact, these "complicating factors" give Hick much more than merely a momentary 'pause.' Rather, they serve to render any 'grading' project of the great post-axial religions, undertaken as it must be from a finite human perspective, doomed from the outset. In light of the wide-ranging and complex histories of each of these great traditions—histories, in each case, comprised of both self-giving benevolence and 'sainthood' on one hand, and self-centered malevolence and depravity on the other—each religion can only be viewed as "a unique mixture of good and evil." Given this assessment, Hick's conclusion is not surprising:

> It may be the case that, from the point of view of omniscience, one tradition stands out as morally superior to all others. But if so this is not evident from our partial human perspective. It is not possible, as an unbiased judgment with which all rational persons could be expected to agree, to assert the overall moral superiority of any one of the great religious traditions of the world.[73]

And so, despite Hick's recognition and implementation of a universal religious criterion, the "large complicating factors" involved with assessing the major world religions leave their parity intact and, with it, the pluralist hypothesis untouched.

Help from the Buddha: Hick's Response to the Problem of Conflicting Religious Truth-Claims

The above analysis of Hick's neo-Kantian proposal has demonstrated the manner in which he deals with the most troubling inter-religious truth-claim conflict. Hick has also refined his approach to other types of doctrinal conflict over the years. Specifically, he has turned to several aspects of Buddhist thought as resources in his attempt to vitiate a number of such problems. Hick now employs the Buddhist notions of *upaya* (i.e., "skilful means") and *avyakata* (i.e., "undetermined/unanswerable questions"); both concepts are derived from the Buddha's teachings in the *Majjhima Nikaya*.[74]

A discussion of Hick's utilization of the notion of *upaya* can set the stage for explicating his use of *avyakata*. It is within the context of his soteriocentric view of religion that he appropriates the notion of "skilful means." Tradition has it that the Buddha communicated the notion of *upaya* in the Parable of the Raft. This parable tells of a man who constructs a raft in order to cross a river. Upon crossing successfully, the man is so thankful for the raft that he is tempted to hoist it on his back and haul it along with him over the dry land. But the Buddha points out that this would be counter-productive to his journey. Transposed into the religious realm, the message is clear. The raft (i.e., doctrinal concepts) has served its (soteriological) purpose; it can now be discarded. Using it in its broadest sense, Hick employs this idea to emphasize that one's religious knowledge and concepts are, at best, a means to a soteriocentric end; at worst, they can hinder progress toward that end.[75]

Again, it is within this soteriocentric context that Hick unfolds his appropriation of the Buddhist concept of *avyakata vis-à-vis* religious doctrine. He identifies two types of doctrinal questions. First, "unanswered questions" involve those doctrinal questions "to which there is a true answer although we do not in fact know that answer," since we lack the type and/or degree of knowledge a definitive answer would require.[76] Second, "unanswerable questions" concern doctrinal issues that, by the very nature of the case, can never be broached in anything but terms of utter mystery, since they involve "realities transcending the systems of categories available in our human thought and language."[77] Again, with the Buddha, Hick affirms that finding answers to either type of question is practically extraneous to the vital question of human salvation. Armed with these two classifications, Hick applies them to his three types of inter-religious doctrinal conflict, the names of which have undergone some refinement since their debut in the early 1970s: "historical truth-claims," "trans-historical truth-claims," and "conceptions of the ultimate reality."[78]

Hick concludes that the first type—conflicts between historical claims—are, ultimately, of the "unanswered" variety. Given the great differences in time and culture, we simply do not have enough reliable information upon which to adjudicate between the various religions' conflicting historical truth-claims. Interestingly, Hick concludes that there "aren't in fact many such conflicts between the religions because, generally speaking, each tradition cherishes its own separate strand of remembered history."[79] When pressed, he has stated that he can only think of *two* such instances in religious history![80] The third type, doctrinal conceptions of the divine Reality, are, given Hick's neo-Kantian proposal, clearly of the "unanswerable" variety. Since they make claims concerning a *noumenal* Reality to which we have no access whatsoever—we can only know its phenomenal manifestations—such conflictive doctrinal claims are not only unadjudicable, but are really not even literally conflictive given their mythological nature (more on this below). Finally, the second type, transhistorical doctrinal claims (e.g., creation claims, eschatologies, etc.), can be either "unanswered" or "unanswerable" in nature. Hick offers the question of the nature of the universe (i.e., eternal or temporally finite?) as an example of the former, and the question of the nature of eschatologically perfected humanity as an instance of the latter.[81] In this manner, Hick relegates virtually any assessment of inter-religious doctrinal disputes to the realms of the virtually impossible and practically unnecessary.

In accord with these gleanings from Buddhist thought, Hick's notion of *myth* has developed in both complexity and expanse. To begin with, it is important to note that Hick has retained his earlier definition of "myth": a myth is "true" to the degree that it "tends to evoke an appropriate dispositional attitude to X."[82] Next, Hick introduces a distinction between two different types of myth: the first type, "expository myths," involve doctrinal matters "that can also be [expressed] non-mythologically, though generally with markedly less imaginative impact."[83] Thus expository myths pertain to those matters that fall within the bounds of "unanswered questions." Hick offers the stories of the Judeo-Christian Adamic fall, Buddha's flight to Sri Lanka, and the archangel Gabriel's dictation of the Qur'an, as well as the doctrines of transubstantiation and reincarnation, as examples of expository myth.

Hick spends the most space and ink, however, developing his second sense of myth: namely the mythological character of language about the divine Reality and any and all religious thought/doctrine related to It. Here, one has clearly entered the realm of "mysteries" and "unanswerable questions." Since all human language is bound to the phenomenal realm, such language and its conceptual categories can have no literal—or even analogical—purchase *vis-à-vis* the divine noumenon. But since all religious language is *intended* by the believer to be about the ultimate divine Reality, it must be, at best, mythological in nature. That is, although the doctrines of the world religions—contrary to the belief and intention of their adherents—provide no true factual information about the divine, they can nonetheless be deemed "mythologically true" *if* they serve to "evoke in us attitudes and modes of behavior which are appropriate to our situation *vis-à-vis* the Real."[84] Thus the value of myth is purely practical—as opposed to cognitive—in nature.

Hick emphasizes that this second type of myth runs along a formal continuum from the concrete/narrative to the abstract/philosophical—all of it is equally mythological. Thus, the sophisticated philosopher of religion is no closer to a "literal," non-mythological understanding of the divine Reality than is the most simple, naive religious believer. In this manner, *almost* the entire world of religious and theological thought and discourse is reduced to non-cognitive myth:

> we can identify the various systems of religious thought as complex myths whose truth or untruth consists in the appropriateness or inappropriateness of the practical dispositions which they tend to evoke.[85]

One must qualify the last claim with an "almost," since Hick must attempt to retain *something* of religious cognitive value lest he fall prey to the non-cognitive/non-realist camp against whom he has struggled—as a "critical realist"—for the last four decades. For Hick and his pluralist hypothesis, it appears that all that is salvageable as something more than non-cognitive myth are the following two claims: (1) there exists a divine noumenal Reality that reveals Itself as the unknowable ground of all religious experience, (2) humanity is destined for a "limitlessly good" future existence, a concept supported by the "cosmic optimism" shared by all the great world religions.[86] Hick continues to employ his long-standing notion of eschatological verification, if in a qualified version, as a means of safe-guarding the realist intent of these two claims. When asked recently if he has abandoned the idea of eschatological verifiability, as opposed to falsifiability, *vis-à-vis* his pluralist hypothesis, Hick responded:

> Yes and no. Yes, in the sense that the Real, as the ultimate nature of reality, is not postulated as an entity that could ever be observed, even in a final eschatological state—so the idea of direct experiential verification does not apply here. But No, in the sense that the structure of reality, as it affects us human beings, can be progressively experienced and found to be such that the pluralistic hypothesis is the best picture of the universe that we can form....[87]

By maintaining a realist claim regarding the two eschatologically verifiable doctrines that form the core of his pluralist hypothesis, Hick distinguishes his 'religious understanding of religion' from the naturalistic, non-realist alternative. Yet, because *all* the world religions can agree with these two doctrines (even though the manners in which they would flesh them out with substantive content would seriously clash), and because all the other doctrinal conflicts have been vitiated by classifying them as myths—and thus granting them at least potential, complementary parity, Hick can also maintain his unitive religious pluralism.[88] Thus, to Hick's mind, pluralism's classic problem of conflicting religious truth-claims has finally been solved via his pluralist hypothesis:

> My conclusion, then, is that the differences between the root concepts and experiences of the different religions, their different and often conflicting historical and trans-historical beliefs, their incommensurable mythologies, and the diverse and ramifying belief-systems into which all these are built, are compatible with the pluralistic hypothesis that the great world traditions constitute different conceptions and perceptions of, and responses to, the Real from within the different cultural ways of being human.[89]

If Hick is right, he has attained the best of both worlds: a radically pluralistic religious realism.

Tying Up Loose Ends: Of Mythology, Eschatology, and Cosmic Optimism

In spite of these adjustments, Hick's pluralist model continued to draw accusations, including the charge of covert theism. Here, one of Hick's most cordial, insightful, and enduring critics comes to the fore of the discussion: the Roman Catholic inclusivist, Gavin D'Costa. According to D'Costa's early critique in the mid-1980s, despite the adoption of the neo-Kantian proposal, Hick's Copernican revolution is, in fact, tantamount to "just another, but rather confused, Ptolemaic epicycle."[90] The reason for this assessment is two-fold, and both aspects serve to raise, once again, the specter of covert theism.[91]

First, although Hick has adopted the neo-Kantian mechanism and tradition-neutral terminology, and has discontinued his explicit 'God of universal love' defense, such moves only serve to intensify the question of just what *grounding* his pluralist move now carries. Once one ontologically disengages the Christian God of love from the noumenal Real, the impetus for the pluralist shift should be eliminated as well. The fact that this is not the case for Hick reveals that he is still harboring a covert theism and a Christological one at that. It is fundamentally *Christological* in that God's universal love—the pluralist assumption—is definitively revealed only in Jesus Christ. Thus, in D'Costa's words:

> without this premise [i.e., the 'God of universal love'], the Copernican enterprise will collapse. With this premise, and its inevitable *Christological* implications, the Copernican revolution looks rather like yet another ingenious Ptolemaic epicycle![92]

Second, and even more explicitly, D'Costa pointed out that Hick's post-Copernican conception of the eschaton remained fundamentally *theistic*. This type of charge was such that it not only challenged Hick's pluralist model, but his life-long concern to maintain a robust religious realism. As noted earlier, since the 1950s, Hick had argued for the notion of 'eschatological verification' as an answer to those positivistically-influenced philosophers who questioned the very meaningfulness of God-talk. Hick's contention was that as long as the eschaton offered an opportunity for theistic verification, one could justifiably hold to such a belief, based on personal, subjective religious experience, in the interim. For this reason, Hick was disposed toward maintaining a conception of the eschaton that offered a final clarification of the religious question. And so, even several years after his pluralist move, one finds Hick on the last page of his global thanatology arguing for an eschatological vision that:

> implicitly rejects the *advaitist* view that Atman *is* Brahman, the collective human self being ultimately identical with God, in favor of the more complex *vishishtadvaitist* interpretation of the Upanishads, which is in turn substantially in agreement with the christian conception of God as personal Lord, distinct from his creation.[93]

Thus, in D'Costa's summary words:

> on Hick's premises, religious truth claims are verified in the eschaton and his Co-pernican eschaton is distinctly theistic, thereby smuggling "God" from the *centre* to the *end* of the universe of faiths—thereby creating the same problems prior to the epicycle.[94]

At the same time, D'Costa noted a parallel strand of implicit theism running through Hick's post-Copernican theodicy.[95] Although it was developed in his pre-pluralist days,[96] Hick continued to apply his "Irenaean theodicy" on this side of the Copernican divide whenever the problem of evil cropped up.[97] The problem here, again, is that his Irenaean theodicy is fundamentally grounded upon the notion of a personal God of universal love. Hick himself makes this quite clear:

> On this view the human, endowed with a real though limited freedom, is basically formed for relationship with God and destined to find the fulfillment of his or her nature in that relationship....*given the theistic postulate*, it seems to me to offer a very probable account of our human situation.[98]

Thus, as D'Costa points out, despite his best efforts to the contrary, Hick the pluralist is again found writing as if the ultimate Reality is—in the end—best described in terms of personalistic theism.

Hick was quick to bring critical adjustments to each of these areas highlighted by D'Costa and others. Given the timing, it is difficult to say when he was responding to explicit criticisms and when he was simply reworking the model on his own, given its implicit logic. In either case, it is safe to say that by the time of his 1986–7 Gifford Lectures, Hick had offered substantive responses to the above criticisms, each of which served to seriously modify not only his pluralist model, but his life-long theological project as well. Four important moves can be identified.[99]

First, in a 1985 "Postscript" to a reprint of his earlier article "Eschatological Verification Reconsidered," Hick significantly reworks the explicitly theistic eschatological scenarios portrayed both in the original essay and in *Death and Eternal Life*:

> [I]t seems likely that the different expectations cherished within the different traditions will ultimately turn out to be partly correct and partly incorrect. It could be that in a mind-dependent *bardo* phase immediately after death these expectations will be fulfilled in the experience of believers—Christians, Hindus, Muslims, and so on each encountering what their different traditions have taught them to anticipate. But as they advance beyond that phase…[they] will themselves develop, becoming gradually more adequate to the reality.…[I]t may well be that the final state will prove to be beyond the horizon of our present powers of imagination.[100]

More recently, Hick addresses this issue in *Interpretation of Religion*. He begins by easily demonstrating how the notion of eschatological verification could work in accordance with the theistic religions. The problem, of course, arises with the question of how to preserve a place of parity for the various non-theistic traditions' post-mortem scenarios, while nonetheless providing the requisite elements necessary for the (eschatological) verification of prior religious claims. In answer to this question, Hick offers an example of how it might work for an Advaita Vedanta scenario:

> If, then, in the eschaton all consciousnesses have united into a single consciousness, and if this was predicted in a theory propounded by some of the individual consciousnesses before they united, it would seem that the unitary consciousness may be said to have verified that theory in its own experience. The eternal Self will know (and indeed knows now) that It is the one ultimate Reality underlying the illusorily finite egos.[101]

With moves such as this, Hick purports to put to rest any charges of covert eschatological theism.[102] At the same time, however, it appears that such developments have the unavoidable effect of seriously disrupting Hick's perennial basis for meaningful God-talk (or 'Real'-talk), and thus his life-long religious realism. Hick can no longer claim that the eschaton will bring with it (or not) the verification of a particular religion's truth-claims. Instead, the most he can now posit is that his eschatological verification principle will ultimately decide the truth of a generally "religious," as opposed to a "naturalistic," interpretation of the presently always religiously ambiguous universe.[103] It is telling that in light of this decisive adjustment, D'Costa has generally desisted from leveling the charge of implicit theism at Hick's model. Instead, he has replaced it with the equally disturbing charge—for the realist Hick—of "transcendental agnosticism."[104]

A second critical shift, one parallel to the above, is made explicit in Hick's *An Interpretation of Religion.* In a section devoted to an analysis of the "naturalistic option," Hick once again calls forth his Irenaean theodicy—with its personalist-theistic presumption—as a response to the problem of evil.[105] However, twelve chapters later, in the course of a discussion on the fundamentally mythological character of religious language, he attaches an appendix entitled "Theodicy as Mythology." Here, Hick effectively neutralizes the charge of covert theism *vis-à-vis* his Irenaean theodicy—but only at the expense of divesting it of any and all realist implications. He writes:

> Such a theodicy is mythical in the sense that the language in which it speaks about the Real, as a personal being carrying out intentions through time, cannot apply to the ultimate Reality in itself. But such a theodicy nevertheless constitutes a true myth in so far as the practical attitudes which it tends to evoke amid the evils of human life are appropriate to our present existence in relation to the Real.[106]

Thus, theodicy becomes merely a matter of the phenomenal—that is, "mythical" *vis-à-vis* the Real—realm of religion; in relation to the Real itself it says *nothing*, since here, by definition of course, nothing substantial ever can be said. Or, as D'Costa has nicely put it: "The outcome of the escape from particularity can only be to nothing in particular."[107]

Hick has also constructed a response to one particular form of the covert theism charge that has plagued him from the beginning: namely the claim that the Christian 'God of universal love' is, and always has been, the true animating force behind his pluralist enterprise. As noted earlier, by the early 1980s, Hick had discontinued his overt use of this defense for his pluralist move.

However, since he had never explicitly replaced it with a more feasible, tradition-neutral motivational vehicle, suspicions continued to run high that, in fact, it still lurked within his model, even if at a subterranean level.[108] With the publication of *An Interpretation of Religion*, however, Hick brought a new resource into play—namely the *inter-religious* notion of "cosmic optimism," which serves as short-hand for the common soteriological sensibility and hope found within all of the post-axial traditions.[109] Hick explains the importance of this shift:

> whilst the Christian concept of a loving personal divine Father is indeed, in my view, incompatible with traditional Christian exclusivism, when we are concerned with the religious life of humanity as a whole we have to look beyond this to the more basic affirmation of the ultimate goodness of the universe from our human point of view. And so I have used Jewish, Christian, Muslim, Hindu and Buddhist sources to establish the 'cosmic optimism' of the great post-axial streams of religion. The belief in a sovereign and loving Creator is only one of the forms that this belief takes.[110]

Thus, with the adoption of the idea of "cosmic optimism" as a motivating force, Hick maintains the basic "goodness" of the universe, while distancing his pluralist philosophy—and especially his conception of the Real—from a specifically Christian and/or theistic manifestation of this general theme. It is worth noting here that 'Cosmic optimism' has also become, for Hick, constitutive of the critical divide between the religious and the naturalistic interpretation of religions. Thus, Hick's notions of a common soteriological structure of religions, cosmic optimism, and the connected claim that "the structure of the universe is such that this limitlessly better possibility is actually achieved" (both now in a limited fashion, and more fully in the eschaton) represent all that is left of Hick's once robust realist truth-claims.[111]

Finally, in accordance with the shifts noted above, Hick has fine-tuned his understanding of the Real—the divine noumenal Reality that is the source and ground of all human religious experience—so as to further safeguard him from the charge of privileging *any* particular phenomenal manifestation. He stresses more strongly than ever that the Real is beyond *all* human conceptual-linguistic categories:

> we cannot apply to the Real *an sich* the characteristics encountered in its *personae* and *impersonae*. Thus it cannot be said to be one or many, person or thing, conscious or unconscious, purposive or non-purposive, substance or process, good or evil, loving or hating. None of the descriptive terms that apply within the realm of

human experience can apply literally to the unexperienceable reality that underlies that realm....We cannot even speak of this as a thing or an entity.[112]

Thus, even the one general conceptual point of common ground among the religions—the common ethical ideal of agape/karuna—cannot be applied directly to the Real: "It is good, then, not in itself but in relation to the deepest concerns of human beings."[113] In light of this state of affairs, Hick suggests that a fitting symbol for the ultimately Real can be found in one particular development of the Buddhist notion of *sunyata* ("emptiness"), which can actually signify "an anti-concept excluding all concepts."[114]

With such adjustments as these, it would appear that Hick has successfully warded off a variety of charges to which the earlier versions of his pluralist model were vulnerable. Unfortunately, a number of Hick's critics either have not noticed these more recent modifications, or else simply have not adequately appraised their effectiveness.[115] In any case, trotting out now-obsolete forms of critique can only serve to impede the critical assessment of Hick's present model. Hick is correct that unless his critics thoroughly shift their focus "to the more fully developed pluralist hypothesis in *An Interpretation of Religion*," significant headway in the discussion will not be made.[116] For this reason, I will confine my own critical discussion in the final chapter of this study to those aspects of Hick's thought that allow for direct ties to his post-*Interpretation of Religion* model of religious pluralism.

Theological Implications of Hick's Mature 'Neo-Kantian' Model: A Christological Sounding

John Hick is a philosopher of religion. He has struggled to clarify the fact that his pluralist hypothesis is first and foremost a component of a wider religious field theory of religion, offered from a tradition-neutral philosophy of religion perspective. However, John Hick is also a Christian, and a "Christian theologian" at that. As such, Hick sees it as his "primary responsibility to contribute to the rethinking of absolutism within my own tradition."[117] Since Christian 'absolutism' is chiefly fueled by the orthodox doctrine of the deity of Christ, the incarnation continues to be the principal target of Hick's doctrinal "reinterpretation" project.[118]

The essential core of Hick's 'incarnation-as-myth' approach to understanding Jesus has undergone little real change since its genesis in the 1970s. This becomes quite clear as one compares his early pluralist Christology with his more recent (1993) volume devoted to this topic, *The Metaphor of God Incarnate: Christology in a Pluralistic Age*.[119] Hick has described the "main conclusion" of this book as follows:

> that the idea of divine incarnation in its standard Christian form, in which both genuine humanity and genuine deity are insisted upon, has never been given a satisfactory literal sense; but that on the other hand it makes excellent metaphorical sense.[120]

Again, in essence, there is little new in this general conclusion when compared to his earlier thought. However, as one makes her way through the book, she will quickly recognize changes, both of form and content, in a number of areas of Hick's argument. First, Hick opens the book by noticing just "how strongly and even frenetically polemical" the 1970s debate was that surrounded the *Myth of God Incarnate* volume. In a moment of confession, he acknowledges that "we authors of *The Myth* were as polemical as our critics."[121] It is Hick's hope that, with the passage of time, it is now possible to continue the discussion in a "more temperate mood." And toward this end he offers *The Metaphor of God Incarnate* as his contribution to the on-going discussion, one that seeks to "pose the central question afresh in a less stark and more nuanced way."[122] Thus, Hick would have us consider the more moderate tone and careful presentation of his recent work on Christology.

Hick's critique of traditional Chalcedonian incarnational Christology remains largely unchanged. He continues to proffer the three lines of counterargument mentioned earlier: First, neither the teaching nor the apparent experience of the historic Jesus serves to authorize the claim of a literal incarnation.[123] Hick's understanding of the historical Jesus is most clearly indebted to the work of E. P. Sanders and Paula Fredericksen. This locates Hick within a definite school of thought within the contemporary Jesus Quest. With these two scholars, he emphasizes the Jewishness of Jesus, and the importance of Jesus as an apocalyptic prophet. Second, in retrospect, one can trace the historical process by which Jesus came to be thought of as 'God,' and can fully explain it in terms of human instigation.[124] Finally, no rendition of the traditional model of 'fully God and fully human,' taken literally, has ever been shown to be *meaningful*; all attempts to do so err by privileging either the human or divine over the other.[125]

With regard to this last point, although a number of Christian scholars have attempted to meet Hick's challenge to present a "viable understanding of the incarnation" for theological and philosophical examination, Hick remains unconvinced.[126] It should be noted that Hick's charge against a literal understanding of the incarnation is *not* that it is necessarily logically self-contradictory. Rather, he simply argues that, to date, no attempt to render it philosophically meaningful has succeeded. In principle, however, he is open to such a possibility:

> the more philosophically ingenious christologies have become the less religiously realistic they seem to be. This conclusion can never of course be final, for it must always be theoretically possible for a new theory to be conceived that is free from serious objection. [However,] I do not think that the theoretical possibility of a successful theory in the future should now be allowed to hold up the development of [pluralist christologies].[127]

In addition to these three now-standard arguments against a literal incarnation, Hick has come to emphasize a fourth: "historically the traditional dogma has been used to justify great human evils."[128]

Another development in the presentation of Hick's Christology arose in the early 1980s. Since this time, Hick has consistently cited the work of Donald Baillie and Geoffrey Lampe as departure points for his own Christological project.[129] In Baillie's "paradox of grace" approach to understanding the incarnation, as well as in Lampe's Spirit Christology, Hick sees indicators of a fruitful path toward a pluralist Christology. Their proposals point toward the conclusion that Jesus, instead of being 'divine' in any uniquely ontological sense, is best understood as the highest human exemplar of one indwelt and motivated by the Spirit of God so as to fully realize the divine-human relationship intended by the Creator.

The conclusions of Baillie and Lampe serve to set the stage for Hick's own "inspiration" Christology.[130] For Hick, inspiration is simply another way of saying "grace."[131] He is clear on the "kind" vs. "degree" question: "Incarnation in this sense has occurred and is occurring in many different ways and degrees in many different persons."[132] In his most critical departure from both Baillie and Lampe, Hick challenges their apparently *a priori* assumption that the Spirit's connection to Jesus was somehow fuller or more absolute than in anyone else. Rather, this question can only be settled by assessing the historical data regarding each religious claimant. In light of our lack of the necessary detailed information, as well as the inherent "difficulties and uncertainties" of historical judgments in general, the question of which religious person(s) throughout history have been the most Spirit-influenced becomes practically unanswerable.[133] Thus Jesus, along with all other religious figures, becomes de-absolutized not only in an ontological/constitutive sense, but even in terms of functioning as a universal religious norm.

One also notices that Hick has substituted the term 'metaphor' for 'myth' in his recent Christological proposal. This terminological change does not seem to signal any substantive modification of Hick's thesis. Rather, it appears that he is merely attempting to root his former notion of the incarnation as 'myth' in more recent discussions that have focused upon the metaphorical nature of language in general, and religious language in particular.[134] Whether or not Hick has been successful here is a matter of debate.[135]

Finally, Hick has continued his attacks on the traditional notions of the Trinity and the atonement. Specifically, he demonstrates that his "inspiration" Christology would suggest that we reject a "social" view of the Trinity in favor of a purely "modal" understanding. In regard to atonement theory, any sort of 'objective' element should be discarded (e.g., Christus victor or vicarious substitution models). Rather, Jesus' death is better viewed in purely 'subjective' terms (e.g., revelatory or exemplar models).[136] Needless to say, Hick's more recent criticisms of traditional incarnational Christologies, and his own constructive proposal of an alternative Christology have not gone unchallenged.[137]

Notes

1   See e.g., Philip Almond, "John Hick's Copernican Theology," *Theology* 86 (1983): 36–41; Peter Byrne, "John Hick's Philosophy of World Religions," *Scottish Journal of Theology* 35 (1982): 289–301; Duncan Forrester, "Professor Hick and the Universe of Faiths," *Scottish Journal of Theology* 29 (1976): 65–72; Paul Griffiths and Delmas Lewis, "On Grading Religions, Seeking Truth, and Being Nice to People," *Religious Studies* 19 (1983): 75–80; Kubias, "John Hick's Epistemology"; J. J. Lipner, "Does Copernicus Help? Reflections for a Christian Theology of Religions," *Religious Studies* 13 (1977): 243–58; idem., "Truth-claims and Inter-religious Dialogue," *Religious Studies* 12 (1976): 217–30.

2   See e.g., Sir Norman Anderson, "The Incarnation and Comparative Religion," in *The Mystery of the Incarnation*, 60–81; L. Philip Barnes, "Towards a Theology of World Religions: An Outline and Assessment of the Work of John Hick," *Churchman* 97 (1983): 216–31; Hywel D. Lewis, "Appendix B: A Note on Professor Hick's Views," *Jesus in the Faith of Christians* (London: Macmillan, 1981), 107–10; J. J. Lipner, "Christians and the Uniqueness of Christ," *Scottish Journal of Theology* 28 (1975): 359–68; Kenneth Surin, "Revelation, Salvation, the Uniqueness of Christ and Other Religions," *Religious Studies* 19 (1983): 323–43; Max Warren, "The Uniqueness of Christ," *Modern Churchman* 18 (1974): 55–65. See also John Coventry, "The Myth and the Method," *Theology* 81 (1978): 252–61.

3   "Copernican Revolution," in *God and the Universe of Faiths*, 131.

4   Ibid., 131–32. Hick had already made this point explicit in the 1972 article, "Christian

View of Other Faiths," 38.

5   Almond, "John Hick's Copernican Theology," 39; see also Forrester, "Professor Hick and the Universe of Faiths," 69.

6   See Almond, "Hick's Copernican Theology," 37–38; Lipner, "Does Copernicus Help?" 253–54.

7   Coward, *Pluralism*, 30.

8   See D'Costa's summary discussion, *Hick's Theology of Religions*, 152.

9   "Mystical Experience as Cognition," 52.

10   Chubb, "Presuppositions of Religious Dialogue," 295.

11   See, for instance, the essays comprising chapters 3, 5, and 6 in Hick, *God Has Many Names*.

12   E.g., see *God Has Many Names*, 91, 110; *Philosophy of Religion*, 3rd ed., 118; *Interpretation of Religion*, 236–37.

13   *God Has Many Names*, 110.

14   See Hick, "The Theology of Religious Pluralism," 336–37.

15   *Interpretation of Religion*, 240.

16   The lecture is available on audio tape as "Christian Faith and People of Different Faiths," Goodkind of Sound, Rt. 3, Box 365AA, Sylva, N.C. 28779.

17   Twiss, "The Philosophy of Religious Pluralism: A Critical Appraisal of Hick and His Critics," *Journal of Religion* 70 (1990): 534–36, 567–68.

18   *Interpretation of Religion*, 240.

19   Ibid., 242.

20   "Copernican Revolution," 131 (emphasis in text).

21   "Toward a Philosophy of Religious Pluralism," *God Has Many Names*, 90–91.

22   See "Theology of Religious Pluralism," 336; also *Philosophy of Religion*, 3rd ed., 118; "On Conflicting Religious Truth-Claims," 488. See Hocking, *Living Religions and a World Faith*, 7. On the specific chronological development of Hick's terminology at this time see D'Costa, *John Hick's Theology of Religions*, 158, n. 23.

23   See Hick, "Interpretation and Reinterpretation in Religion," in *The Making and Remaking of Christian Doctrine: Essays in Honor of Maurice Wiles*, ed. Sarah Coakley and David Pailin (Oxford: Clarendon, 1993), 71; idem, "Response to Douglas Geivett and W. Gary Phillips," in *More Than One Way?* 250.

24   See (1) "The Real in Itself and as Humanly Experienced," 236–40; and (2) "Kant's Epistemological Model," 240–46.

25   Ibid., 236–37; see also *Christian Theology of Religions*, 57–58.

26   *Interpretation of Religion*, 237.

27   Ibid., 238.

28   Hick, "Ineffability," *Religious Studies* 36 (2000): 35. In this article, Hick responds to several who have criticized his appeal to ineffability.

29   Ibid., 239 (emphasis added).

30   See respectively Hick, "The Philosophy of World Religions," *Scottish Journal of Theology* 37 (1984): 232; *Interpretation of Religion*, 237–9.

31   Otto, *Naturalism and Religion* (New York: Putnam's Sons, 1907); Oakes, "Noumena, Phenomena, and God," *International Journal for Philosophy of Religion* 4 (1973): 30–8.

32   This term derives from William Forgie's "Hyper-Kantianism in Recent Discussions of Mystical Experience," *Religious Studies* 21 (1985): 208. Forgie does not, however, apply

his critique to Hick.

33   *Interpretation of Religion*, 245.

34   "The Real and its Personae and Impersonae," in *Disputed Questions*, 177–78.

35   *Interpretation of Religion*, 241.

36   Ibid., 240. Here, Hick cites Peter Berger and Thomas Luckmann, *The Social Construction of Reality* (Garden City: Doubleday, 1966); Michael Arbib and Mary Hesse, *The Construction of Reality* (Cambridge: Cambridge University Press, 1986); and the work of Clifford Geertz.

37   Cited in *Interpretation of Religion*, 240–41. See also Hick, "Ineffability," 35–40.

38   Ibid., 244.

39   Ibid., 240, 244.

40   See Immanuel Kant, *The Critique of Pure Reason*, abridged ed., Norman Kemp Smith, trans. (London: Macmillan, 1952): 26–27, 72.

41   *Interpretation of Religion*, 243–44.

42   See *Second Christianity*, 81; "Religious Pluralism and Absolute Claims," 199–201. This formerly central analogy still shows up occasionally in Hick's more recent—especially *theological*—work; see "Non-Absoluteness of Christianity," 23; Hick, "Straightening the Record: Some Response to Critics," *Modern Theology* 6 (1990): 190.

43   The last straightforward appeal to this defense that I have located, outside of the context of an explicitly intra-Christian dialogue, is in his 1983 article "The Theology of Religious Pluralism," 338.

44   C. Robert Mesle reports that in "correspondence and discussion" Hick has as much; see Mesle, *John Hick's Theodicy: A Process Humanist Critique* (New York: St. Martin's, 1991), 89.

45   See e.g., Hick, "Towards a Philosophy of Religious Pluralism," *Neue Zeitschrift für Systematische Theologie und Religionsphilosophie* 22, 2 (1980): 131–49 (reprinted in *God Has Many Names*, 88–115); "A Philosophy of Religious Pluralism"; "The Philosophy of World Religions."

46   *Interpretation of Religion*, 1. See also Hick, "A Religious Understanding of Religion: A Model of the Relationship Between Traditions," in *Many Mansions: InterFaith and Religious Intolerance*, ed. Dan Cohn-Sherbok (London: Bellew, 1992), 122–36.

47   Müller (from *Natural Religion*) cited in Eric J. Sharpe, *Comparative Religion: A History*, 2nd ed. (La Salle, Ill.: Open Court, 1986 [1975]), 39.

48   "A Religious Theory of Religion," *Religion Defined and Explained* (New York: St. Martin's, 1993), 85.

49   This issue has been summarily explored in an unpublished paper by Chester Gillis entitled "John Hick as Philosopher of Religion," (20 pp.), to which some of my thoughts in this area are indebted.

50   Ibid., 5.

51   E.g., see *Christian Theology of Religions*, 43–4.

52   See e.g., "Straightening the Record," 190–91; *Christian Theology of Religions*, 72.

53   See *Philosophy of Religion*, 4th ed., 56–67.

54   E.g., see "On Grading Religions," in *Problems of Religious Pluralism*, 86; *Interpretation of Religion*, 36–55.

55   "Sketch for a Global Theology," in *God Has Many Names*, 83.

56   *Interpretation of Religion*, 240 (emphasis added).

57   Ibid., 56.
58   "Toward a Philosophy of Religious Pluralism," in *God Has Many Names*, 106.
59   "God Has Many Names," 57; see *Interpretation of Religion*, 56.
60   *Interpretation of Religion*, 3–4. This criticism of Hick's theory will be explored further in chapter five.
61   "On Grading Religions," in *Problems of Religious Pluralism*, 79–80 (emphasis added).
62   "On Grading Religions," 69, 86; this essay was originally published in *Religious Studies* 17 (1981): 451–67.
63   See especially "Religious Pluralism and Salvation," 365–77; *Interpretation of Religion*, chs. 2, 3, 17, 18.
64   *Interpretation of Religion*, 300.
65   Ibid., 303.
66   Ibid., 300.
67   *Interpretation of Religion*, 325. See also *Christian Theology of Religions*, 77–78.
68   *Interpretation of Religion*, 340.
69   "On Grading Religions," in *Problems of Religious Pluralism*, 84–85.
70   See e.g., "The Outcome," 148 (wherein Hick also adds "warlock worship, and faith in witchcraft and in astrology" to his list of questionable religious traditions); "A Concluding Comment," 453; *Interpretation of Religion*, 326; *Christian Theology of Religions*, 79.
71   Hick, "Possibility of Religious Pluralism: A Reply to Gavin D'Costa," 162.
72   Ibid., 326, 327.
73   Ibid., 337.
74   As early as 1983, Hick is found making reference to the Buddha's doctrine of 'undetermined questions' as a helpful resource for the problem of inter-religious doctrinal disputes; see "On Conflicting Religious Truth-Claims," 489. Hick makes use of the notion of "unanswerable questions" in *Interpretation of Religion*, 343–7; see also *Christian Theology of Religions*, 52, 72. Hick has developed these ideas in "The Buddha's Doctrine of the 'Undetermined Questions'," *Hermeneutics, Religious Pluralism and Truth*, ed. G. D. Pritchard (Winston-Salem: Wake Forest University, 1989), 1–17, and "Religion as 'Skilful Means': A Hint from Buddhism," *International Journal for Philosophy of Religion* 30 (1991): 141–58. Both essays are reprinted in Hick's *Disputed Questions in Theology*.
75   See "Religion as 'Skilful Means'"; *Christian Theology of Religions*, 114–16.
76   "Buddha's Doctrine," in *Disputed Questions in Theology*, 106.
77   Ibid., 108.
78   Ibid., 108–16; see also *Christian Theology of Religions*, 51–56; *Metaphor of God Incarnate*, 140–46.
79   *Christian Theology of Religions*, 55.
80   Ibid. Namely, (1) the conflict between Judaism and Islam regarding Isaac and Ishmael, and (2) the conflict between Christianity and Islam on the question of whether or not Jesus actually died on the cross.
81   Ibid., 111–12.
82   *Interpretation of Religion*, 348.
83   Ibid., 348.
84   Ibid., 351.
85   Ibid., 353. More recently Hick has reaffirmed this understanding: "all theological

discourse…is to be understood, in the last analysis, as mythological in character" ("Response to Mesle" in Mesle, *John Hick's Theodicy*, 116. Hick compares his general claim here to the theological vision of Gordon Kaufman as delineated in *The Theological Imagination* (Philadelphia: Westminster, 1981); see *Interpretation of Religion*, 361, n. 5.

86   *Interpretation of Religion*, 356, 361 (n. 8).

87   *Christian Theology of Religions*, 76.

88   *Interpretation of Religion*, 359.

89   Ibid., 375–76.

90   "John Hick's Copernican Revolution," 329.

91   It is worth noting that D'Costa begins by distinguishing his own form of this charge from those "earlier critics who pointed out that it was a Christian God at the centre of the universe of faiths" (ibid., 327). In saying so, D'Costa implicitly acknowledges that Hick's adjustments of his model had effectively served to vanquish at least some forms of this charge.

92   *Theology and Religious Pluralism*, 32.

93   *Death and Eternal Life*, 464.

94   *Hick's Theology of Religions*, 170.

95   See D'Costa's "John Hick's Copernican Revolution," 328–9; "Pluralist Paradigm in the Christian Theology of Religions," 217–18; *Hick's Theology of Religions*, 162–70. See also Gerard Loughlin's defense of Hick at this point ("Paradox and Paradigms: Defending the Case for a Revolution in Theology of Religions," *New Blackfriars* 66 [1985]: 127–35), and D'Costa's response in the same volume ("An Answer to Mr. Loughlin," 135–7).

96   See Hick's *Evil and the God of Love*; idem., "The Problem of Evil in the First and Last Things," *Journal of Theological Studies* 19 (1968): 519–602; idem., "God, Evil and Mystery," *Religious Studies* 3 (1968): 539–46.

97   See e.g., Hick's "An Irenaean Theodicy," in *Encountering Evil: Live Options in Theodicy*, ed. Stephen Davis (Atlanta: Knox, 1981), 39–52; *Interpretation of Religion*, 118–22.

98   "An Irenaean Theodicy," 52 (emphasis added).

99   For Hick's own recounting of this period, both in terms of his critics and his own responses see "Straightening the Record," 187–95.

100   *Problems of Religious Pluralism*, 124.

101   *Interpretation of Religion*, 182–3.

102   See Hick's "Straightening the Record," 191, where he forthrightly admits the inherent "contradiction" between his earlier position in *Death and Eternal Life* and his current pluralistic hypothesis, and his repudiation of the former in this regard. See also *Interpretation of Religion*, 177–88 for his related discussion.

103   "Postscript" to "Eschatological Verification Reconsidered," in *Problems of Religious Pluralism*, 125; see also *Christian Theology of Religions*, 72–76 for Hick's most recent replies to criticisms about his new understanding of eschatological verification.

104   See D'Costa, "John Hick and Religious Pluralism: Yet Another Revolution," in *Problems in the Philosophy of Religion*, 3–18; idem., "Christian Theology and Other Religions: An Evaluation of John Hick and Paul Knitter," *Studia Missionalia* 42: *Theology of Religions: Christianity and Other Religions* (1993), 161–78. Heim ("The Pluralistic Hypothesis, Realism, and Post-Eschatology," *Religious Studies* 28 [1992]: 207–19) and I ("Religious Pluralism and the Divine") have made similar arguments. Similarly, in his 1992 Harvard

Ph.D. dissertation, "Knowing the Real," Kenneth Rose has focused much of his critique upon the claim that Hick's pluralistic hypothesis has served to drain the life's blood from his earlier eschatological verification position, and so has put his religious cognitivism/realism in jeopardy.

105   *Interpretation of Religion*, 118–22.

106   *Interpretation of Religion*, 359–60. Hick's understanding of "myth" is essentially unchanged since his early pluralist move; compare *God and the Universe of Faiths*, 166–67; "Jesus and the World Religions," 178.

107   D'Costa, "Christian Theology and Other Religions," 167. See Hick's discussion on these matters in "Myth, Mystery and the Unanswered Questions," in *Interpretation of Religion*, 343–61.

108   See e.g., Chester Gillis' charge—in a 1989 publication—that Hick takes as his "starting point" the concept of "God as loving creator" (*A Question of Final Belief*, 170).

109   See *Interpretation of Religion*, 56–69, 380; also *Christian Theology of Religions*, 104–06.

110   "Straightening the Record," 190.

111   Hick, "Religious Realism and Non-Realism," in *Disputed Questions in Theology*, 12.

112   *Interpretation of Religion*, 246, 350; see also *Christian Theology of Religions*, 60–65.

113   *Interpretation of Religion*, 338.

114   Ibid., 246; see also *Christian Theology of Religions*, 60–61.

115   For an example of an unjustified charge of covert theism in regard to Hick see Keith Ward, "Truth and the Diversity of Religions," *Religious Studies* 26 (1990): 15; similarly, with regard to covert non-theism, see William Rowe, "John Hick's Contribution to the Philosophy of Religion," in *God, Truth and Reality*, 22.

116   "Straightening the Record," 194.

117   Preface to *Disputed Questions in Theology*, viii.

118   See Hick's "Interpretation and Reinterpretation in Religion," 57–72.

119   See also the less comprehensive, but more recent, clarification and defense of his pluralistic Christology in *Christian Theology of Religions*, 82–103.

120   *Metaphor of God Incarnate*, 12.

121   *Metaphor of God Incarnate*, 2, 15–22.

122   Ibid., 3.

123   See *Metaphor of God Incarnate*, chs. 2 & 3. Hick acknowledges that his portrait of Jesus "falls within the tradition of 'liberal' interpretation established by Schleiermacher, Strauss, Harnack and others" wherein the fundamental importance of Jesus is traced to "his strong and continuous awareness of God as *abba*, 'father'" (18).

124   See *Metaphor of God Incarnate*, ch. 4.

125   In his 1977 contribution to *The Myth of God Incarnate*, "Jesus and the World Religions," Hick likened the problem of explaining how Jesus could literally be both fully God and fully human to explaining how "this circle drawn with a pencil on paper is also a square" (178).

126   "Is there a Doctrine of the Incarnation?" 50. For Hick's critique of several attempts see "The Logic of God Incarnate," *Religious Studies* 25 (1989): 409–23; *Metaphor of God Incarnate*, chs. 5–7.

127   *Metaphor of God Incarnate*, 104.

128   *Metaphor of God Incarnate*, ix. For Hick's discussion of this point see *Metaphor*, ch. 8; and "Non-Absoluteness of Christianity."

129   See e.g., the published results of a 1981 conference paper: Hick, "A Recent Development

within Christian Monotheism," *The Concept of Monotheism in Islam and Christianity*, ed. Hans Koechler (Vienna: Braumueller, 1982), 60–70. The two works cited by Hick are Baillie's *God Was in Christ* (New York: Scribner's, 1948), and Lampe's *God as Spirit* (New York: Oxford University Press, 1977); for a summary of Lampe's approach see his "The Holy Spirit and the Person of Christ," in *Christ, Faith and History: Cambridge Studies in Christology*, ed. S. W. Sykes and J. P. Clayton (Cambridge: Cambridge University Press, 1972), 111–30.

130 See "Non-Absoluteness of Christianity," esp. 31–4; "An Inspiration Christology"; "Rethinking Christian Doctrine in the Light of Religious Pluralism," in *Christianity and the Wider Ecumenism*, ed. Peter Phan (New York: Paragon, 1990), 89–102; "Trinity and Incarnation"; *The Metaphor of God Incarnate*, 106–110.

131 *Metaphor of God Incarnate*, 111; "Non-Absoluteness of Christianity," 32.

132 "Non-Absoluteness of Christianity," 32.

133 *Metaphor of God Incarnate*, 110.

134 Hick makes this connection clear: 'myth,' the essential definition of which has not changed for Hick since the 1970s, is further described as a "much extended metaphor" (ibid., 105). Among others, Hick cites the following works: Max Black, *Models and Metaphors* (Ithaca, N.Y.: Cornell University Press, 1962); George Lakoff and Mark Johnson, eds., *Metaphors We Live By* (Chicago: University of Chicago Press, 1980); Sallie McFague, *Metaphorical Theology* (Philadelphia: Fortress, 1982); Paul Ricoeur, *The Rule of Metaphor* (Toronto: University of Toronto Press, 1978); Janet Soskice, *Metaphor and Religious Language* (Oxford: Clarendon, 1985).

135 Both Chester Gillis and Gerard Loughlin have argued that Hick is working with an outmoded and seriously flawed theory of metaphorical language. Both suggest that his indebtedness to the 'empiricist' philosophical tradition fosters a faulty pre-understanding of the nature and capabilities of metaphor. See Gillis, *A Question of Final Belief*, 164–70; Loughlin, "Squares and Circles: John Hick and the Doctrine of the Incarnation," in *Problems in the Philosophy of Religion*, 189–93.

136 "Non-Absoluteness of Christianity," 32–33. Both of these moves closely parallel those of Lampe in *God as Spirit*. For Hick's critique of Richard Swinburne's defense of an objective atonement see *Metaphor of God Incarnate*, ch. 11.

137 See e.g., Gerald O'Collins, "The Incarnation Under Fire," *Gregorianum* 76 (1995): 263–80; Gillis, "John Hick's Christology," *Bijdragen* 49 (1988): 41–57; Gregory H. Carruthers, *The Uniqueness of Jesus Christ in the Theocentric Model of the Christian Theology of World Religions: An Elaboration and Evaluation of the Position of John Hick* (Lanham, Md.: Univertsity Press of America, 1990); Loughlin, "Squares and Circles"; Molly Truman Marshall, *No Salvation Outside the Church? A Critical Inquiry* (Lewiston, N.Y.: Mellen, 1993), 164–69, 183–94; Douglas McCready, "The Disintegration of John Hick's Christology," *Journal of the Evangelical Theological Society* 39 (1996): 257–70; Jürgen Werbick, "Heil durch Jesus Christus allein? Die 'Pluralistische Theologie' und ihr Plädoyer für einen Pluralismus der Heilswege," in *Der einzige Weg zum Heil?* ed. Michael von Brück and Jürgen Werbick (Freiburg: Herder, 1993), 11–61; Edmund Arens, "Perspektiven und Problematik pluralistischer Christologie," *Münchener Theologische Zeitschrift* 46 (1995): 329–43; Marilyn McCord Adams, "Chalcedonian Christology: A Christian Solution to the Problem of Evil," in *Philosophy and Theological Discourse*, ed. Stephen D. Davis (New York: St. Martin's, 1997), 173–98.

5   Critical Responses to Hick's Religious Pluralism

There is one thing that virtually all of Hick's partisans and critics alike agree upon: no one has produced a more intellectually sophisticated and provocative apologetic for the pluralist paradigm. Witness the fact of how few general critiques of the pluralist paradigm leave Hick out of their discussion. It is safe to say that no other pluralist proponent in the western world today is as often cited and critiqued as Hick. Thus, it is widely recognized that if one is going to challenge the pluralist interpretation of religious diversity in general, Hick's model must be reckoned with. Given this fact, it is not surprising to find that the criticisms of Hick's pluralist religious interpretation of religion are many and varied. These criticisms can be categorized under three general rubrics: (1) Is it pluralistic? (2) Is it Christian? (3) Does it work?[1]

The first question—Is it pluralistic?—points to those criticisms that suggest Hick's so-called pluralism is less than pluralistic in its conclusions, and actually fosters a homogenizing effect that undermines the true diversity of the world's religions. An important set of criticisms connected to this issue calls into question the viability of Hick's tradition-neutral 'religious' interpretation of religions. The second question—Is it Christian?—suggests those criticisms which claim that to adopt Hick's hypothesis is to abandon Christianity in anything like its historic sense. The focus here are the various theological critiques that have arisen within Hick's own intra-Christian context. Finally, the third question—Does it work?—raises the issue of whether Hick's neo-Kantian proposal, on purely internal, philosophical grounds, is ultimately successful.

Is it Pluralistic? Hick's Hypothesis and the Homogenization of the World's Religions

A host of related criticisms of Hick's religious pluralism revolve around the manner in which the religions of the world are treated under Hick's hypothesis. The common theme that links these criticisms together is the charge that, ironically, Hick's so-called 'pluralism' is actually serving what is ultimately a "homogenizing agenda."[2]

The primary concern appears to be that, in order for Hick's thesis to work, it must reduce the obvious, important, and self-conscious *differences* among the world's religions to little more than practical trivialities. Only then, once the apparent irreconcilable differences have been neutralized, can he subsume them under the umbrella of his pluralist hypothesis. One interesting fact about this criticism is that it has been directed at Hick's model by soteric exclusivists/particularists,[3] inclusivists,[4] and pluralists alike.[5] Several specific criticisms fuel this general line of critique.

Is Hick's Soteriological Criterion Successful?[6]

The soteriological criterion as religious homogenization Hick's view of religious salvation/liberation has become a magnet for criticism. This criticism follows naturally from the prior discussion of the homogenizing effect of Hick's thesis, as well as its inability to accurately reflect the religions' self-understandings (see below), and its tendency to fall into the trap of descriptive reductionism. In fact, a number of critics have identified Hick's salvation/liberation motif as a significant conceptual culprit behind the monizing effect of his pluralist hypothesis.[7] More specifically, several scholars independently have argued that one of the most scandalous effects of Hick's soteriological model is its blatant and deceptive homogenization of the radically different visions of salvation, the vast variety of ultimate aims and objectives, found within the world's religions.[8] Kenneth Rose summarizes the concern:

> Hick's quasi-Kantian approach fails, I think, because it attempts to meet the threat of relativism implicit in religious pluralism with a monistic, soteriological criterion that forces all of the diverse religions to submit to the sole criterion of soteriological efficacy, as conceived by Hick. Given this circumstance, it is evident that Hick has never really embraced religious pluralism as *truly pluralistic*, but has merely replaced one monism with another.[9]

It has been further suggested that Hick's universalizing soteriological criterion is ultimately and inevitably to be traced to a modern, Western, post-Enlightenment worldview. As such, there is good reason to wonder whether it is as universal a criterion as Hick suggests.[10] Hick has distinguished between 'pre-axial' (or 'extra-axial') religions and the great world faiths born during the 'axial' period, and has claimed that his soteriological criterion is representative of the latter type. However, it is not clear that the categories are this nice and neat. Within the so-called axial traditions themselves, there is, to this day, often a mixture of folk and philosophical (i.e., 'village' and 'world') streams of thought, wherein complex and multi-layered visions of salvation exist. Suffice to say that they are not always identifiable as mere variations of Hick's proposed criterion. In this regard, Hick may be seen as propounding a form of what some scholars would regard as a methodologically suspect thesis, in the tradition of certain evolutionary-driven 19th-century history-of-religions theories.[11] Even within the classical expressions of some axial religions, there is some question as to whether 'the transformation from self- to Reality-centeredness,' and the moral and spiritual fruit that evidences such a turn, would be recognized as the primary soteriological criterion. In classical (magisterial) Protestant theology, the 'justification by faith' doctrine would tend to claim that saintliness (i.e., 'sanctification'), is a by-product, rather than a constituent element, of salvation itself.[12]

In his 1995 volume *Salvations*, S. Mark Heim devotes himself to constructing an approach to religious diversity that can acknowledge and celebrate the wide diversity of religious understandings of salvation. In a chapter given to an assessment of Hick's pluralist hypothesis, Heim raises the question: "What's not pluralistic about the pluralistic hypothesis?"[13] In answering this question, Heim traces a monizing impetus in Hick's thesis back to two foundational "assumptions." The second of these assumptions is germane to the topic at hand:

> The second sweeping assumption in the pluralistic hypothesis is that if real human transformations are taking place in various religious traditions—identified by moral behavior—then in fact *one identical salvific process is taking place in all of them.*[14]

Heim eventually articulates his own vision of "pluralistic inclusivism," a brand of inclusivism (in Heim's case, Christian inclusivism) wherein he entertains the possibility that the radically different aims and goals of the world's religions are "maintained through [different] historical and eschatological states of religious fulfillment."[15] Whether or not Heim's own model can be rendered intelligible in the end is a matter for debate. However, it is ironic that we find here an *inclusivist* who claims to take religious soteriological diversity much more seriously than can Hick's pluralist hypothesis. Heim offers this insight on the soteriologically homogenizing effect of Hick's thesis:

> were Hick not so intent that the traditions should express the same truth, they would have more room to be simultaneously accurate in their concrete description of varying religious paths and aims. If God and the Dharma are each real, for instance, then the Muslim and Buddhist traditions are both much more concretely

correct than Hick would allow. Because of the practical benefits he sees in the assumption of an identical religious end, Hick is willing at this crucial point to opt for a religious truth that brooks no rivals because it defines away all alternatives....Desiring to affirm the many religious ways, Hick hones them to a highly abstract point of identity—salvation—and locates their validity at that point....Since he admits that the 'soteriological criterion' can only be applied by selecting out certain similar aspects in what are empirically *different* concrete forms of religious life, it is crucial to ask whether he provides convincing grounds to presume that there is but one end of all the faith paths and that he has described it more adequately than any existing tradition.[16]

Soteriocentrism as a 'Common Core' Theory of Religion In the introduction to his *Interpretation of Religion*, Hick offers a 'family resemblance' concept of religion wherein "[i]nstead of a set of defining characteristics there is a network of similarities overlapping and criss-crossing like the resemblances and differences...among the members of a natural family."[17] In the process, he specifically rejects a "common essence" view of religion, where a single and central element (e.g., a common experience) identifies the heart of religion and thus unifies all of its manifold expressions.[18] In spite of this disclaimer, a number of critics have charged Hick with holding to a type of 'common core' theory of religion. In pursuing the question of what evidence could ever lead to such a conclusion in the face of Hick's protests to the contrary, the common response points back to Hick's soteriocentrism. Clarke and Byrne capture the essence of this charge:

> There are oddities in [Hick's claim to support a family resemblance definition of religion] which strike us immediately when we ask how, if the class of religions has no essential unity, can it be the subject of the generalizations that Hick so obviously wants to make about it?... A sense of tension in Hick's account is confirmed when we examine what he suggests about the character of post-Axial religions later in the book. What unites them is not simply that they arose coincidentally. They exhibit a strikingly similar soteriology....[In his discussion of criteriology] we find Hick wielding the characteristic weapon of core or essence theorists of religion, namely a distinction between genuine and fake versions of the 'kind' religion....This shows Hick's essentialism and his closeness to the tradition which locates an essence to religion in ethics.[19]

Some have gone so far as to suggest that Hick's position is akin to the 'perennialist' vision of religion, the epitome of a 'common core' approach. Rose, for example, makes the claim that "[d]espite constructivist appearances, Hick thus turns out to [be] a crypto-perennialist."[20]

In assessing this issue, one must take seriously the fact that Hick ostensibly rejects a 'common core' approach in favor of a 'family resemblance' definition. Likewise, it is important to recognize that a significant part of his hypothesis emphasizes the wide-ranging differences between the religions. However, the differences arise in Hick's theory only at the phenomenological level. At the noumenal level there is one Reality common to all true religion. Moreover, this commonality does penetrate to the phenomenological level in the form of what one could call a 'common soteriological core.' Hick himself has admitted as much: "[The various religions do] exhibit a *common structure*, which is soteriological in the broad sense that it offers a transition from a radically unsatisfactory state to a limitlessly better one."[21] Similarly, in response to the question of whether the religions are asking different soteriological questions, Hick concludes that "these questions, whilst *specifically* different, are *generically* the same."[22] Thus, although it requires careful nuancing, the charge that Hick's theory is tied to a 'common core' theory of religion seems accurate on these counts.

The Question of Empirical Evidence Hick's theory is also charged with accusations similar to those directed at certain varieties of the 'phenomenology of religions' method of religious studies, an approach with which Hick's perspective does share some interesting connections. First, like Rudolf Otto and other phenomenologists, Hick's theory includes an emphasis on the primacy of religious experience, and an anti-reductionistic attitude toward the divine. Second, Hick explicitly affirms that the work of the great phenomenologist Mircea Eliade, "was based upon the premise" that serves as a foundational assumption of Hick's own project: the irreducibility and uniqueness of the sacred.[23] Third, Hick's own religious theory of religion, as presented in *An Interpretation of Religion*, begins with a three-chapter section on "phenomenology." Throughout the next four sections of this volume, Hick appeals to the conclusions of his phenomenological study as the *a posteriori*, empirical grounding for his subsequent theoretical work.

Douglas Allen has summarized the standard charges against the phenomenology of religion method. The parallels between this critique and criticisms of Hick's approach are hard to miss:

> most phenomenologists of religion insist they are using an empirical approach, which is free from *a priori* assumptions and judgments....These phenomenologists usually maintain that their discoveries of essential typologies and universal structures are based on empirical, inductive generalizations.

One of the most frequent attacks on the phenomenology of religion is that it is not empirically based, and that it is therefore arbitrary, subjective, and unscientific. Critics charge that the universal structures and meanings are not found in the empirical data and that the phenomenological discoveries are not subject to empirical tests of verification.[24]

Similarly, some critics have charged that Hick's claim of a unifying soteriological structure among the post-axial religions is simply an exercise in circular argumentation.[25] D'Costa, for instance, expresses his concern that Hick's thesis "refuses to take seriously the genuine differences between the understanding of ethics within the world religions, let alone within a single tradition."[26] Ronald Nash, argues that Hick's treatment of feminist thought leads him to acknowledge a "bizarre exception" to his post-axial soteriocentric principle, one that encourages a "transformation from weakness to self-centeredness."[27]

Hick has responded to the 'circular argumentation' critique by agreeing that there is a circularity here, but that it is an instance of the type of benign circularity that inevitably accompanies "*any* comprehensive view....There are no non-circular ways of establishing fundamental positions."[28] William Wainwright, however, challenges Hick at this point. On one hand, he acknowledges that there is always a benign circularity involved in justifying epistemological decisions. On the other hand, he emphasizes that, in such cases, "accounts of these epistemic practices' play a crucial role in their justification. If Hick is right, however, and the Real can't be described, nothing like this is possible with respect to the *pluralist's* criterion (*viz.*, love/compassion)."[29]

Others have gone so far as to suggest that, in empirical fact, Hick's claim that the world's great religions are equally effective vehicles of 'salvation' is arbitrary, completely unverifiable, and, perhaps, simply wrong.[30] Kenneth Rose writes of "Hick's arbitrary belief" in the co-equal salvific efficacy of the religions: "There is no compelling reason to credit this belief, even if, for reasons of civility, we cannot or do not wish to say *which* of the traditions is relatively more or less salvific, enlightening, or humanizing." Kenneth Surin has gone so far as to say that, contra Hick:

only an incarnational faith can be salvific (in the strict sense of the term). Non-incarnational faiths may enlighten man, they may ease his anguish, they may make him more compassionate, they may make him a more moral being, but in the last resort only an incarnational faith embodies the true way to salvation. Now, in as much as Christianity is—historically—the only such faith, the following conclusion seems inescapable: Christianity is, strictly speaking, the only religion of salvation.[31]

A Contentless Soteriology? Another, although related, criticism of Hick's salvation/liberation motif is the claim that, ultimately, it is little more than a vacuous formulaic cipher, lacking any definite content.[32] Of Hick's soteriological definition, 'the transformation from self-centeredness to Reality-centeredness,' Netland writes:

> it appears that Hick is adopting a kind of "lowest common denominator" soteriology, resulting in a strictly formal formula that ignores central aspects of the soteriology of the various religions....One suspects that soteriology comes close here to being reduced to common morality; but this is something that a host of religious figures from many traditions would emphatically reject.[33]

Once this abstract soteriological structure is viewed within the context of its proper function—an orientation process toward the unknowable Real *an sich*— things become ever more murky. C. Robert Mesle poses a relevant question:

> What can it mean for a human life to be centered on something totally devoid of any positive qualities, something which is not good or loving or active? I see no ethical value in such a move. Why not simply advocate growth from self-centeredness to *other-centeredness*, and acknowledge that religious traditions often help people make this shift?[34]

At this point, Paul Griffiths suggests that Hick is in something of a double-bind. If the soteriological criterion is left as a purely formal concept, "then it cannot do the work it was intended to do."[35] On the other hand, to specify its content by giving it real substance is to journey down a path that finally leads to the privileging of one type of soteriological vision over another.[36]

Soteriocentrism and Epistemological Grounding   A final criticism of Hick's soteriocentric thesis involves the perennial question to be faced by any pragmatic theory of (religious) truth: that of epistemological grounding.[37] With Hick's complete lack of cognitive revelational and/or doctrinal content *vis-à-vis* the Real, the question arises of how he can ever hope to grant the heart of his soteriocentric program—the notion of 'orientation toward the Real'—anything in the way of substance, beyond a vague linguistic symbol? As D'Costa notes:

> Hick's emphasis on praxis still begs the question of the *basis* for the *recognition* of what *constitutes* a turning from "self-centeredness to Reality-centeredness"—which leads back to doctrinal formulations and their validity...[38]

If, in fact, the properties of the Real are entirely beyond our ken, how does Hick know that the only appropriate response to it is a turn toward it and away from self-centeredness? Or how can Hick say that what we would call malicious and evil behavior is an inappropriate response to the Real, when he has already claimed that it cannot be said to be either "good or evil"?[39]

In assessing the criticisms of Hick's soteriocentrism, practical considerations must play a role. For instance, one important pragmatic concern emerges in asking *how* Hick's proposal could ever justifiably circumscribe questionable religious experiences and soteriological programs. For his own part, Hick has explicitly stated that his criterion is able to identify and filter out such soteriologically defective religious perspectives. He writes: "not by any means every religious movement…is salvific: not Nazism, or Satanism, or the Jim Jones or the Waco phenomena, for example."[40] Just how Hick can make this judgment is not at all clear, however. For example, consider Satanists, or 'Christians' who operate under the banner of the Aryan Brotherhood. Both of these religious groups could seemingly agree with (1) Hick's two remaining realist (doctrinal) claims of a transcendent Reality and a limitlessly good future existence—though both would no doubt disagree with Hick on just what "good" might turn out to be, and (2) Hick's definition of salvation, where self-centeredness truly is abandoned for 'Reality-centeredness'—the latter being apprehended in the phenomenal persona of the Devil and the 'God of the Bible' (understood, of course, as the original Creator of white supremacy) respectively. It is true that some forms of Satanism (e.g., Anton LaVey's Church of Satan) do not profess belief in a literal Satan, but rather use the term as something of a cipher for the more carnal instincts within human nature. In this case, Hick's criterion would serve to disqualify the religious phenomenon, since self-centeredness is explicitly encouraged. Other forms of Satanism, however, take the Devil quite seriously, and, in terms of worship, would seem to constitute another instance of turning from oneself to another (phenomenal) Reality.

Hick would no doubt counter this claim by suggesting that the "observable moral and spiritual fruits" of these religious traditions are such that they would be disqualified by his criterion.[41] However, this is a rather arbitrary response in light of the fact that he is willing to overlook countless examples of tainted spiritual fruit within other of the world's religious traditions, and deem them soteriologically effective nonetheless. If self-centeredness and horrendous evils can co-exist with Reality-centeredness and soteriological effectiveness in Hinduism, Buddhism, Judaism, and Christianity, then why not in Satanism, Nazism, and the Jonestown, Waco, and Solar Temple movements? Empirically speaking, Hick's religious criterion of 'transformation from self-centeredness to Reality-centeredness' is simply too vague to circumscribe such generally repugnant religious phenomena. It would seem, then, that Hick's decisions in these matters are driven not by the criterion itself, but rather by the fact that such phenomena are universally recognized by most people to be religiously offensive. The vacuousness of this criterion allows Hick to circumscribe any religious phenomena that happen not to appeal to him (or others), and at the same time claim that the major religious traditions of the world, while filled with similar evils, are roughly equally effective vehicles of human salvation. Thus, both on theoretical and practical grounds, Hick's soteriological criterion founders at points crucial to his wider hypothesis.

Is Hick's Pluralism a form of Arrogant Western Imperialism?[42]

It has become a common-place among many adherents of the pluralist paradigm that exclusivist theologies of religions are something less than morally exemplary. W. C. Smith has captured this sentiment well: "Exclusivism strikes more and more Christians as immoral."[43] Hick himself has pointed a moral finger at "Christian absolutism," arguing that it has served to validate "centuries of anti-Semitism, the colonial exploitation by Christian Europe of what we today call the third world, and the subordination of women within a strongly patriarchal religious system..."[44] Thus, perhaps the most ironic charge leveled against the pluralist paradigm in recent years is the claim that it represents an arrogant imperialist approach, rooted in a totalizing modern Western mentality.[45] Dirk Louw, among others, has directed this criticism toward Hick's pluralist model in particular:

> *Prima facie* Hick does not indulge in the absolutism and imperialism for which he criticizes genetic confessionalists....However, in his effort to transcend the relativism of exclusivism and inclusivism, he introduces a [soteriological] criterion for the judging and even grading of religious traditions which defeats the object of his enterprise....He is therefore guilty of the very same absolutism and imperialism for which he criticizes exclusivists and inclusivists.[46]

Several arguments have served to buttress such charges.

The Pluralist Assumption of a Privileged Vantage-point[47] Hick's thesis has been criticized on a number of counts for assuming a vantage-point that is, in reality, unattainable. One criticism in this vein focuses upon Hick's single, early use of the now-famous 'blind men and elephant' parable as an illustration of the pluralist perspective.[48] Criticisms have tended to point out that the analogy presupposes that the parable teller is privy to a universal perspective from which to determine that the blind men are only partially correct. Thus, according to Philip Almond, "the central assumption of the parable is that Hick is in a position to see whereas the blind religions are not."[49] Recognizing, perhaps, that the analogy was bringing more trouble than it was worth, Hick has wisely discontinued its use.[50] (It would now be equally wise for Hick's critics to resist bringing up this parable in the context of their discussions of his mature hypothesis. Hick has moved far beyond blind men and elephants in terms of the sophistication of his model and precision of expression.) However, this has not brought an end to the general charge of an assumed privileged vantage-point on the part of Hick's thesis.

More recently, Hick has come under fire from 'postmodern' quarters for adopting a 'modernist,' Enlightenment position that assumes the possibility of a universal and objective philosophical perspective from which to analyze the world's religions. D'Costa expresses this sentiment well when he writes of Hick's replacement of "one form of 'arrogance' with another in that his pluralism implicitly claims a vantage point on truth, so that all religious claims are deemed mythological, whether or not adherents recognize this."[51] Likewise, Garrett Green finds in Hick's claim that all the great religions mediate the Real in a co-equally authentic fashion an "implicit arrogance" that "assumes a position outside and above the religions."[52]

No one has expressed this criticism of Hick's thesis with more moral indignation and rhetorical flair than Gerard Loughlin.[53] Using something of a postmodern (Foucaultian) 'archaeological' method, Loughlin unearths what he believes to be a programmatic plot on Hick's part to erase any evidence of the ruptures in his thought over the years by representing them (via new prefaces to new editions, etc.) in ways that smooth over the actual discontinuities. Nonetheless, Loughlin believes that he has caught Hick in the act of attempting to 'master' his own texts through sheer authorial force, a purely 'foundationalist' enterprise that now stands 'unmasked.' In the course of his argument, he touches on the criticism at hand:

> Thus it would appear that Hick is not as far up the mountain as might be supposed; his global vision not as comprehensive or far-seeing as his rhetoric suggests....[Hick's perspective] betrays the Anglo-American locus of Hick's vantage-point; it is the viewpoint of old empires....Pluralism is a subtle rhetoric, its

very frankness a deception. Only pluralism names the object of its mastery. It claims to name the truth of plurality and to be the *ism* that captures its actuality; the 'system' that masters the fact. In blurring the distinction between *plurality* and *pluralism*, by subsuming the former within the latter, pluralism seeks to erase all that may resist the theory that so names the plural. It seeks to forget what is here plural, the variety and difference of religion; the otherness of strangers.[54]

Pluralism as a Western Liberal Enlightenment Project of the Capitalist Leisure Class[55]
Others have completed this critique by mapping the historical, political and socio-cultural contexts from which the pluralist paradigm emerged and within which it is always-already imbedded. According to John Apczynski's analysis:

> [Hick's] interpretation of religion is a rather parochial one that has been shaped by a contemporary version of the liberal intellectual tradition. Its modern origins include Enlightenment rejection of all forms of tradition-constituted reason in favor of a universal conception of rationality appealing to methods and principles deemed unexceptionable by any reflective person.…[H]is implicit commitment to the liberal intellectual tradition effectively detaches him from the substantive truth claims of every tradition so that in the final analysis the truth of none of them matters.[56]

Similarly, Frans Van Beeck has noted that the pluralist paradigm is "so obviously manufactured in the liberal-Christian and post-Christian West."[57]

In fleshing out the contextual backdrop of Hick's pluralist project, others have emphasized that it is an "ideological construct" that "presupposes a particular and privileged social reality."[58] For instance, Peter Van Ness's logic runs as follows: As Hick's pluralist hypothesis is a philosophical construct, and as philosophizing requires leisure (Aristotle), and as one man's leisure comes at the expense of the many's exploitation (Marx), Hick's project is immediately suspect. He concludes:

> So long as the ideological meaning of the idea of pluralism is denied and the remedial effects of an ideological critique resisted, pluralism will likely serve as a projection onto social reality of intellectual errors wrought by pure theorizing.[59]

Kenneth Surin has taken up the postmodern critique, honed it to a fine edge on the wheel of a materialist hermeneutic of suspicion, and used it to identify, with a surgical precision, what he sees as global-capitalist roots of Hick's project.[60] Surin states that the first thing to notice about Hick's "ahistorical affirmation of a 'common human history' is that it is irredeemably ideological."[61] In identifying the constituent elements of this ideology, Surin decides that it is "no mere coincidence that 'global' theologies have appeared at the precise historical moment when capitalism has entered its global stage."[62] Surin pursues this insight to the following conclusion:

> In [Hick's] scheme, the different religions are only different ways of saying or experiencing or striving for the 'same' thing, that is, 'Reality-centeredness.' In the process, the 'otherness' of the Other is traduced, and the real possibility of any kind of dialectical confrontation between the different religious traditions is extinguished. The faiths have the structure of commodities: they are fungible, homogenous entities which are to be consumed according to the preferences of the individual consumer. 'Pluralism', thus conceived, shamelessly reinforces the reification and privatization of life in advanced capitalist society. Such is the political cosmology of 'religious pluralism.'[63]

He goes on to call for a move to a "post-pluralistic" position, one which rejects the totalizing meta-narratives of the pluralist enterprise, as well as the aspirations to "dominance and hegemony" that fuel them.[64]

In response to this line of criticism, and as Hick has rightly pointed out, he is unfairly caught coming and going. While some charge him with remaining trapped in a defunct 'modernism,' others accuse him of slipping into a 'postmodern' relativism.[65] Clearly, 'postmodernism' is in the eye of the beholder! Hick is on the right track when, in response to certain postmodern critics, he reminds us to restrain the 'hermeneutic of suspicion' from becoming a 'hermeneutic of paranoia.'[66] An example of this sort of so-called 'paranoia' is reflected in Loughlin's article "Prefacing Pluralism." In his response to Loughlin, Hick rightly argues that Loughlin's attempt to (in Hick's words) weave "an extraordinary—even fantastic—literary conspiracy theory…[i]n a jargon that threatens to detach the mind from reality" is quite unjustified.[67] That Hick has changed his mind over the years is true. That he has consciously tried to mastermind a literary cover-up of this fact, as Loughlin suggests, is nonsense. It may well be the case that Hick's common claim over the years that his critics have misunderstood and/or misrepresented him has worn itself thin as an apologetic tool. However, in Loughlin's case the point is well taken.[68]

On the other hand, there is no question that Hick's project is fundamentally indebted to a modern Western liberal worldview. If certain Jewish-Christian movements forced the early church to ask the question 'Must a Gentile become a Jew to become a Christian?' so Hick and his fellow pluralists have forced the issue: 'Must a traditional believer become a Western liberal academic to become a responsible Christian?' As in the first century, so today, clearly the answer must be a resounding 'No.'

Does Hick's 'Religious' Theory of Religion Do Justice to the World's Religions?

A number of critics have argued that Hick's religious interpretation of religion is deeply flawed. Some attack certain elements or perceived shortcomings within the theory. Wainwright, for example, suggests that, even if Hick's pluralist model was the best explanation for religious diversity, "it does not follow that it is a better hypothesis *tout court*. Inclusivism may be an essential part of a larger hypothesis such as traditional Christian theism that has more explanatory power than either the pluralistic hypothesis or a Christianity that has been modified to conform to it."[69] Others suggest that, by definition, any large-scale 'religious' theory of religion is doomed from the start. For instance, Owen Thomas raises the question, with regard to Hick's interpretation of religion, of "whether or not a meta-position is possible which transcends all positions."[70] The following arguments form the central pillars of this line of criticism.

The De-valuing of Religious Doctrine and Doctrinal Conflicts[71] First, there is the charge, in the words of Gavin D'Costa, that Hick's hypothesis is indebted to "an implicit ontology (agnosticism) which refuses to take seriously the genuine plurality of ontological claims in the world religions." More recently, D'Costa has argued that "while Hick's intentions are noble and serious, his project, like Kant's, finally divests all religions of any revelatory power and achieves precisely the opposite of its stated goal."[72] In a similar vein, Surin has concluded that Hick's:

> 'religious pluralism' is a comprehensive and homogenizing historical scheme which assimilates to itself, and thereby tames and domesticates, the practices and beliefs of the different religious traditions.[73]

It has been the observation of many that Hick's theory of religion, bolstered by his pluralist hypothesis, all too quickly dismisses the very real and robust inter-religious doctrinal differences in a way that most religious persons themselves could never countenance.[74] By rendering virtually all questions about the truth of religious doctrines to be ultimately either 'unanswerable' or 'unanswered,' Hick reduces the practical import of religious doctrine to the realm of the purely pragmatic. Thus, doctrinal 'truth' regarding the ultimate divine Reality ends up having *nothing* to do with the question of whether cognitively-oriented claims accurately correlate to that Reality, but rather only whether the doctrines under consideration "evoke in us attitudes and modes of behavior which are appropriate to our situation *vis-à-vis* the Real."[75] Doctrinally speaking then, one could ask the question of whether Hick, in an attempt to accommodate all the world's religions, "unwittingly ends up in danger of accommodating none."[76]

Ironically, such moves with regard to his understanding of the nature of doctrinal truth-claims align Hick with the type of 'personalistic'—as opposed to 'propositional'—understanding of religious truth that he originally rejected in the work of W. C. Smith in the early 1970s. Even among those sympathetic to something like Hick's religious epistemology (e.g., the Reformed epistemologists), there is a strong tendency to avoid the *cognitive* religious relativism suggested by his model. Rather, they would tend to take the assessment of David Hume quite seriously, that "in matters of religion whatever is different is contrary."[77] Thus, for example, Alston concludes that Hick's attempt to escape the real difficulties posed by conflicting religious truth-claims is ultimately unsuccessful in "eliminating at least a stubborn residue of incompatibilities."[78] It is instructive that Hick has seen fit to correlate his views here, notwithstanding the differences between their "conceptual system[s]," with the proposal of George Lindbeck in *The Nature of Doctrine*. Specifically, Hick favorably compares his view with Lindbeck's notion that a religion is like a "vast complex proposition," and that it "is a true proposition to the extent that its objectives are interiorized and exercised by groups or individuals in such ways as to conform them in some measure in the various dimensions of their existence to the ultimate reality and goodness that lies at the heart of things."[79]

Paul Griffiths touches on a related aspect of this line of critique when he writes that Hick's view:

> is an a priori position, a position, that is, constructed without much interest in the empirical details of what religious communities actually tend to assert, value, and practice. This is evident from the fact that no empirical evidence as to the extent of incompatibilities among doctrine-expressing sentences is usually allowed to count against its truth.[80]

Griffiths and others have gone on to demonstrate how it is possible to take religious doctrines—and doctrinal conflicts—seriously in an inter-religious context, without falling into either of the perennial twin threats of intolerant triumphalism or doctrinal (conceptual) relativism.[81]

In assessing this criticism, it is helpful to have a particular example in mind.

Here, one can turn to the question of how Hick's understanding of the relationship between religious beliefs and salvation compares to that of most religious persons.[82] For Hick, while matters surrounding conflicting doctrinal claims may be philosophically interesting, they "cease to be a matter of religious life and death."[83] Bluntly stated:

> they are not of great *religious*, i.e., soteriological, importance. For different groups can hold incompatible sets of theories all of which constitute intellectual frameworks within which the process of salvation/liberation can proceed.[84]

However, most religious persons, certainly those of the theistic traditions, would question a premise basic to Hick's pragmatic thesis: namely that certain central religious beliefs (i.e., both 'dogmas' and 'doctrines') and salvation are so easily separable, with the former being at best an *upayic* "skilful means" that is essentially disposable if not an outright hindrance. Such a reductivist understanding of religious beliefs will be seen as religiously—i.e., soteriologically— destructive by most religious persons. In reducing virtually all religious truth-claims to either 'unanswered' or 'unanswerable' questions-cum-myth, the question arises of whether Hick has not simply undergone a type of conversion (conceptual if not religious; in part if not in whole) to an essentially Buddhist philosophy of religious doctrine. While few religious adherents (beyond the pure Gnostic, if there is such an ideal typical creature) would suggest that knowledge/doctrine *alone* can save, it is equally clear that few (certainly no Christians in anything like the historic sense of the term) could countenance the rejection of right knowledge/belief from sharing a critical role in the soteriological process.

On the other hand, and in fairness to Hick, it should be noted that one does find statements in his corpus that ostensively claim an intimate, even unbreakable, link between doctrine and salvation. Hick offers an analogy:

> I suggest that in fact the truth-claim and the salvation-claim cohere closely together and should be treated as a single package. The valuable contents of this package, the goods conveyed, consist in salvation or liberation; and the packaging and labeling, with the identifying of the sender and the directing of the package to the recipient, are provided by the doctrine. Thus doctrines are secondary and yet essential to the vital matter of receiving salvation, somewhat as packaging and labeling are secondary and yet essential to transmitting the contents of a parcel.[85]

Hick's distinction between the 'facts of faith' (i.e., dogmas) and 'doctrines' should seemingly also lead to an indivisible connection between at least some religious beliefs and the soteriological process. If (1) religious experience is soteriological in focus and primary in importance, and (2) if "facts of faith" are "disclosed in the *religious experience* of a particular tradition," then it would seem, on Hick's own account, that certain central religious beliefs and salvation/liberation cannot be separated.[86] But then Hick's final response to inter-religious dogmatic conflicts and the issue of their comparative truthfulness—namely, that we must finally acquiesce to the fact that such questions are ultimately 'unanswered' or 'unanswerable'—cannot sit well with the majority of the world's religious persons. Thus, Hick's proposal for reconciling conflicting religious beliefs appears to be at odds with what he considers to be the central phenomenon of religion: *religious experience*. It may be that we are simply hitting here on an unresolved tension in Hick's thought. In any case, this is an issue that calls for clarification on Hick's part, if not outright reformulation.

The Distortion of the 'Self-Understanding' of the Religions[87] A number of Hick's critics have called his theory into question on the grounds that it serves to radically distort the self-understanding of the very religions that he claims to interpret.[88] Harold Netland has emerged as a leading critic in this vein:

> [I]nsofar as Hick's theory of religious pluralism is intended to be a comprehensive theory about the nature of various religious traditions its adequacy will be a function of (1) the accuracy with which it reflects, and the ease with which it accommodates, the data from different religions, and (2) the internal consistency and plausibility of the theory itself....But perhaps the vulnerability of the theory is most apparent in its failure to account satisfactorily for significant elements of major religions. Hick's treatment is frequently reductionistic and he freely reinterprets troublesome doctrines so as to accommodate them within his theory....Thus, if there are significant elements of religions which clash with Hick's analysis, this prima facie counts against his theory.[89]

In his recent dissertation devoted to the analysis of Hick's religious pluralism, Kenneth Rose follows this line of criticism when he charges Hick's theory with being "reductionistic."[90] To Rose, this is a "serious fault," since:

> not many adherents of specific religions would likely, upon reflection, agreeably allow their beliefs, or interpretation of the mystery of existence, to be subjected to the reductionism inherent in Hick's pluralistic hypothesis.[91]

In assessing this criticism, one must step briefly into an on-going debate within the field of religious studies. This is not the place to enter into an extensive analysis of the discussion and debates surrounding the question of the proper mode of investigating and theorizing about human religious life. However, a few words can be said in order to elucidate both the legitimate concern behind this criticism and the misunderstanding inherent within it. To avoid confusion in this area, one must distinguish between two senses of the term 'interpretation' that are often conflated and obscured.[92] The first use of the term, and the one for which the term 'interpretation' is best reserved, is the task of providing a descriptive account of religious phenomena, including the first-order beliefs associated with a particular religious tradition. The second sense, better referred to as 'explanation,' involves the second-order task of offering an explanation—or 'theory'—of religious phenomena in terms of an over-arching explanatory scheme. The descriptive task of 'interpreting' a religion's first-order beliefs and practices must be judged by the degree to which the adherents of that religion would recognize and confirm the interpretation. To fail to render an interpretation that can be affirmed by an adherent is to fall into the "fallacy of descriptive reductionism."[93] However, the second and distinct task of providing a trans-tradition explanatory model that can explain religion as a whole *may or may not* accord with the self-understanding of any particular religious tradition under analysis. In fact, unless the explanation emerges as the self-conscious expression of a particular religious tradition, it is a safe bet that it will not agree with any given tradition; and even if it does, it will then not agree with any other tradition's explanatory model. Thus, religious explanation necessarily trades in what can be called 'explanatory reductionism.'[94] However, unlike 'descriptive reductionism,' to label it a form of reductionism is not to criticize the exercise. Rather, it is simply an expression of the inherent nature of all large-scale explanatory models of religion. *No* explanatory model of religion can evade this methodological necessity, since, by definition, every model must be constructed from the vantage point of one certain human perspective (i.e., disciplinary, philosophical, religious, etc.).

At this point, the criterion proposed by Netland and others is seen to be important yet circumscribed. If, in the process of explicating his pluralist hypothesis, Hick falls into a *descriptive reductionism*, one would have to judge his theory to be flawed at this point. Such descriptive reductionism may be what some of these critics have in mind. For instance, many have charged Hick with 'reducing' the radically diverse concepts of 'salvation' among the religions to a vague and essentially contentless unifying cipher. This is an important indictment, and one which has been addressed above. However, at least as I read the charges, it appears that often this legitimate *interpretive* criticism has been dislocated from its proper domain (i.e., religious description) and illegitimately applied to Hick's second-order *explanation* of religion. In such cases, the charge is simply misguided, being founded on a conceptual confusion. After all, Hick's meta-theory of religion can hardly be faulted for doing what a meta-theory is, by definition, designed to do.[95]

On the Very Possibility of a Tradition-Neutral 'Religious' Theory of Religion Several scholars of religions have raised the issue of whether or not Hick's tradition-neutral *universal religious* theory of religion can actually do what it must to be successful. Clarke and Byrne's thoughts on this question get to the heart of the issue:

> Hick's 'critical realism'…is suppose to avoid the disadvantages of a confessionally based theory of religious history and those of an external, illusionist theory. Trying to steer a middle path and retain some advantages of both approaches is bound to meet with the objection that no one can have his cake and eat it.…Combining some kind of commitment to the reality of the sacred while avoiding all first-order theological claims may in the end be an impossible task.[96]

It has been argued that no one can be 'religious in general,' and Hick himself would agree in the sense that all religious experience of the Real takes place within the concreteness and particularities of a specific religious tradition.[97] However, Hick's second-order philosophical theory about the religions and the discourse that supports it does depend upon an abstraction of 'religion' in general. There is also the question of how such generalizations are even possible given the inherent ambiguities of Hick's 'family resemblance' definition of religion. Clark and Byrne pose the issue: "…how, if the class of religions has no essential unity, can it be the subject of the generalizations that Hick so obviously wants to make about it?…If the class of religions is irreducibly diverse Hick's project appears to be in jeopardy."[98]

Finally, some would argue that a religious theory of religion is, by definition, problematic.[99] For instance, beginning with the assumption that 'theories,' by definition, involve hypotheses that can, at least in principle, be falsified, Russell McCutcheon suggests that a religious theory of religion is something of a misnomer. He argues that one important difference between religious and scientific discourses is that "only the latter are falsifiable."[100] McCutcheon concludes:

> What is missed in the confusion is that religious accounts are the *data* for scholars

who develop sociological, psychological, socioeconomic, and so on, theories of religion. Accordingly, religious accounts are not competing theoretical accounts.[101]

To begin to explore this question is to enter into a thorny debate currently underway in the field of religious studies today. Specifically, the issue revolves around the question of the relationship between 'religious studies' and 'theological studies'.[102] As Hick is involved in both, sometimes in ways that seem to conflate the two, he can hardly avoid this issue. In any case, Hick's project assumes the viability of a 'religious' theory of religion that is, at the same time, 'theologically' neutral. At the very least, a clear explanation of just how this sort of project can be accomplished without blurring important methodological distinctions and disciplinary boundaries—if such an explanation is possible—is called for.

Hick's Pluralist Hypothesis as a Rival Religion   Another challenge to Hick's religious interpretation of religion is the claim that this theory would itself function as a religious worldview for its adherents. Practically speaking, once adopted it becomes not simply a meta-theory about the religions, but a rival to the religions.[103] In this vein, Art Hurtado suggests that Hick's theory "ceases to be an interpretation of religion and becomes another religious interpretation of the world.... Hick's pluralist hypothesis is simply another potential band of color in the Rainbow of Faiths."[104]

Part of the issue here is the question of whether an adherent of one of the world's religions can adopt Hick's perspective and yet remain as convinced and committed a member of their religious tradition as before. Several scholars have answered this question with a resounding 'No': people simply do not think and live the way Hick's theory would demand. Once a religious person sees that their doctrines—including their conception of ultimate reality—are at best 'mythologically true,' they can no longer be expected to put the same stock in them that they once did. First, simply 'knowing' that a mysterious noumenal Real lies 'behind' the always partial and limited conception of God/ the Absolute found in one's own tradition will cause many believers (certainly those who lack the philosophical sophistication to understand the complex nuances of the neo-Kantian thesis itself) to lose faith in their traditional concept of the religious ultimate. Despite Hick's well-meaning philosophical protestations, many will naturally turn their necessarily vague conception of 'the noumenal Real'—which now has become, of course, another phenomenal manifestation—into an object of worship.[105] George Mavrodes has put his finger on the problem:

The Real is religiously attractive because of the deep religious orientation toward what is real. The suggestion, therefore, that there is something still *more* real than the religious object will be intolerable to many believers. Their move, in response to [Hick's transcendentalizing of the Real], is likely to be that of identifying the religious object with the allegedly more basic reality. And thus the [Real is always]…in danger of being eaten and absorbed by some allegedly lower [phenomenal] deity.[106]

Second, one must consider that the cognitive and practical realms of human life are inherently interconnected. Thus, ironically, once Hick's theory is accepted, "the transformational power of their religious tradition would be undermined for most ordinary believers."[107]

These sorts of considerations have led some to the conclusion that, ultimately, Hick's interpretation of religion is simply another form of religious inclusivism. Heim writes:

[Hick's meta-theory is] a friendly reductionism, which sees a true *religious* meaning of the faiths obscured by metaphorical language. He asserts that the real truth of religion…is explicitly grasped only in his meta-theory. He argues the faiths grope toward this truth in their own conditioned, particular manners; like all inclusivisms, he comes to fulfill and not to destroy.[108]

It has been argued that one clear example of Hick's inclusivism involves the way in which his religious interpretation views the various naturalistic worldviews. In this regard, Hick has written that, viewed from the vantage-point of his religious interpretation of religion:

the basic intent of the Marxist-Leninist, Trotskyist, Maoist, and broader socialist movements…has to be interpreted as a dispositional response of the modern sociologically conditioned consciousness to the Real.[109]

Thus, Hick classifies "the secular faith of Marxism," in terms of 'soteriological' structure, as a post-axial faith, and suggests that it falls within his family resemblance definition of religion. He is able to "fully agree" with the statement that possibly "atheists are being saved by God even though they are unaware of his existence."[110] It would seem that Hick, similar to an inclusivist, understands those who operate within naturalistic worldviews as 'anonymous religionists,' despite the naturalist's reading of the situation to the contrary. Heim pointedly formulates the challenge:

Hick can be criticized here for falling away from the pluralist principles he has expounded: if the humanist "faith" in toto is salvifically effective, why insist that its tenets are false and Hick's are true, that humanism's salvific effect is, so to speak, parasitic on the truth of religion? Hick surely condemns such a claim from one religion to another. Would it not be more consistent with Hick's general approach to say that, like the *persona* and *impersona* of the Real, naturalistic and religious views are two equally good ways of relating to a great unknown?...Hick can be criticized for revealing that despite protests to the contrary he is actually an inclusivist through and through....[111]

Faced with this charge of 'inclusivism,' Hick has responded: "And why not? But of course to have an inclusivist view in one area does not mean that one must also have an inclusivist view in another."[112] This is a very interesting response. It suggests that Hick sees no problem with 'inclusivism' per se, but only that he is not convinced that it is the best approach within the inter-religious arena. For Hick to say this is to seemingly bring into question years of his own attacks on 'inclusivism' as somehow inherently narrow-minded (i.e., 'Ptolemaic') and arrogant. However, when the issue is religion vs. religion, as opposed to religion vs. naturalism, Hick continues to criticize inclusivism in the same terms he always has. For instance, he has recently claimed that "inclusivism is an inherently unstable position comparable with the epicycles that were added to the old Ptolemaic astronomy." Are we to believe that in one setting inclusivism is "unstable," while in the other it is "appropriate"? How this could be the case is not at all clear.[113]

A second response on Hick's part is even more revealing: "Respect for humanists does not entail thinking their belief system is true...this is an appropriate inclusivism."[114] Here is the very claim that exclusivists and inclusivists have been making with regard to inter-religious dialogue! If Hick can respect and participate in fruitful dialogue with naturalists while believing them to be 'anonymous religionists' so to speak, then why can't Christian inclusivists, say, do the same with Buddhists or Muslims?

These sorts of concerns have led some to see in Hick an evangelist of a new missionary religious faith.[115] Hick himself would strongly object. He has clearly stated that, according to his theory, there could never be a "cult of the Real *an sich*," that "worship of the Real" as such is simply not possible. Rather, "[r]eligious believers do not worship the Real in itself, but always some particular manifestation of it."[116] This may be the case for Hick's theory. However, the question remains of whether less philosophically sophisticated religious believers can keep first-level religious and second-level philosophical concepts and discourse as compartmentalized and tidy as can Hick. While we may not see the Church of the Unknowable Real springing up any time soon, there is something to the concern that Hick's theory of religion (with its noumenal 'Real') violates boundaries by inherently competing with other religions for the hearts and minds of their adherents regarding the question of ultimate Reality.

Hick's Pluralism as a Hindrance to Genuine Inter-Religious Dialogue[117]   Another ironic criticism of Hick's approach is that, ultimately, it serves to eliminate true inter-religious dialogue.[118] Hick holds to the common pluralist assumption that the retention of doctrinal claims of superior and/or exclusive soteriological effectiveness, etc. necessarily hamper inter-religious dialogue.[119] Glyn Richards has succinctly summarized this pluralist view: "Open-mindedness in dialogue, therefore, involves the total rejection of exclusivism with its apologetic and proselytizing attitude, which might be regarded as a form of arrogance and presumptuousness and an attempt to limit the love of God."[120]

A number of critics of the pluralist paradigm have argued that such a view disallows real and robust inter-religious dialogue from the start by demanding that each religious adherent modify their potentially offensive beliefs prior to coming to the table. From this perspective, the *a priori* pluralist requirements for dialogue trade the heart and soul of a religion—its doctrinal self-understanding—for what amounts to a "superficial and brittle" unity.[121] Thus, Eric Springsted speaks for many when he argues that the true concern of religious dialogue "is not, as Hick sees it, in removing those beliefs and values that appear to hinder dialogue because of their uniqueness but in engaging in dialogue *given those beliefs and values*."[122] Along these lines, Julius Lipner contrasts "Reduction Dialogue" (i.e., Hick's pluralistic approach) with "Committal Dialogue," and argues for the value of the latter approach. Jon Levenson has pointed out the inherent exclusivism and practical shortcomings of the theory of inter-religious dialogue that requires one to leave their traditional beliefs of (exclusive) religious truth outside the door:

> Self-censorship of this sort is not so problematic for those whose positions tend toward liberalism or relativism, but it will take a heavy toll on that minority of committed traditionalists willing to enter into dialogue. It means they will either have to stay out of the dialogue or express within it something less than what they regard as the whole truth.…But why must dialogue preclude the opportunity for each community to witness in an open, courteous, and equitable way to what it regards as the truth…?"[123]

If true dialogic encounter between robust living religions is the goal, rather than a superficial, lowest-common-denominator agreement, then it is difficult for Hick's pluralism to escape this criticism.[124] In the end, it is primarily the attitudes of the partners, and not the presence or absence of exclusive religious truth-claims, that will determine the success of a dialogical experience.

Is it Christian?: The Christological Question

As a philosopher of religion, Hick has constructed his pluralist hypothesis as a response to the problematic of religious diversity. As a Christian theologian, Hick has attempted to identify and modify the orthodox tenets of his own faith that the pluralist hypothesis has flagged as inherently and irredeemably exclusivist in nature. Critical responses to these attempts have highlighted a number of points at which Hick's approach can be seen as betraying the very religious community he purports to serve. Thus, for many within the Christian community, a commitment to Hick's religious pluralism inherently involves at the same time a "retreat from Christianity."[125] Gavin D'Costa has suggested the possibility that, viewed through the question of truth criteria and revelation, "pluralists cannot properly be regarded as Christian," while James Kraft has concluded that Hick's pluralism fails as a properly Christian approach to interfaith issues.[126]

There are those exclusivist and inclusivist Christians who claim that Hick has misunderstood and/or misrepresented their own positions.[127] Some have argued, contra Hick, that the Christian faith demands that the Triune God be understood, not as one possible phenomenal manifestation of an always unknowable ultimate Reality, but as a revelation of that Reality as it is in Itself. Jacques Dupuis writes: "For Christian faith, then, the Triune God cannot be viewed as a manifestation or an appearance, among others, of an Ultimate Reality....It is not a penultimate sign of the Real *an sich*; it is the Ultimate Reality itself."[128]

Further concerns regarding Hick's doctrine of God range from his 'Sabellian' anti-Trinitarianism to the foisting of a modern western 'democratic' ideology upon God such that "God must behave in an equal democratic way towards all people" so that none are left with any kind of "religious advantage."[129] Ironically, just as Hick is mounting a strong criticism of the doctrine of the Trinity, something of a renaissance is taking place in trinitarian quarters today. In particular, there is a wide-ranging appreciation of a robustly social trinitarianism that, nonetheless, avoids the potential dangers of tritheism.[130] Others have suggested that Hick's perspective neglects the Christian doctrine of sin, and falls instead into a form of modern-day Pelagianism.[131] By far and away, however, the bulk of criticism against Hick's treatment of the Christian faith focuses upon his Christological reinterpretation. In short, many Christian thinkers of various stripes have argued that the rejection of the ontological deity of Jesus Christ, as demanded by Hick's pluralist Christology, is theologically intolerable. In previous chapters, the influence of the various developmental stages of Hick's approach to religious diversity has been traced through a series of Christological soundings. This chapter will conclude with a survey and assessment of criticisms directed at his pluralist Christology.

Responses to Hick's Critique of Orthodox Christology

Doctrinal Development, Biblical Criticism, and the Historical Jesus[132]   Numerous scholars have challenged important aspects of Hick's first two lines of critique of orthodox Christology—namely, (1) that modern biblical criticism has shown that the Jesus of history most likely did not originate the idea that he was divine, and, rather, (2) that the genesis and development of this myth can be traced through the first few centuries of the early church. First, some have argued that Hick's uncritical dependence upon modern historical-critical methodology has caused him to give up a basic theological tenet of the Christian faith: the authority of the Bible.[133] Others have noted that Hick's critique does not allow for the historic Christian notion of divine revelation, wherein the identify of Christ is progressively unfolded.[134] Gerard Loughlin has chastened Hick for adopting an "irreducibly 'empiricist' or 'positivist' conceptuality" that *a priori* allows the orthodox Christian doctrine of the incarnation no conceivable quarter.[135]

There are those who, having granted Hick the premise that faith in Jesus Christ as the divine Son of God must be rooted in the historical record, have gone on to challenge his conclusions. Generally, they have argued that the supposed critical 'consensus' regarding the historical Jesus in the post-Bultmannian world of New Testament studies is anything but a consensus.[136] More specifically, some have pointed out that Hick chooses to overlook important evidence in the New Testament pointing toward Jesus' implicit, if not explicit, claim to identification with Yahweh God.[137] Conservative scholars have consistently defended some of the more explicit passages, passages that Hick regards as creations of the post-Easter church, as authentically reflecting the perspective of the pre-Easter Jesus.[138]

Related to this, Hick has been challenged by some to "face the Easter witness" of the resurrection and its implications for Jesus' identity.[139] The claim that the deification of Jesus in the early church is simply one more example of a common religious phenomenon has likewise been challenged. Here, the primary difference that has been emphasized involves the speed with which the supposed deification myth would have arisen around a recently deceased historical person, and that within a monotheistic Jewish culture.[140]

Finally, it has been asserted that for Hick to reject the orthodox understanding of the incarnation simply because the full articulations of this doctrine did not arise for several centuries after Jesus is to commit "the genetic fallacy of supposing that, once one has said *how* a belief has come to expression, one has said all that is to be said."[141]

The Meaning of the Incarnation[142] Hick's claim that, taken literally, the historic Christian doctrine of the incarnation is meaningless has likewise not gone unchallenged. Some have wondered about the sublime depth of knowledge about God required to make such a pronouncement. Loughlin writes:

> in order to advance this claim—that the doctrine of the incarnation is manifestly absurd—Hick has to know a lot about God and about what it is to be a human person. But the implicit claim to so much knowledge is highly questionable.[143]

D'Costa has emphasized this point as well. He argues that the definitions of 'God' and 'human' are hardly givens, and that, for the Christian, they are disclosed decisively only through Jesus Christ. However, Hick's incompatible definitions are somehow known by him prior to the incarnation.[144] For many theologians, this is simply not a properly Christian approach to the question. One could expand upon this criticism by demonstrating the complexities and difficulties of conclusively showing the fundamental incoherence of two concepts. Reality is often filled with more mystery than we initially imagine, and epistemological humility is all too often a rare commodity.

On one hand, there are those who have responded by arguing that to speak of the incarnation is, by definition, to be forced into "a paradoxical dialectic."[145] Anders Jeffner, for instance, calls for Hick to acknowledge the category of "indirect cognitive meaning." He writes:

> The indirect meaning expressed by the Nicene principle of incarnation can be seen as cognitive but absolutely impossible to formulate in direct propositions....The idea of ineffable cognitive meaning seems to me possible to defend....Such an

apophatic or negative theology seems to me to be an unavoidable part of a Christian doctrine and a reasonable way of handling the Nicene principle of incarnation.[146]

Thus, to ask that the Chalcedonian vision of Christ's incarnation be literally expressible in a philosophically understandable form is to ask it to do something it was never designed for.[147] Naturally, this line of thought will hardly be impressive to Hick, since it plays right into his hand. In his eyes, this type of response only confirms what he has been saying for the last three decades: that the incarnation is best understood as myth/metaphor.

On the other hand, various scholars have taken up Hick's gauntlet in a more direct fashion. Some simply want to claim that the idea of the incarnation can be shown to be non-contradictory.[148] Others take the next step and offer what they consider to be a philosophically defensible explanation of the incarnation. The two most promising approaches, and thus the two that Hick spends the most time criticizing, are the 'kenotic' and the 'two minds' models.[149] It must suffice to note at this point that a variety of philosophers of religion and theologians have come to the opposite conclusion from Hick with regard to the explanatory power and philosophical success of one or the other of these models. R. B. Nicolson, for instance, concludes that Thomas Morris' 'two minds' model "goes a long way towards showing us that a Chalcedonian type of Christology is not necessarily incoherent, impossible, or logically untenable."[150] With others coming to judgments on these matters so contrary to Hick's, there are good grounds upon which to question Hick's claim that the incarnation is, literally speaking, meaningless. These grounds are further strengthened by a final consideration. Here, Nicolson's musings are instructive:

> [However a] major problem with Chalcedonian christology and the associated soteriology is that effectively it makes human life and human salvation only fully explicable in Christian terms; it is exclusivist, and leaves the major part of the human race out of account....We are left with a christology which is, if Morris is right, perfectly logical but not perfectly moral.[151]

Nicolson's observation re-opens the question of the connection between a Chalcedonian Christology and an exclusivist theology of religions. With this, it is time to survey the most common criticisms of Hick's alternative Christological proposal, the first of which follows from Nicolson's insight—and one that clearly resonates with Hick.

Criticisms of Hick's Pluralist Christology

Hick's A Priori Pluralist Bias against a Literal Incarnation A number of Hick's interlocutors have suggested that, rather than Hick's conclusions on Christology leading him toward pluralism, the motivating line of influence has moved in the opposite direction. Clark Pinnock has, perhaps, put the issue most starkly:

> Hick wants to leave the impression that his Christology is based primarily upon historical (i.e., Jesus did not teach this doctrine) and theological (i.e., it never did make sense) considerations. It seems more likely that this analysis is a rationalization of the position his system requires....A belief in the Incarnation and Trinity would spoil everything. Therefore, the effort to get rid of the Incarnation has less to do with evidence than with the ideology....The bias against the Incarnation is invincible going in.[152]

Again, Hick himself has consistently stated that if the classical doctrine of the incarnation is true then the pluralist paradigm is doomed. For Hick, if Jesus is literally the divine Son of God, then "the only doorway to eternal life is Christian faith."[153] Given this conviction, the pressure upon Hick to conclude against a literal incarnation is tremendous. In short, the pluralist paradigm, to which he is already committed, demands it. Thus, in light of this bias, it is suggested that Hick's conclusions on Christology should have little force upon those not already committed to a pluralist model.[154]

Deficiencies of Hick's Incarnation-as-Myth/Metaphor Model[155] From the time of the publication of *The Myth of God Incarnate*, various critics have charged Hick (along with his fellow mythographers) with an inappropriate and/or ambiguous use of the term 'myth.'[156] Nicholas Lash, for example, drew attention at this time to the "crudeness and imprecision" of the mythographers' distinction between 'literal' and 'metaphorical' language.[157] Lash writes:

> Running through several of the contributions to *The Myth of God Incarnate* there is an assumption that 'literal' discourse is 'objective', fact-asserting, whereas imaginative, metaphorical, symbolic or mythological discourse is 'subjective', expressive of attitudes. This assumption is most clearly evident in John Hick's essay....Its oddness becomes apparent when we reflect on the fact that ninety per cent of commonsense and scientific discourse is saturated with metaphorical usage. The assumption embodies, I suspect, a highly questionable account of the supposedly contrasting activities of 'reasoning' and 'imagining'....[158]

For the last two decades, this type of criticism has plagued Hick's Christological project. His understanding of myth and metaphor have been appraised as "severely limited," "captive to a crude positivism," "reductive in a bad sense" and indicative of a "puzzling insensitivity about the nature of truth."[159] Chester Gillis has emphasized the important implications this line of criticism could have for Hick's project. If they are correct, "then Hick's entire [Christological] system is flawed because it is based upon a faulty interpretation of language forms."[160] In brief, the central charge here is that Hick fails to recognize that the language of myth and metaphor is not simply an ornamental or emotive way of expressing what can be more precisely stated in 'literal' propositions. Rather, they involve a "cognitively creative process" that issues in a unique expression which, once 'translated' into another language form, can at best only be approximated. Thus, "[m]etaphor, precisely as metaphor, discloses or manifests."[161] Once the false dichotomy hidden within Hick's theory of myth/metaphor—that 'literal' language deals with cognitive and factual content, while 'mythological' and 'metaphorical' trade in something else—is exposed and rejected, the Christological question immediately resurfaces: "Could not the phrase 'the Son of God' as applied to Jesus be both metaphorical and metaphysical?"[162]

Loughlin raises the issue in an alternative fashion: "We cannot conceive of emotive 'import' apart from a cognitive content which elicits it. If Jesus is in no sense the Son of God it is difficult if not impossible to understand why the attitude that such a statement might evoke could be in any sense appropriate to Jesus."[163]

Hick's 'New' Pluralist Christology as 'Old' Liberal Christianity   One of the common criticisms of Hick's pluralist Christology is that it represents little more than a modified 19th-century Protestant liberalism.[164] Thus, Gregory Carruthers offers the somewhat ironic conclusion that Hick's contemporary Christology, being "uncritically grounded in principles and attitudes of the late nineteenth century" is already "dated." He goes on to clarify this comment: "Hick is reliant on nineteenth century history of religions for his mistaken view that the doctrine of the Incarnation was an alien intrusion into Christianity.[165]

Some have pushed this line of critique even further, both historically and theologically. Of Hick's most recent treatment of Jesus, Gerald O'Collins writes:

> *The Metaphor of God Incarnate* illustrates a persistent characteristic of liberal
> Christology: it pretends to represent a new, Copernican-style revolution in Christian
> thought. So much for the old Ebionites, Adoptionists and Arians, none of whom

ever rate a mention in this book....Modern liberal Christologies are philosophically and (in some ways) biblically ahead of their ancient Adoptionist and Arian counterparts. But can Neo-Arianism hope to succeed where Arianism failed?[166]

Hick's appeal to a 'Spirit' (or 'Inspiration') Christology would find growing support in various theological circles today. But the conceptual options regarding Spirit Christology are many. Hick's conception of Spirit Christology (following the broad lines of G. W. H. Lampe's proposal leads to a generally neo-modalist approach wherein the hypostatic Trinitarian distinctions are denied.[167] However, a number of contemporary Spirit Christologies have demonstrated that this fruitful line of thought can be pursued while maintaining the Trinitarian distinctions in a robust fashion. Ralph Del Colle, for instance, argues that, far from attenuating the possibilities of inter-religious dialogue, a Spirit-Christology that maintains the integrity of the hypostatic distinctions between divine Son and Spirit "should be able to enrich the possibilities" of such dialogue.[168]

In light of this summary of theological critiques, it is clear that, for a significant number of Hick's fellow Christians, the answer to the question 'Is it Christian?' is something less than affirmative. In this regard, Terrence Merrigan has poignantly articulated the fears of many:

> What is at stake is not simply purging Christianity of antiquated elements with a view to the encounter with the world's religions, but the survival of Christianity as a distinctive faith tradition with a claim to represent a divinely sanctioned narrative, praxis, and spirituality.[169]

I shall now turn to the final chapter of this study and, with it, the final critical question that Hick's hypothesis must face—'Does it work?'

Notes

1   The last two of these three questions represent what Knitter has identified as the two primary lines of criticism against the pluralistic paradigm; "The Pluralist Move and Its Critics," *The Drew Gateway* 58 (1988): 10–6. Hick's own categorization of the major criticisms of his model can easily be fit into this tripartite schema; see *Christian Theology of Religions*, chs. 2–5.

2   Alister E. McGrath, "The Christian Church's Response to Pluralism," *Journal of the Evangelical Theological Society* 35 (1992): 487. In context, McGrath's comment is directed at the pluralist paradigm in general; it is clear, however, that he includes Hick in this assessment. See also Loughlin, "Prefacing Pluralism."

3   E.g., see Nash, *Is Jesus the Only Savior?* 94–95; Douglas R. Geivett, "John Hick's Ap-

proach to Religious Pluralism," in *The Challenge of Religious Pluralism*, 50–51.

4   E.g., see D'Costa, "Taking Other Religions Seriously: Some Ironies in the Current Debate on a Christian Theology of Religions," *The Thomist* 54 (1990): 519–29; Heim, *Salvations*, 23–35. It would seem that Christoph Schwöbel and Terrence W. Tilley would also
fit this category; see Schwöbel, "Particularity, Universality, and the Religions: Toward a
Christian Theology of Religions," in *Christian Uniqueness Reconsidered*, 32; Tilley, review of *Interpretation of Religion*, *Theological Studies* 51 (1990): 137.

5   E.g., see Gordon D. Kaufman, "Religious Diversity and Religious Truth," 163, n. 2; idem.,
"Religious Diversity, Historical Consciousness, and Christian Theology," in *Myth of
Christian Uniqueness*, 5, 15, n. 2; Raimundo Panikkar, "The Jordan, the Tiber, and the
Ganges: Three Kairological Moments of Christic Self-Consciousness," in *Myth of Chris-
tian Uniqueness*, 109–11; Langdon Gilkey, "Plurality and Its Theological Implications," in
Myth of Christian Uniqueness, 41; John B. Cobb, Jr., "The Meaning of Pluralism for Christian Self-Understanding," in *Religious Pluralism*, 172; Rose, "Knowing the Real," 168.
It should be noted that most pluralists who level this criticism against Hick can just as
easily be tagged with the charge. Kaufman's 'modernizing' world culture, Gilkey's "divine mystery," and even Panikkar's categories of "politicization" and neo-Vedanticism
each serve to conceptually organize, and thus control, the radical diversity of human
religious life. See respectively, Kaufman, "Christian Theology and the Modernization of
the Religions," 106–9; Gilkey, "The Pluralism of Religions," in *God, Truth and Reality*,
122; Panikkar, "The Jordan, the Tiber, and the Ganges," 101–05.

6   For Hick's response to this line of criticism see *Christian Theology of Religions*, 37–41, 106–08.

7   See e.g., Heim, *Salvations*, 23–35; J. A. DiNoia, "Varieties of Religious Aims," in *Diversity
of Religions*, 51–55; Colin Grant, *A Salvation Audit* (Scranton: University of Scranton
Press, 1994), 212–13; Dirk J. Louw, "The Soteriocentrism of John Hick," *South African
Journal of Philosophy* 14 (1995): 19–23; D'Costa, "Elephants, Ropes and a Christian The-
ology of Religions," *Theology* 88 (1985): 265–67; Rose, "Knowing the Real, 168; Clendenin,
Many Gods, 107–9.

8   In addition to the sources to follow, see also John B. Cobb, Jr., "Beyond 'Pluralism'," in
Christian Uniqueness Reconsidered, 83; Netland, *Dissonant Voices*, 160; Louw,
"Soteriocentrism," 22; John Clayton, review of *An Interpretation of Religion*, *Journal of
Theological Studies* 43 (1992): 804.

9   "Knowing the Real," 168.

10   This question is answered in the negative by David E. McKenzie, "Kant, a Moral Criterion, and Religious Pluralism," *American Journal of Theology and Philosophy* 6 (1985): 56.

11   See Douglas Davies' insightful discussion, "Salvation in Preliterate Societies," in *Meaning and Salvation in Religious Studies*, SHR 46, (Leiden: Brill, 1984), 101–20.

12   So argues Rebecca Pentz, "Hick and Saints: Is Saint-Production a Valid Test?" *Faith and
Philosophy* 8 (1991): 96–103.

13   *Salvations*, 23.

14   Ibid., 26 (emphasis added). The first monizing assumption is that "the realm of ultimate
reality consists of a single, noumenal element which Hick calls 'the Real'" (p. 23).

15   Ibid., 152.

16   Ibid., 34–35 (emphasis in text). Similar concerns are voiced by DiNoia, "Varieties of Religious Aims," 51–55; Peter Fenner, "Religions in the Balance," *Sophia* 30 (1991): 16–20. In

a similar vein, Steven G. Smith ("Bowl Climbing: The Logic of Religious Question Rivalry," *International Journal for Philosophy of Religion* 36 [1994]: 27–43) has suggested that to take religious diversity seriously is to realize that the issue is not merely a plurality of different religious answers to "a certain great Question," but rather a radically diverse set of religious questions (p. 43).

17   *Interpretation of Religion*, 4; Hick takes this definitional paradigm from Wittgenstein.

18   Ibid. For an excellent discussion of 'family resemblence' versus 'essentialist' understandings of religion (from a 'family resemblence' perspective) see Benson Saler, *Conceptualizing Religion: Immanent Anthropologists, Transcendent Natives, and Unbounded Categories* (New York: Brill, 1993).

19   "A Religious Theory of Religion," in *Religion Defined and Explained*, 89. For similar assessments of Hick's program see Fredericks, "A Universal Religious Experience?" 67, 73; Terrence Merrigan, "Religious Knowledge in the Pluralist Theology of Religions," *Theological Studies* 58 (1997): 695–96, 698; Wells, "Taking Pluralism Seriously: The Role of Metaphorical Theology within Interreligious Dialogue," *Journal of Ecumenical Studies* 30 (1993): 22–23; Wyle Tan, "Religious Pluralism Revisited," *Asia Journal of Theology* 2 (1988): 348; Michael LaFargue, "Radically Pluralist, Thoroughly Critical: A New Theory of Religions," *Journal of the American Academy of Religion* 60 (1992): 693; Art Hurtado, "The 'Real', the Incarnation and Myth in John Hick's Pluralistic Hypothesis," paper presented at the 1998 Southwest Regional meeting of the American Academy of Religion (Dallas, Tex.), 13. Others have concluded that an important distinction remains between Hick's thesis and a classical 'common core' theory; see e.g., Bernard J. Verkamp, "Hick's Interpretation of Religious Pluralism," *International Journal for Philosophy of Religion* 30 (1991): 114; Peter Slater, "Lindbeck, Hick and the Nature of Religious Truth," *Studies in Religion* 24 (1995): 70–71.

20   Rose, "Knowing the Real," 118 (see also 140–41); see also Owen Thomas, review of *Interpretation of Religion, Anglican Theological Review* 73 (1991): 503.

21   "On Grading Religions," in *Problems of Religious Pluralism*, 69 (emphasis added).

22   *Christian Theology of Religions*, 41 (emphasis in text).

23   *Interpretation of Religion*, 15, n. 1.

24   "Phenomenology of Religion," in *Encyclopedia of Religion*, 16 vols., ed. Mircea Eliade (New York: Macmillan, 1987), XI:280.

25   E.g., see William Wainwright, review of *An Interpretation of Religion, Faith and Philosophy* 9 (1992): 264; idem, review of *A Christian Theology of Religions, International Journal for Philosophy of Religion* 42 (1997): 126; Timothy R. Stinnett, "John Hick's Pluralistic Theory of Religion," *Journal of Religion* 70 (1990): 586–87.

26   "Taking Other Religions Seriously," 529.

27   *Is Jesus the Only Savior?* 51. See Hick, *Interpretation of Religion*, 54.

28   *Christian Theology of Religions*, 78.

29   Wainwright, review of *Christian Theology of Religions*, 126.

30   Rose, "Knowing the Real," 172. See also Garrett Green, review of *An Interpretation of Religion, Theology Today* 46 (1990): 462; Kelly James Clark, "Perils of Pluralism," *Faith and Philosophy* 14 (1997): 316; Clark H. Pinnock, "Response to John Hick," in *More than One Way?* 61; Surin, "'Politics of Speech'," 209.

31   Surin, "Revelation, Salvation, the Uniqueness of Christ," 343.

32   See e.g., Netland, *Dissonant Voices*, 225–27; Brian Hebblethwaite, review of *An Inter-pretation of Religion*, *Zygon* 26 (1991): 330; Robert A. Segal, "A Review Essay: Religion as Interpreted Rather than Explained," review of *An Interpretation of Religion*, *Soundings* 74 (1991): 287; Siegfried Wiedenhofer, "Between Particularity and Universality: A Christian View of the Possibility of Ensuring the Identity and Communicability of Cultural and Religious Traditions," paper presented at Frankfurt am Main, Germany, January 15, 1995, 8.

33   *Dissonant Voices*, 226–27.

34   Mesle, review of *An Interpretation of Religion*, *Journal of the American Academy of Reli-gion* 58 (1990): 714 (emphasis in text).

35   Paul J. Griffiths, *An Apology for Apologetics: A Study in the Logic of Interreligious Dialogue* (Maryknoll, N.Y.: Orbis, 1991), 50.

36   See ibid., 48–50.

37   See e.g., Rose, "Knowing the Real," 138–43; Netland, *Dissonant Voices*, 159–60. This criti-cism poses a problem for several models of religious pluralism. I have offered a similar critique of Paul Knitter's model; see "Paul Knitter's Theology of Religions," 241–43.

38   "John Hick and Religious Pluralism," 12.

39   *Interpretation of Religion*, 246. Alvin Plantinga raises similar questions for Hick in *War-ranted Christian Belief* (New York: Oxford University Press, 2000), 43–63.

40   *Christian Theology of Religions*, 44; see also pp. 78–79.

41   *Christian Theology of Religions*, 111.

42   For Hick's response to this line of criticism see *Christian Theology of Religions*, 31–37.

43   "An Attempt at Summation," in *Christ's Lordship and Religious Pluralism*, 202. See also Runzo, "God, Commitment and Other Faiths," 357; Tom F. Driver, "The Case for Plural-ism," in *Myth of Christian Uniqueness*, 207.

44   *Disputed Questions in Theology*, viii; see also Hick, "Non-Absoluteness of Christianity," 18–20.

45   D'Costa has pushed this criticism in a strong way in recent years; see "Christian Theol-ogy and Other Religions," 177; idem, "Whose Objectivity? Which Neutrality? The Doomed Quest for a Neutral Vantage Point from which to Judge Religions," *Religious Studies* 29 (1993): 94; idem, "Impossibility of a Pluralist View." See also Peter Donovan, "The Intol-erance of Religious Pluralism," *Religious Studies* 29 (1993): 217–29; Alister E. McGrath, "The Challenge of Pluralism for the Contemporary Christian Church," *Journal of the Evangelical Theological Society* 35 (1992): 371–72; Lesslie Newbigin, "Religion for the Mar-ketplace," in *Christian Uniqueness Reconsidered*, 137; Brad Stetson, *Pluralism and Par-ticularity in Religious Belief* (Westport, Conn.: Praeger, 1994), 77; M. M. Thomas, "A Christ-Centered Humanist Approach to Other Religions in the Indian Pluralistic Con-text," in *Christian Uniqueness Reconsidered*, 57.

46   "Soteriocentrism," 22.

47   For Hick's response to this line of criticism see *Christian Theology of Religions*, 49–51.

48   In his 1973 essay, "The New Map of the Universe of Faiths" in *God and the Universe of Faiths* (140), Hick concludes his telling of the parable by stating that "of course [each of the blind men's reports about what the elephant was like was] true, but each referring only to one aspect of the total reality and all were expressed in very imperfect analogies." Likewise, Hick suggested, the many different accounts of divine reality are all true, while none of them perfectly captures this reality.

49   "John Hick's Copernican Theology," 37. For similar criticisms see D'Costa, *Hick's Theol-*

ogy of Religions, 141–4; Byrne, "Hick's Philosophy of World Religions," 291–92; Michael Barnes, *Religions in Conversation* (London: SPCK, 1989), 78.

50   See Hick's response to Almond's charge regarding the parable in "The Theology of Religious Pluralism," 336; also *Christian Theology of Religions*, 49.

51   "The New Missionary: John Hick and Religious Pluralism," *International Bulletin of Missionary Research* (April 1991): 69.

52   Review of *Interpretation of Religion*, 462. For similar criticism see Newbigin, *The Gospel in a Pluralist Society* (Grand Rapids, Mich.: Eerdmans, 1989), 10; Dan R. Stiver, review of *The Metaphor of God Incarnate*, *International Journal for Philosophy of Religion* 40 (1996): 181; Peters, *God—the World's Future*, 348–49.

53   See his "Prefacing Pluralism." Loughlin's antagonism toward Hick is even more interesting in light of an earlier article in which he is found defending Hick's pluralist move against D'Costa's criticisms; see "Paradox and Paradigms."

54   "Prefacing Pluralism," 44, 46 (emphasis in text).

55   For Hick's response to this line of criticism see *Christian Theology of Religions*, 37–39.

56   Apczynski, "John Hick's Theocentrism: Revolutionary or Implicitly Exclusivist?" *Modern Theology* 8 (1992): 47–48. See also Milbank, "End of Dialogue," 174–75; Donovan, "Intolerance of Pluralism."

57   Van Beeck, "Christian Faith and Theology in Encounter with Non-Christians: Profession? Protestation? Self-Maintenance? Abandon?" *Theological Studies* 55 (1994): 57. See also Clendenin, *Many Gods*, 96–97; McGrath, "Challenge of Pluralism," 371.

58   Peter H. Van Ness, "Conversion and Christian Pluralism," *Philosophy and Theology* 7 (1993): 348. Peter Donovan ("Intolerance of Pluralism," 220) has drawn attention to the distinction between 'epistemic' and 'ideological' pluralism: While those in the first camp hold that pluralism is "a way to finding truth," ideological pluralists claim that "pluralism is the truth."

59   Van Ness, "Conversion and Christian Pluralism," 348.

60   See Surin, "Towards a 'Materialist' Critique"; idem., "A 'Politics of Speech.'"

61   "Towards a 'Materialist' Critique," 120.

62   Ibid., 120–21.

63   Ibid., 123.

64   "Politics of Speech," 209–10. Although he does not name Hick specifically, Francis Schüssler Fiorenza identifies similar connections between pluralism and the capitalist west; see "Christian Redemption between Colonialism and Pluralism," in *Reconstructing Christian Theology*, 284.

65   See e.g., Robert Cook, "Postmodernism, Pluralism and John Hick," *Themelios* 19 (1993): 10–12. See Hick's "Response to Robert Cook," *Themelios* 19 (1994): 20, and Cook's rejoinder, "Response to John Hick," *Themelios* 19 (1994): 20–1. See also Hick, *Christian Theology of Religions*, 38.

66   *Christian Theology of Religions*, 31.

67   "A Response to Gerard Loughlin," 57.

68   "Response to Loughlin," 57. For examples of Hick's claim of 'misunderstanding' see "On Conflicting Truth-Claims," 485; "Concluding Comment," 452; "Letter to the Editors: World Religions," *Theology* 92 (1989): 297; "Straightening the Record," 187; "Reply [to Loughlin]," in *Problems in the Philosophy of Religion*, 206.

69   Review of *Christian Theology of Religions*, 127–28.

70   Review of *Interpretation of Religion*, 504.

71   For Hick's response to this line of criticism see *Christian Theology of Religions*, 51–56.

72   See respectively "Taking Other Religions Seriously," 527; "Revelation and World Religions," *Divine Revelation*, ed. Paul Avis (Grand Rapids, Mich.: Eerdmans, 1997), 122.

73   "Towards a 'Materialist' Critique," 121.

74   E.g., see Griffiths, *An Apology for Apologetics*, 46–51; D'Costa, "Taking Other Religions Seriously," 519–29; Netland, *Dissonant Voices*, 227–33; Rose, "Knowing the Real," 114–20; Wolfhart Pannenberg, "Religious Pluralism and Conflicting Truth Claims: The Problem of a Theology of the World Religions," in *Christian Uniqueness Reconsidered*, 96–106; Evelina Orteza y Miranda, "Religious Pluralism and Tolerance," *British Journal of Religious Education* 17 (Autumn 1994): 19–34; Clendenin, *Many Gods*, 103–07.

75   *Interpretation of Religion*, 351.

76   D'Costa, "Taking Other Religions Seriously," 520.

77   Hume, " Of Miracles," in his *An Inquiry Concerning Human Understanding*, Charles W. Hendel, ed. (Indianapolis: Bobbs-Merrill, 1955 [1748]), 129.

78   "Religious Diversity," 433.

79   *Nature of Doctrine*, 51; cited in *Interpretation of Religion*, 360–61, n. 4.

80   *Apology for Apologetics*, 47–48. Griffiths comments are directed toward what he calls "universalist perspectivalism"; he explicitly points to Hick as a prime example.

81   Griffiths has been on the cutting edge of this endeavor. See especially his *Apology for Apologetics*; also idem., "Doctrines and the Virtue of Doctrine: The Problematic of Religious Plurality," in *Religions and the Virtue of Religion*, ed. Thérèse-Anne Druart and Mark Rasevic (Washington, D.C.: Catholic University of America, 1992), 29–44; idem., "Denaturalizing Discourse: Abhidharmikas, Propositionalists, and the Comparative Philosophy of Religion," *Myth and Philosophy*, ed. Frank Reynolds and David Tracy (Albany: SUNY, 1990), 57–91; idem., "Philosophizing Across Cultures: Or, How to Argue with a Buddhist" *Criterion* (Winter 1987), 10–14; idem., "Why We Need Interreligious Polemics," *First Things* 44 (June–July, 1994): 31–37.

82   No one has pressed Hick's theory on this point more strongly than Mark Heim; see *Salvations*, 26–35.

83   "Concluding Comment," 452–53.

84   "On Conflicting Religious Truth-Claims," 93–94.

85   "Religious Pluralism and Absolute Claims," 193; see also "Concluding Comment," 450.

86   *Interpretation of Religion*, 372–73; *Faith and Knowledge*, 198–99. See chapter two of this study for discussion.

87   For Hick's response to this line of criticism see *Christian Theology of Religions*, 41–49.

88   See e.g., Clendenin, *Many Gods*, 103–05; Colin Grant, "The Threat and Prospect in Religious Pluralism," *Ecumenical Review* 41 (1989): 54–55; Heim, "Pluralism and the Otherness of World Religions," *First Things* #25 (August–September 1992): 29–35; Netland, *Dissonant Voices*, 221–33; idem., "Professor Hick on Religious Pluralism," *Religious Studies* 22 (1986): 255–57; Rose, "Knowing the Real," 114–26; Sanders, *No Other Name*, 119.

89   *Dissonant Voices*, 221–22.

90   "Knowing the Real," 114.

91   Ibid., 116.

92   As suggested, there is heated discussion in the field of religious studies as to the proper mode of investigating religion. Much of this debate centers on the conflict between 'interpretive' and 'explanatory' approaches. For two very helpful entrances into these matters see Robert A. Segal, *Religion and the Social Sciences: Essays on the Confrontation* (Atlanta: Scholars Press, 1989); and especially idem., *Explaining and Interpreting Religion: Essays on the Issue* (New York: Lang, 1992). See also Daniel L. Pals, *Seven Theories of Religion* (New York: Oxford University Press, 1996); Clarke and Byrne, *Religion Defined and Explained*; Wayne Proudfoot, *Religious Experience* (Berkeley/Los Angeles: University of California Press, 1985), chs. 2, 5. For some helpful thoughts on these matters in the context of a critique of Hick's thought see Segal, "Religion as Interpreted Rather than Explained."

93   Twiss, "Philosophy of Religious Pluralism," 542.

94   Ibid., 543.

95   This point is well stated by Sumner Twiss in his largely sympathetic analysis of Hick's project; see "Philosophy of Religious Pluralism," 541–45. See also Hick's parallel response to this charge in *Christian Theology of Religions*, 41–44.

96   "A Religious Theory of Religion," 96. Keith Ward has voiced his agreement with Byrne and Clarke's skepticism at this point; *Religion and Revelation* (New York: Oxford University Press, 1994), 107–08.

97   Jacob Neusner, "Can You Be 'Religious' in General?" *Religious Studies and Theology* 12 (1992): 69–73.

98   "A Religious Theory of Religion," 89.

99   E.g., Apczynski ("Hick's Theocentrism," 40) argues that "the very project of offering philosophical foundations for a field theory of religion from a religious point of view is misconceived."

100   McCutcheon, *Manufacturing Religion: The Discourse on Sui Generis Religion and the Politics of Nostalgia* (New York: Oxford University Press, 1997), 147. It should be noted in passing that, while some would concur with McCutcheon's assessment of the striking contrasts between scientific and religious epistemologies and/or methodologies, others at work in the contemporary science and religion dialogue would strongly disagree. See e.g., Nancey Murphy, *Theology in the Age of Scientific Reasoning* (Ithaca, N.Y.: Cornell University Press, 1990).

101   *Manufacturing Religion*, 147 (emphasis in text). See also idem., "'My Theory of the Brontosaurus': Postmodernism and 'Theory' of Religion," *Studies in Religion* 26 (1997), 3–23.

102   For a recent exchange that presents the various views on this debate see Ray L. Hart, "Religious and Theological Studies in American Higher Education: A Pilot Study," *Journal of the American Academy of Religion* 59 (1991): 715–827; Schubert M. Ogden, "Religious Studies and Theological Studies: What is Involved in the Distinction between the Two?" *Council of Societies for the Study of Religion Bulletin* 24 (1995): 3–4; and the six articles on the topic in *Council of Societies for the Study of Religion Bulletin* 26 (1997): 50–68.

103   E.g., Hebblethwaite, review of *Interpretation of Religion*, 332; Joseph O'Leary, *Religious Pluralism and Christian Truth* (Edinburgh: Edinburgh University Press, 1996), 20–22; Norman Lillegard, "Philosophers, Theologians, and the Pluralism Problem," *Philosophy and Theology* 7 (1993): 389; Quinn, "Toward Thinner Theologies," 150.

104   "The Real," 12, 14.

105   See Hick, "Response to Mesle," in Mesle, *John Hick's Theodicy*, 134.

106   Mavrodes, "The God above the Gods: Can the High Gods Survive?" in *Reasoned Faith: Essays in Philosophical Theology in Honor of Norman Kretzmann*, ed. Eleonore Stump (Ithaca: Cornell University Press, 1993), 203.

107   Clark, "Perils of Pluralism," 317.

108   *Salvations*, 30 (emphasis in text). Gillis (*Question of Final Belief*, 174) has referred to Hick's program as "another, albeit more sophisticated, form of inclusivism." In assessing such judgments, one's definition of 'inclusivism' (i.e., alethic vs. soteric typologies) is all-important.

109   *Interpretation of Religion*, 306.

110   Ibid., 5, 33, 378; Hick, "Letter to the Editors: Only One Way to God?" *Theology* 86 (1983): 128.

111   *Salvations*, 29. Mesle was one of the first to identify this problem in Hick's theory; see "Humanism and Hick's Interpretation of Religion," in *Problems in the Philosophy of Religion*, 54–85; *Hick's Theodicy*, 90–1; review of *Interpretation of Religion*.

112   *Christian Theology of Religions*, 81.

113   "A Pluralist View," 82.

114   "Response [to Mesle]," *Problems in the Philosophy of Religion*, 83.

115   E.g., D'Costa, "The New Missionary"; Forrester, "Professor Hick," 71–2.

116   "Response to Mesle," in Mesle's *Hick's Theodicy*, 134.

117   For Hick's response to this line of criticism see *Christian Theology of Religions*, 120–4.

118   See e.g., Apczynski, "Hick's Theocentrism," 49–50; David K. Clark, "Can Apologists Enter Genuine Dialogue?" in *Challenge of Religious Pluralism*, 152–62; Clendenin, *Many Gods*, 107; D'Costa, "Theology of Religions," 284–5; Gillis, *Question of Final Belief*, 163–4; Griffiths, *An Apology*, ch. 4; Jürgen Moltmann, "Is 'Pluralistic Theology' Useful for the Dialogue of World Religions?" in *Christian Uniqueness Reconsidered*, 149–56; Ted Peters, "Confessional Universalism and Inter-Religious Dialogue," *Dialog* 25 (1986): 145–9.

119   See Hick, "Five Misgivings," in *The Uniqueness of Jesus: A Dialogue with Paul F. Knitter*, ed. Leonard Swidler and Paul Mojzes (Maryknoll, N.Y.: Orbis, 1997), 81; *Second Christianity*, 90–1.

120   *Towards a Theology of Religions* (New York: Routledge, 1989), 155. See also Eck, *Encountering God*, 197–9.

121   Forrester, "Professor Hick," 71.

122   Springsted, "Conditions of Dialogue: John Hick and Simone Weil," *Journal of Religion* 72 (1992), 25–6 (emphasis in text). For criticisms of Hick's view of dialogue in particular (including his negative assessment of non-pluralist dialogue), see D'Costa, *Hick's Theology of Religions*, 147–50; Forrester, "Professor Hick," 71; Griffiths and Lewis, "On Grading Religions, Seeking Truth, and Being Nice to People," 75–80; O'Leary, *Religious Pluralism and Christian Truth*, 21–2.

123   See respectively Lipner, "Truth-Claims and Inter-Religious Dialogue," 226–7; Levenson, "Must We Accept the Other's Self-Understanding?" *Journal of Religion* 71 (1991): 564.

124   See McGrath, "The Challenge of Pluralism for the Contemporary Christian Church," in *Challenge of Religious Pluralism*, 246.

125   McGrath, "Challenge of Pluralism," 243.

126   See respectively, D'Costa, "Impossibility of a Pluralist View of Religions," 226; Kraft, "What Constitutes a Distinctively Christian Approach to Interfaith Dialogue?" 282–90.

127   E.g., from the exclusivist/particularist perspective: Geivett and W. Gary Phillips, "Re-

sponse to John Hick," *More than One Way?* 71–80; McGrath, "Response to John Hick," in *More than One Way?* 65–70. From the inclusivist perspective: D'Costa, "*Extra Ecclesiam nulla Salus*' Revisited," in *Religious Pluralism and Unbelief*, 130–47; Pinnock, "Conclusion," in *More than One Way?* 146–8; Marshall, *No Salvation Outside the Church?* 184–5.

128   *Toward a Christian Theology of Religious Pluralism* (Maryknoll, N.Y.: Orbis, 1997), 263. See also Merrigan, "Religious Knowledge," 706–7.

129   O'Collins, "Incarnation Under Fire," 278–9.

130   On the theological and practical strengths of a social trinitarian approach, see David Brown, *The Divine Trinity* (LaSalle: Open Court, 1985); Jürgen Moltmann, *The Trinity and the Kingdom* (San Francisco: Harper & Row, 1981); Cornelius Plantinga, "The Hodgson-Welch Debate and the Social Analogy of the Trinity," (Ph.D. diss., Princeton Theological Seminary, 1982); Thomas R. Thompson, "Trinitarianism Today: Doctrinal Renaissance, Ethical Relevance, Social Redolence," *Calvin Theological Journal* 32 (1997): 9–42.

131   E.g., O'Collins, "Incarnation Under Fire," 279; McCready, "Disintegration of Hick's Christology," 267–8.

132   For Hick's response to this line of criticism see *Christian Theology of Religions*, 86–98; also the relevant sections in *Metaphor of God Incarnate* (esp. chs. 2–4).

133   E.g., Gillis, "John Hick's Christology"; Sanders, *No Other Name*, 117.

134   Gillis, "Hick's Christology," 53–4; see also David L. Edwards, "John Hick and the Uniqueness of Jesus," in his *Tradition and Truth: The Challenge of England's Radical Theologians 1962–1989* (London: Hodder and Stoughton, 1989), 239; D'Costa, "Revelation and World Religions," 122; McGrath, "Challenge of Pluralism," in *Challenge of Religious Pluralism*, 244–5; Merrigan, "Religious Knowledge," 706.

135   "Squares and Circles," 202. See also Coventry, "The Myth and the Method," 252–61; Carl W. Ernst, "From Philosophy of Religion to History of Religion," in *Problems in the Philosophy of Religion*, 48. Gillis ("Interpretation of *An Interpretation*," 37) traces Hick's "concern with empiricism" to "a concession to the validity of the whole enterprise of logical positivism" whose criteria are no longer viewed as "well founded or acceptable."

136   McGrath, "Response to Hick," 66; D'Costa, *Hick's Theology of Religions*, 125–33; Lipner, "Uniqueness of Christ," 362–3; O'Collins, "Incarnation Under Fire," 278. For Hick's use of 'consensus' language see *Christian Theology of Religions*, 91; *Metaphor of God Incarnate*, 15 ("modest consensus").

137   O'Collins, "Incarnation Under Fire," 264–7; Netland, *Dissonant Voices*, 246–7. For one of the most recent and provocative arguments that the Jesus of history made implicit claims of identification with Yahweh, see N. T. Wright, *Jesus and the Victory of God* (Minneapolis: Fortress, 1996), ch. 13. For a recent attempt to critically examine Hick's Christology in light of Wright's work, see my "John Hick and the Historical Jesus," in *The Convergence of Theology: A Festschrift in Honor of Gerald O'Collins*, ed. Stephen T. Davis and Daniel Kendall (New York: Paulist, 2001), 304–19. Interestingly, Hick (*Christian Theology of Religions*, 96) has recently conceded something on this count. With regard to these types of passages, he writes: "I agree that it's possible to see an implicit claim to deity here." He now writes as if he is less certain that the biblical evidence is clearly on his side: "If you want biblical confirmation for a conservative position, you can find it, and if you want biblical confirmation for a more liberal position you can find that.... [W]e all use the Bible selectively (whether consciously or not) in the light of our theological outlook."

138   E.g., see David M. Ball, "'I am...': The 'I am' Sayings of Jesus and Religious Pluralism," in Clarke and Winter, eds., *One God, One Lord*, 65–84; Nash, *Is Jesus the Only Savior?* 84.

139   O'Collins, "Incarnation Under Fire," 272. See also Gillis, "Hick's Christology," 53; Marshall, *No Salvation Outside the Church?* 189–90; Stiver, review of *Metaphor of God Incarnate*, 181; Norman Anderson, *The Mystery of the Incarnation*, 70–8.

140   See McCready, "Disintegration of Hick's Christology," 269; Stephen Neill, "Jesus and Myth," in *Truth of God Incarnate*, 58–70.

141   Loughlin, "Squares and Circles," 194. Along this line, Melvin Tinker writes that Hick is "grossly wide of the mark in suggesting a sufficient cause" for the type of language that the monotheistic Jewish church applied to Jesus early on; "Truth, Myth and Incarnation," *Themelios* 14 (1988): 16.

142   For Hick's response to this line of criticism see *Christian Theology of Religions*, 98–103.

143   Loughlin, "Squares and Circles," 197.

144   D'Costa, review of *The Metaphor of God Incarnate*, *Religious Studies* 31 (1995): 137.

145   Loughlin, "Squares and Circles," 200.

146   Jeffner, "The Difficult Limits of Logic," in *God, Reality and Truth*, 139–40.

147   Loughlin, "Squares and Circles," 195.

148   See Norman L. Geisler and William D. Watkins, "The Incarnation and Logic: Their Compatibility Defended," *Trinity Journal* 6 (1985): 185–97; O'Collins, "Incarnation Under Fire," 275–6; Nash, *Is Jesus the Only Savior?* 90; Tan, "Religious Pluralism," 346–7; Tinker, "Truth, Myth," 16.

149   For Hick's exposition and critique of the 'two minds' and 'kenotic' models see *Metaphor of God Incarnate*, ch. 5, and chs. 6–7 respectively. See also Hick's detailed critique of Thomas Morris 'two minds' model in "The Logic of God Incarnate," *Religious Studies* 25 (1989): 409–23. Morris' has set forth his 'two minds' approach in *The Logic of God Incarnate* (Ithaca, N.Y.: Cornell University Press, 1986); for a summary see his "Understanding God Incarnate," *Asbury Theological Journal* 43 (1998): 63–77.

150   "A Logical Defense of Chalcedon?" *Journal for the Study of Religion* 2 (1989): 43. D'Costa (review of *Metaphor of God Incarnate*, 137) has pointed out that Hick has failed to engage a wide number of philosophically sensitive contemporary Christologies, including those of Barth, Rahner, Moltmann, Pannenberg, Kasper, and Jüngel, to name but a few.

151   "A Logical Defense of Chalcedon?" 43.

152   "Response to Hick," 63.

153   "Jesus and the World Religions," 180. More recently see "Five Misgivings," in Swidler and Mojzes, eds., *Uniqueness of Jesus*, 83.

154   E.g., see McGrath, "Challenge of Pluralism," 244; Geivett and Phillips, "Response to Hick," 75; Netland, *Dissonant Voices*, 242; McCready, "Disintegration of Hick's Christology," 270; Millard J. Erickson, *How Shall They be Saved? The Destiny of Those Who Do Not Hear of Jesus* (Grand Rapids: Baker, 1996), 102.

155   For Hick's response to such criticisms see *Christian Theology of Religions*, 90–103.

156   E.g., in his review of *Myth of God Incarnate*, John Macquarrie expressed his deep concerns for the lack of consistency with regard to the use of the term 'myth' among the various contributors; "Postscript: Christianity without Incarnation? Some Critical Comments," in *Truth of God Incarnate*, 140–4.

157   Lash, "Interpretation and Imagination," in *Incarnation and Myth*, 25.

158 Ibid., 21. Similar concerns were expressed around this time by Basil Mitchell ("A Summing Up of the Colloquy: Myth of God Debate," in *Incarnation and Myth*, 236–7).

159 See respectively, Tinker, "Truth, Myth," 15; Marshall, *No Salvation*, 185; Loughlin, "Myths, Signs and Significations," *Theology* 89 (1986): 271; John Rodwell, "Myth and Truth in Scientific Enquiry," in *Incarnation and Myth*, 70.

160 *Question of Final Belief*, 164–5. See also Gillis' critique of Hick's views of myth and metaphor in "An Interpretation of *Interpretation*" (37–8), with which Carl Ernst ("Philosophy of Religion," 48) has concurred.

161 *Question of Final Belief*, 165.

162 Ibid., 168; see also O'Collins, "Incarnation Under Fire," 276.

163 "Squares and Circles," 191; see also Tinker, "Truth, Myth," 16. Along these lines, D'Costa argues that the "sooner the christological debate moves out of this sterile binary option (metaphor or literal) the better"; review of *Metaphor of God Incarnate*, 138.

164 Hick, of course, is not going to be terribly disturbed by this charge. For years, he has been quite comfortable defending the label and substance of "liberal Christianity"; most recently see *Christian Theology of Religions*, 133–4.

165 Carruthers, *Uniqueness of Jesus Christ*, 329–330. See also O'Collins ("Incarnation Under Fire," 278), who characterizes Hick's model of Jesus as an "updated" version of "older low Christologies."

166 "Incarnation Under Fire," 279. Similarly, Gillis ("Hick's Christology," 52) notes that in our modern context where something Christologically "new and other" is sought after, "even the old heresies do not appear so heretical anymore."

167 Lampe, *God As Spirit: The Bampton Lectures, 1976* (Oxford: Clarendon Press, 1977).

168 Del Colle, *Christ and the Spirit: Spirit-Christology in Trinitarian Perspective* (New York: Oxford University Press, 1994), 210. See also Clark H. Pinnock, *Flame of Love: A Theology of the Holy Spirit* (Downers Grove, Ill.: InterVarsity, 1996), 79–111.

169 "Religious Knowledge," 707.

6 'Does it Work?': A Critical Examination of Hick's Pluralist Hypothesis

This chapter will address the final critical question to be faced by Hick's pluralist hypothesis: 'Does it work?' The issue at hand here is whether or not Hick's pluralist hypothesis is actually successful on its own terms. As in the previous chapter, various issues and concerns that have led Hick's critics to answer this question in the negative will be catalogued.[1] However, in this chapter, the cataloging of other's criticisms will be subservient to the development of my own critical analysis of Hick's thought. Here, my focus shall be the more specific question of whether Hick's neo-Kantian hypothesis, the conceptual power-house of his pluralist model, is able to provide an adequate solution to the 'conflicting conceptions of the divine' problem. I will argue that, in the end, it does not.

My critique will involve a two-pronged argument. First, I will argue that ultimately, and despite his protestations to the contrary, Hick's neo-Kantian hypothesis cannot avoid falling victim to a form of theological non-realism. I am not suggesting that Hick's hypothesis is bereft of realist elements. Rather, with William Alston, I would want to talk about "two Hicks," which Alston describes as "the Kantian *empirical realist-transcendental idealist*, and the *semi-expressivist-instrumentalist*," and which I shall herein characterize as religious realism and non-realism respectively.[2]

Second, I will argue that one reason Hick seems able to avoid such a conclusion is found in the fact that his theory retains a shrouded and very subtle, yet all-important, strand of covert theism at its core. These two arguments, taken together, pose a philosophical dilemma, either horn of which Hick's theory must avoid if it is to do the work that he claims it does: namely, provide a *realist* interpretation of religion that is *entirely neutral* with regard to the question of whether ultimate Reality is theistic or non-theistic in nature. I will suggest, then, that Hick's hypothesis in its present form is driven by its own logic onto both of these horns at crucial junctures, and so contains the essence of its own destruction.

The Implicit Non-Realist Tendencies of Hick's Neo-Kantian Hypothesis[3]

The Real in Itself vs. the Real as Humanly Experienced

Hick's thesis depends upon the all-important and radical distinction between the Real as it is in Itself and the Real as humanly experienced. He garners support for this distinction from the Christian tradition, and specifically from the classical notion of divine infinity.[4] I shall argue that the tradition does not support anything like Hick's extreme disjunction. I shall further argue that Hick's radical distinction at this point inevitably leads him in a decidedly non-realist direction.

Issues Regarding the Concept of Divine 'Infinity' First, it is important to note that the classical notion of divine infinity entails nothing like the type of radical epistemological rift embodied in Hick's model. It is clear from its use—at least within orthodox Christian tradition (and one could, I think, make a similar case for other traditions as well)—that the idea of divine infinity does allow for some positive characterizations of the divine. Here, infinity is generally taken to mean not a radical and complete "denial of limitation" in every sense of the term,[5] but rather (for example) "that [the divine] possesses the fullness of all possible perfections."[6] In fact, within the Christian tradition—including those very theologians that Hick appeals to for support—limitation of the divine, both inherent (e.g., the inability to sin) and self-imposed (e.g., the creation of the finite world and free creatures in relation to which the divine is delimited), is admitted without question.

It is important to note here that even the more minimalist views of religious language, such as a fairly agnostic reading of Aquinas' analogical predication or, more so, the Areopagite's *via negativa*, still deal in the production of knowledge concerning the divine.[7] Hick's attempt to correlate his proposal with the Thomistic model of analogy by offering the latter as a 'thought model' suggestive of his own hypothesis must finally be regarded as an apologetic failure. Certainly arguments have been made for relatively agnostic readings of analogy in general, and Aquinas' model of it in particular.[8] However, even among those who interpret Aquinas in such a fashion, virtually no one would suggest that his understanding of analogy, or his dictum "Things known are in the knower according to the mode of the knower," imply anything like the type of radical subjectivity and agnosticism called for by Hick's model.[9] And on the other side of the interpretive field, there are those who see predication

in general and/or Aquinas' analogical view in particular, as offering the possibility of a significant linguistic/conceptual correspondence between the human and divine.[10]

To return to the idea of infinity, one can argue that the implications of
applying this notion to the divine are anything but obvious, contrary to Hick's
specific and radical claims. As Timothy J. Pennings points out, since the term
'infinite' has multiple meanings, "inferences from the statement 'God is infinite'
are not automatic." Bringing the discussion into the realm of mathematics for
analogy's sake, he continues:

> For example, consider the argument: The set of real numbers between 0 and 1 ([0,
> 1]) is infinite and infinite means unbounded, so the set [0, 1] is unbounded. The
> conclusion is false. The problem is that two different meanings of the word 'infinite'
> were used. Similarly, saying God is infinite is ambiguous.... [One should be] wary
> of drawing inferences from the statement as is often done. That is, arguments of
> the form 'God is infinite, therefore...' should be viewed skeptically.[11]

First, even if the notion of infinity is unproblematically applicable to the
divine in a literalistic, philosophical sense, it is far from self-evident that the
concepts of a finite being are then rendered *a priori* incommensurable with it.
Only by positing further undemonstrated assumptions—e.g., that a finite being is limited to finite concepts, and/or that the concepts associated with an
infinite being are themselves infinite—does this argument follow.[12] Second,
even among those who recognize some type of serious incommensurability
based on divine infinity (and here, Hick merely represents one example from
the radical end of the spectrum), there is little agreement on either the degree
of incommensurability or its specific effects on predication potential. In this
light, it would appear that 'infinity' predicated of the divine is best understood
as referring figuratively (*vis-à-vis* the mathematical infinite) to Its mystery and
transcendence rather than literally to any particular unlimitable quality that
would *a priori* preclude some degree of conceptual commensurability.[13] And
if this is the case, then 'divine infinity' becomes not a *cause of or reason for*
incommensurability, but, at most—though not necessarily—an *expression of*
such.[14] Again, all of this is not to deny that the concept of divine infinity entails both mystery and transcendence. However, the most this would necessarily suggest, contrary to Hick, is that the divine can never be *exhaustively* known.
To admit that we can never know *all* of the divine is a far cry from claiming
that we can never know *anything* of the divine.[15] In this regard, Frederick Ferre's

words of warning are fitting: "It is fitting for an Isaiah to exult in the 'incompara-bility' of Jehovah; it is, however, the destruction of faith and of thought for oth-ers to overinterpret this poetic superlative and treat it as a logical doctrine."

Third and finally, a proper understanding of infinity also reveals the confu-sion inherent in Hick's view of divine ultimacy, a view which *a priori* disallows the divine the possibility of co-existence with any delimiting state of affairs. Para-doxically, such a view only gains ultimacy at the expense of divine sovereignty and flexibility. Moreover, it is difficult to see just what meaning it can have given the apparent existence of a finite cosmos, which—unless one opts for a pan- (or panen-) theistic notion of the divine—entails an external (if self-imposed) de-limiting of the Real. All of this goes to show that Hick's model, rather than merely representing a recognition of the relative epistemological humility that is called for by the various religions, exemplifies instead a hyper-subjectivism and/or ag-nosticism that outstrips any parallels in the religions by postulating a complete conceptual incommensurability between the human and divine.

Speaking the Ineffable Real   Many have argued that Hick's neo-Kantian hy-pothesis is naturally connected to a robust view of divine ineffability. If so, then the pressing question arises: How can Hick himself know or say *anything* about the unknowable noumenal Real?[16] Hick has recognized the potential threat here. In response, he has attempted to avoid a 'strong ineffability' posi-tion by claiming that one can make formal, logically-generated (versus sub-stantive) statements concerning the Real.[17] However, upon analysis, one must question even this last remaining manner in which Hick aspires to speak of the noumenal Reality. Apart from the question of whether in fact Hick's model *can* escape a 'strong' notion of ineffability, a serious problem remains: namely, the fact that Hick's expressed instances of supposedly formal properties betray definite signs of a smuggled foreign substance. To speak of purely formal prop-erties is to speak solely in terms of relation, with absolutely no substantive content whatsoever. But clearly to say that X has the property of 'being a refer-ent of a term' *does* deliver some amount of substantive content. If nothing else, it reveals that X "can be identified by some human language user," and such a property breaks the bounds of the purely formal.[18] Hick's confusion of logical and substantive claims is even more apparent when he describes the Anselmian definition of God—"that which no greater can be conceived"—as a formal statement.[19] As Keith Ward notes, 'greater' carries with it such connotations as value, being rationally desirable, etc., all of which are substantial properties.[20]

Thus, we are left wondering if Hick's model is justified in saying *anything* about the divine worth saying. Such a position serves to raise the specter of the Feuerbachian challenge:

> To deny all the qualities of a being is equivalent to denying the being himself....The denial of determinate, positive predicates concerning the divine nature is nothing else than a denial of religion, with, however, an appearance of religion in its favor, so that it is not recognized as a denial; it is simply a subtle disguised atheism....Dread of limitation is dread of existence.[21]

Hick faces a dilemma here. If, in reaction to Feuerbach's challenge, he allows for *some* substantive knowledge of the Real, the heart of his pluralist program is betrayed. Thus, it would seem that Hick is destined to walk a neo-Kantian no man's land that lies somewhere in an imaginary space between religious realism and a thoroughly subjectivized non-realism.

Kant and Hick's Neo-Kantian Hypothesis

John Hick's neo-Kantian proposal represents a complex attempt to allow for a pluralist interpretation of religions, while still safeguarding his realist core belief that religious experience, ultimately, is a non-illusory experience of transcendent Reality. I suggest that his particular nuanced use of Kant, far from side-stepping common Kantian criticisms, only serves to magnify them: specifically, his proposal represents an intensification of Kantian subjectivity—transposed to the religious realm—and thus threatens any realist core with immanent collapse.[22] Four lines of critique can be mentioned here.

Arbitrary Use of 'Sociology of Knowledge' Theory First, those disciplines from which Hick garners supporting evidence—particularly the sociology of knowledge school—in and of themselves suggest a fully constructivist/non-realist interpretation of religion. While Hick makes use of such thought in one sector of his theory—i.e., in his relativization of phenomenal manifestations, he arbitrarily refuses it admission into those quarters of his model where it could do some serious non-realist damage—i.e., the insular sanctum that safely houses his postulated noumenal Real. Thus, Hick is found walking a thin, imaginary tightrope, with threats to his religious realism, or pluralism, on either side.

Hick's Use of Kant[23] Second, Hick's various attempts to distance himself from Kant serve to heighten, rather than diminish, the subjectivist menace. The general transposition of Kant's schema from sensory to religious experience is not merely "very non-Kantian" in a benign sort of way.[24] Rather, it is a transfer to an experiential realm where there is significantly less 'empirical' consensus or control. Thus, from the outset, one can expect that Hick's religious project will justly be exposed to subjectivist suspicions even beyond those directed at Kant's sensory-centered program.[25]

The Intensification of Kantian Subjectivism   A third critical problem involves Hick's category-analogues. As J. William Forgie has shown, 'hyper-Kantian' readings of religious experience such as Hick's serve to intensify the already present Kantian subjectivist threat in at least two ways.[26] As noted earlier, while Kant's categories—as *a priori* knowledge—are by definition strictly universal and necessary, applying to all persons of all places and times, Hick's analogues are entirely culture-relative and contingent in nature. Hick explicitly acknowledges this first prong of Forgie's critique, but his only response is that such a deviation constitutes no rival system to Kant, since it is applied in a different experiential realm. Here he seems to miss the damaging subjectivist implications at the heart of the charge.[27] Forgie's observation can be further developed through the additional insight that, given our "age of eclecticism," fueled by the modern spirit of individualism, religious "traditions" themselves have been rendered unstable and contingent.[28] Thus a second level of contingency reveals itself in Hick's category-analogues. Add to all of this the phenomenological observation that—even within the *very same* religio-cultural system—one can often witness radically *different* experiences of the divine, just where Hick's model would seem to suggest a similar schematization. Each of these observations serve to further implicate Hick's proposal with a radical subjectivism, and hence skepticism.

Another—and potentially more devastating—observation of Forgie's goes unaddressed by Hick. Forgie notes that in Kant's model, the categories 'shape' experience and thus insure that it will take certain forms. But the categories themselves do not provide the *content* of the experiences they form.[29] In 'hyper-Kantian' models, however, the subject-based category-analogues (and one could add 'form-analogues') *do* contribute to the phenomenological content of the experience.[30] And when it comes to Hick's model in particular, the contribution is clearly significant. This hyper-Kantian twist forces the conclusion that the human subject's religious category-analogues, schematized by their religio-cultural systems, *can* account for both the form and content of religious experience. And thus one is forced to ask what, in fact, differentiates Hick's neo-Kantian constructivism from the essentially identical reductionist, non-realist models?[31]

Kantian Interpretation, Hick's Hypothesis, and the Non-Realist Threat Fourth and finally, considering the complexity—many would add internal inconsistency—of Kant's 'things in themselves' vs. 'appearances' schema, and the various interpretations, counter-interpretations, and accusations with which one finds it embroiled, anyone seeking to make use of it today must be prepared to enter the philosophical fray.[32] As suggested above, Hick's relocation of the schema to the religious realm does not safeguard him from such questions, but rather actually exacerbates them. Thus, Hick's claim to immunity from having to enter into the thicket of Kantian interpretation debate is unconvincing.

One way in which Hick has attempted to avoid the radical subjectivist threat is by maintaining—as does his reading of Kant—that "the phenomenal world *is* [the noumenal world] as it appears to our human consciousness."[33] Such an emphasis is characteristic of a 'one world' or 'double aspect'—as opposed to a 'two worlds'—reading of Kant. In other words, the noumenal/phenomenal distinction signifies not two ontologically independent realms or 'worlds,' but rather merely the one objective world considered from two *perspectives*: as it is in itself, vs. as it appears to human consciousness. Clearly Hick does (and must) associate himself with such a perspectival understanding of the noumenal/phenomenal schema, given the nature and claims of his model.

The problem is, however, that his specific restructuring of the Kantian program (which itself already stands in a questionable relation to a pure and simple 'one world' interpretation)[34] exhibits just the type of developments that would serve to render such an interpretation implausible. Specifically, in a perspectival interpretation, to speak of the unknowability of the noumenal is simply to speak tautologically: it is to consider an object of a subject's knowledge as *apart* from that knowledge, and so—by definition—as unknowable.[35] What, then, leads Kant to postulate the real existence of such a noumenon behind the phenomenal apprehension when, in fact, it is strictly unknowable? In large part, the answer to this question is that aside from such a postulation:

> it would be impossible to give any plausible account of the source of 'the empirical differences in shapes and sizes' of the objects of everyday experience....Only what is common to all representations is, for Kant, supplied a priori by the subject in the act of representing. So the thing in itself must be posited and assumed to determine in some sense the raw material for any possible object of knowledge.[36]

But when a similar question is asked of Hick's neo-Kantian model—namely upon what basis he can make a realist claim concerning the divine noumenal

Real—a comparable defense is not available. The simple reason for this is that, unlike Kant, Hick's subject-based categories themselves—as discussed earlier—contribute significantly to the supposed 'raw material' of religious experience. Thus, virtually *everything* of content—including the specific and varied 'shapes and sizes' so to speak—of the religious phenomenal manifestations can be accounted for by the religious concepts and sentiments found in the religio-cultural systems and/or in the individuals themselves. In Hick's hypothesis—again, unlike Kant's—there is *nothing* residual that *requires* the postulation of an 'unknowable' (divine) noumenon; everything can be adequately explained, via the human form/category-analogues, apart from and without the noumenon.

Hick would no doubt respond that such a charge ignores his claim that a transcendent source of 'information' is always an essential constitutive element of religious experience. But a counter-question reveals the practical insignificance of this claim: what 'information,' given the complete incommensurability between human conceptual capacities and the divine, could ever make a distinguishable—and thus practical—difference? Or, again, upon what basis should one ever suspect that "religious experience" includes an irreducibly extra-subjective element when, in fact, it can already be accounted for *in its entirety* as a purely projective exercise? Even on his own terms, the most Hick can allow for from the divine side of the experience is an undefinable apprehension "at some deep level" of the human psyche, which is, of course, always then "expressed in forms supplied by his or her mind."[37] Such non-informative 'information' hardly offers hard data in the religious experience. And thus, Hick's appeal to a non-human, transcendently-derived component in religious experience does not vitiate the radical subjectivism of his proposal.

Thus, it would appear that the noumenal Real in Hick's system is rendered a purely unnecessary and unjustifiable construct. While it *may* exist, like almost anything in the realm of the 'conceivably possible,' there is certainly no reason to think that it *does*. Clearly Gavin D'Costa's characterization of Hick's position as a "transcendental agnosticism" is quite accurate.[38] It is critical to see here that there is virtually nothing that Hick can do to remedy this unfortunate situation; he is precariously situated between the proverbial Scylla and Charybdis. For the only way out of the non-realist constructivism implied in this critique is to reinvest the noumenal Real with the ability to deliver a decisive—and identifiable—amount of raw experiential content, above and beyond any human-based contributions. But this is exactly what Hick cannot do if his neo-Kantian model is to serve and protect his pluralist agenda. And so, with Don Cupitt, one may rightly ask in regard to Hick's "thin-line" religious realism, what, really, prevents him from taking "just one more step and [saying] that religion is wholly human"?[39] Again—and this is critically important—Hick's typical response to this challenge, that *religious experience* provides the basis for such realist hopes, has been shown to be effectively undermined by the implications of his own neo-Kantian proposal.

The Non-Realist Critique: Response and Rejoinder

Professor Hick has graciously responded to my concerns of inherent non-realism both in his book *A Christian Theology of Religions* and in a published article: "Religious Pluralism and the Divine: A Response to Paul Eddy."[40] In this section I shall summarize Hick's response to my critique, and offer a rejoinder in return.

On Divine Infinity and Ineffability Regarding my first two areas of criticism—i.e., the issues surrounding divine infinity and ineffability—Hick offers three lines of response. First, he begins by acknowledging that the Christian tradition has, as a rule, affirmed both that God is ineffable, and yet possesses "determinative characteristics." Hick also makes the claim that the concept of divine ineffability has been "theologically" driven, while the idea that God can be grasped in human concepts such as 'personal' has arisen from devotional and liturgical contexts. How these two strands (in essence the cognitive and the experiential) fit together has been left as "a cloudy mystery."[41] Hick goes on to reassert that this cloud can be dispelled and the paradox unraveled by adopting the Kantian distinction of "the-Real-in-itself and the-Real-as-humanly-thought-and-experienced."[42] Specifically, the former would account for the apophatic strand within the Christian tradition, while the latter would make sense of the cataphatic inclination. Incidentally, Hick reaffirms (against my proposal) that he does accept the traditional implications of the divine infinity doctrine, namely that God cannot be 'limited' to being "personal, purposive, etc."[43] However, it should be remembered that the Christian tradition attributes ineffability to what Hick's theory would consider the phenomenal 'God,' not some (noumenal) 'God beyond God' (i.e., the Real) as does Hick's system. The implications of this observation will be explored below.

In response, first, it is not at all clear that the classical Christian idea that the Triune God can be understood in some real, if limited, sense through human categories is merely an experientially based sentiment developed in devotional and liturgical settings. The conclusion that God is, for instance, a 'personal' and a 'good' Being is no less a derivative of cognitive theologizing than it is of experiential devotion. For Hick to claim otherwise is to create a false dichotomy, one that serves his apologetic purposes well, but that is not true to the available evidence. Second, to correlate the Real in Itself with apophaticism and the Real as humanly thought and experienced with cataphaticism is to ontologically privilege the former over the latter. While setting up the distinction this way would be acceptable to certain forms of Hinduism (i.e., as in Hick's early use of the Saguna-Nirguna distinction), it is not an accurate explanation of the way in which the Christian tradition has understood the apophatic-cataphatic relationship. To set up the sharp distinction of noumenal-as-apophatic versus phenomenal-as-cataphatic is problematic on other grounds. Aquinas has argued that the "idea of negation is always based upon an affirmation;...unless the human mind knew something positive about God, it would be unable to deny anything about Him."[44] If this is true, then, on his own terms, Hick's ability to say *anything* about the noumenal Real is in jeopardy.[45] Thus, contrary to Hick's claim, I would suggest that while his neo-Kantian noumenon-phenomenon motif is one possible way of trying to explain the apophatic-cataphatic phenomenon in the Christian tradition, it is neither the only way nor the best way. A theory that does not inherently privilege one over the other is to be preferred.

Incidentally, Hick nowhere responds to my suggestion that the best way to understand the tradition as a whole is to consider the attribute of divine 'infinity' as a metaphorical (vis-à-vis the strictly mathematical concept) term that signals divine transcendence and thus demarcation (i.e., limitation) over against the created order. Such a use of the term *does* allow for the positive characterizations and theologically necessary distinctions regarding God that are found in the tradition.[46] If one is called to grant any particular worldview the presumption of coherence until otherwise demonstrated, then this reading of the use of infinity within the Christian tradition appears to be a bit more charitable to that tradition than Hick's. Not only does it avoid the appeal to impenetrable mystery (or incoherence), but it safeguards the theistic core of the Christian worldview from the threat of pantheism that is inherent in any system that predicates 'infinity' of ultimate reality in a literal (i.e., quasi-mathematical) sense.[47]

Next, Hick responds to my criticisms that touch on the issue of ineffability vis-à-vis the Real. He begins by acknowledging that my questioning of his categorization of Anselm's dictum (i.e., 'that than which no greater can be conceived') as a purely formal statement is on target, and that he stands corrected on this point.[48] However, he continues to press hard the distinction between "substantial" and "purely formal and logically generated" attributes in order to be able to say *something* about the noumenal Real.[49] Specifically, he maintains that the statement that the Real is "able to be referred to" is a purely formal one with no substantive content that would violate his (what he considers to be) moderate ineffability doctrine.[50] Interestingly, unlike the Anselmian example, Hick does not respond to my question of how this statement can be purely formal when it seems that to say that some ineffable 'X' (i.e., the Real) is 'able to be referred to' is to say that "'This object is such that it can be identified by some human language user,'" which is to say something, however little, of substance.[51] Rather, he simply replies that, "despite Eddy's disagreement," the substantive vs. formal distinction seems to him "entirely sound."[52]

In response, I would want to emphasize that, generally speaking, I affirm the validity of this *theoretical* distinction. It is in the practical application of it that problems arise. Specifically, I question whether a number of the particular ways in which Hick himself speaks about the ineffable Real are, in fact, instances of purely formal statements. It seems to me that, at several turns, a covert 'substance' lies buried within what Hick presents as merely formal statements. I have already mentioned what appears to be one clear case: namely, the statement 'able to be referred to,' which seems to inherently signal the substantive property of being identifiable.[53] Another instance arises when Hick claims that humans 'experience' the Real.[54] William Wainwright has noted that to say "'x veridically experiences y' entails 'y causally acts upon x.'" To say this, it seems, is to predicate causal activity of the Real. But causal activity is "a substantial concept."[55]

This parallels Alvin Plantinga's observation regarding Hick's statement that "we live inescapably in relation to" the Real.[56] He notes that this statement is either formal or not. If so:

> then it would have no connection with religion. So it isn't. But if it isn't, then (1) we have still another positive property had by the Real: the property of being such that we live in relation to it....If the real has no positive properties of which we have a grasp, what is the reason for thinking we live in relation to it?[57]

Thus, it remains for Hick to demonstrate how these sorts of statements are merely formal ones (and thus how he can speak of the Real even in these limited ways) when indications suggest otherwise.

Incidentally, in response to Plantinga's question of what reason Hick has for thinking that we are in relation to the Real, Hick would most likely answer that the Real functions as an hypothesis that accounts for the diversity of ostensibly authentic religious experience throughout the world. However, at this juncture, Hick's thesis appears to be in danger of falling to an invalid logical assumption: namely, the so-called 'quantifier-shift' fallacy.[58] Ward explains:

> If X is indescribable to me, and Y is indescribable to me, it does not follow that X is identical with Y. On the contrary, there is no way in which X could be identical with Y, since there are no criteria of identity to apply.... To assert identity is thus to commit the quantifier-shift fallacy, of moving from 'Many religions believe in an ineffable Real' to 'There is an ineffable Real in which many religions believe'.[59]

Ward goes on to note that if Hick appeals here to the principle of simplicity a problem still remains. The truth is, we have no idea whether ultimate reality is simple or complex. In the end, we are simply "not entitled to assert identity or difference of ineffable objects."[60] A fundamental problem for Hick is foreshadowed by Aquinas' insights on the necessary relation between negative and positive statements, noted above. Simply put by Rose: "we don't seem to be able to say anything at all about that to which *no* substantial properties apply."[61] All of this has caused a number of Hick's interlocutors to conclude that nothing can be said of the ineffable Real worth saying, thus rendering it practically useless and ultimately redundant.[62]

On Kant and the Neo-Kantian Hypothesis In his response to my concerns regarding the neo-Kantian aspects of his hypothesis, Hick begins by emphasizing that he is not bound to every aspect of Kant's own noumenal/phenomenal thesis, and that his deviation from Kant's own use of these concepts is irrelevant to the issues at hand.[63] I do, generally and in theory, agree with Hick on this count. My argument is not simply *that* he deviates from Kant. Rather, it is the manner in which he does so that seems to me to be problematic. Hick is certainly entitled to adopt a neo-Kantian approach to religious epistemology. However, in doing so, he is called to recognize the implications this has for his hypothesis. Hick states that he cannot accept my suggestion that his neo-Kantian model leads to the conclusion that "the entirety of religious experience is supplied by the experiencer."[64] But he never explains just how he can avoid such implications. Once again, and to re-emphasize a point from my original argument, Hick's particular modification of Kant is not benignly non-Kantian. Rather, his hypothesis involves specific elements that serve to exacerbate and intensify the subjectivism already inherent in Kant's program.[65]

To summarize: The use of a constructivist sociology of knowledge theory, the shift of Kant's noumenal/phenomenal conceptual apparatus from the public realm of sensory experience to the private realm of religious experience, the contingent and culture-relative nature of his category-analogues (as opposed to Kant's necessary and universal categories), and the fact that (again, unlike Kant's analogous program) the entirety of religious content can be explained by an appeal to the religio-cultural systems and/or the individual religious believers themselves (and thus apart from a supposed noumenal Reality) all serve to radically subjectivize Hick's approach so as to threaten his realist project. These are the elements of Hick's project that beg to be reconciled with his religious realism. It is noteworthy that, in his response to my arguments at this point, Hick does not engage with any of these four lines of criticism *per se*. Rather, he simply re-asserts that his is a critical realist perspective which balances both realist and constructivist aspects.[66] That Hick aspires to such a position I have no doubt. My suggestion is that his neo-Kantian hypothesis, despite his most enthusiastic intentions, is unable adequately to support a critical *realist* program.

In his response, Hick notes that the pluralist hypothesis holds that:

> the universal presence of the Real is affecting us all the time and that when we allow this impingement upon us to come to consciousness, it takes the varied forms of what we call religious experience. The 'givenness' of the experience is thus the impact upon the human spirit of the Divine....[67]

However, even granting Hick's use of the term 'information' in what he calls a "cybernetic" sense—i.e., as "any impact of our environment upon us" as opposed to "items of information"—the question still remains: why think that such a noumenal source of cybernetic information exists when, in fact, the totality of religious data and experience can be entirely accounted for by the subjectivist elements in Hick's theory?[68]

Hick's claim regarding the Real's 'impact' upon the human spirit raises other questions as well. First, there seems to be significant confusion within Hick's hypothesis as to whether or not human subjects 'experience' the Real *per se*. On one hand, Hick writes that "the noumenal Real is experienced" by different religious persons differently.[69] On the other hand, he claims that the Real is the "unexperiencable ground...of the encountered gods and experienced absolutes witnessed to by the religious traditions."[70] This confusion may simply represent the need for Hick to be more careful in the explication of his ideas. However, it may suggest that Hick has fallen into a dangerous conceptual equivocation with respect to a central aspect of his hypothesis.

The complexities and problems involved in similar areas of Kantian interpretation point toward the latter alternative. As previously noted, interpretation of Kant's noumenal/phenomenal distinction has gone in two directions: the 'one world' (or 'double aspect') view and the 'two worlds' view. Again, the question centers on whether Kant's distinction signifies the one objective world considered from two *perspectives* (i.e., as it is in itself, vs. as it appears to human consciousness), or two independent 'worlds.' Hick's hypothesis would seem to depend upon the success of something analogous (i.e., in the religious realm) to the 'one world' view. And, at times, he clearly indicates such an orientation. His claims that we do experience the Real would align with this perspective. However, at other points, Hick seems to favor a 'two worlds' approach, which would lead to his claim that the Real is fundamentally unexperiencable. Philip Quinn has found Hick equivocating between these two views within the space of three sentences.[71] Thus, he correctly concludes that Hick must "choose between the two models in order to achieve consistency at this point."[72]

According to Quinn, simply making this decision and tidying up his explication of the hypothesis will not suffice. In addition to these things, Hick's thesis must also make a further assumption. Specifically, Hick "must make the strong negative assumption that no positive attributes of any of the phenomenal Reals of the great religious traditions can be an attribute of the noumenal Real."[73] In line with this observation, Alston has detected in Hick's hypothesis a form of the age-old confusion between epistemic and ontological categories. He writes:

> Even if we agree with Hick that there are no rational considerations that show one religion to have the truth about the Real, or to be more likely to do so, it doesn't follow that none of the beliefs of the various religions can be *true* of the Real, in the sense of representing the Real as it is. It only follows that we cannot make a rational determination of which of those beliefs, if any, have that status....Once again, epistemic status has been illegitimately conflated with truth status.[74]

Finally, Hick's claim that the transcendental Real impinges upon human subjects has triggered a different, though not unrelated, criticism from Kenneth Rose. He writes:

Hick is not consistent in holding to this *transcendental* conception of the noumenal Real, since he also conceives the noumenal Real as an element in the *causal* complex that generates religious experience....[C]ausality cannot be predicated of a transcendental postulate, which is a merely notional entity. That is, if the noumenal Real is a causal agent, it cannot at the same time be a transcendental postulate. The difference between these two positions is striking and, it would seem, unbridgeable....[It does not] make sense to claim that an unexperienced *transcendental* postulate "*impacts*" human consciousness, as Hick does.[75]

Next, Hick suggests that my invocation of Feuerbach's critique is "double-edged," since "the naturalistic [i.e, non-realist] option can be invoked against the non-pluralist as easily as against pluralist religious views."[76] But I believe that Hick has missed the thrust of my concern. The question is not whether naturalists will reject both our views as subjectivist projections; they will of course.[77] Rather, the issue that I pose is the Feuerbachian challenge *per se*: "To deny all the qualities of a being is equivalent to denying the being himself....Dread of limitation is dread of existence."[78] It is Hick's inability to say *anything substantive* about the ultimately Real that places his hypothesis in danger, a conundrum that the non-pluralist does not face. In the end, Hick argues that:

Paul Eddy's basic error then, in my view, is his failure to keep clear the distinction between grounds for believing that there is a transcendent divine reality, and reasons for thinking that such a reality is differently conceived, experienced, and responded to from within the different religious traditions.[79]

He goes on to explain that, with respect to his own thought, his experience-based religious epistemology provides the grounds for belief in a transcendent divine Reality. However, for Hick, this forces the development of his pluralist hypothesis wherein one and the same transcendent Reality is differently experienced within the various religions, since all religious traditions are within their epistemic rights to make the same kind of appeal to experience as does Hick.

In response, I would want to affirm with Hick the qualitative difference between these two questions, and the importance of not conflating them. However, it appears to me that within Hick's own account they become inextricably connected. By criticizing Hick's pluralist hypothesis, I realize that I am also calling into question his religious epistemology. But, in terms of developed argumentation, that is another question for another day.

I would maintain that Hick's response to my criticisms has done little to vitiate the concerns they represent. In terms of his own hypothesis, there is nothing beyond fiat assertion that necessitates the postulation of the type of noumenal Reality that Hick offers. The radically subjectivizing elements of his hypothesis should, one would think, beckon Hick into the realm of religious non-realism. Interestingly, Hick refuses to follow that path. Rather, he continues to maintain the stance of an ardent, if 'critical,' religious realist. Why this is so and how it is possible are questions that beg to be addressed. A number of Hick's critics have suggested that by simply modifying his hypothesis just enough to enable some form of positive predication with respect to the Real, he could logically avoid the threat of non-realism.[80] What they seem to miss here, and a point that Hick never forgets, is that with the promise of even the slightest positive knowledge of the Real comes the inevitable—and entirely unacceptable (to the full-blooded pluralist like Hick)—state of affairs wherein one religious tradition's conception of that Reality will be shown to be superior to another tradition's. True to his robust pluralism, Hick refuses to allow such a religiously destabilizing element any quarter within his hypothesis, and yet claims to retain a realist stance. To shed light upon just what lies behind this seemingly impossible conceptual balancing act, I shall turn to my second and final primary line of critique.

The Covert Mono-Theistic Tendencies of Hick's Neo-Kantian Hypothesis

Hick's attempt to develop a tradition-neutral religious philosophy of religions, culminating in the mature form of his neo-Kantian hypothesis, has been traced within chapters three and four of this study. Hick's mature hypothesis continues to attract charges that, despite his attempts to avoid this, it still implicitly assumes and thus privileges either a theistic or a non-theistic worldview. On one hand, there are those who are concerned that Hick's neo-Kantian hypothesis and its noumenal Real that salvifically orients the religious adherents of the world sounds suspiciously like "a Western conception of a personal God."[81] On the other hand, some critics continue to suggest that important aspects of his pluralist model betray "a strong affinity with Eastern pantheistic conceptions of reality," and are thus "antagonistic to the core principles of Christianity."[82] This criticism is related to the concern expressed by some that the noumenal Real of Hick's pluralist hypothesis is not able to adequately make sense of some of the world's significant religions. Harold Netland, for instance, argues that, with regard to Shinto, it "is not clear that the notion of religious ultimacy is even applicable." Keith Ward has pushed the problem even further by suggesting that, for Tibetan Buddhism, "there is no Being, no Absolute, at all."[83] In spite of his best attempts, I will argue that Hick's efforts to safeguard his pluralist model from the these types of criticisms—specifically the perennial charge of covert monotheism—are ultimately unsuccessful. Several lines of evidence are relevant here.

Hick's Hypothesis as Covert 'Mono'-theism

I will begin with the first half of this compound charge: Hick as "*mono*"-theist. It is important to note that, throughout his pluralist project, Hick has unswervingly referred to the ultimate Reality in fundamentally *singular* terms and categories. To be fair to Hick, it must be said that he has tried to circumvent the possible problematic implications of this practice. He writes:

> if we are going to speak of the Real at all, the exigencies of our language compel us to refer to it either in the singular or the plural. Since there cannot be a plurality of ultimates, we affirm the true ultimacy of the Real by referring to it in the singular....The Real, then, is the ultimate Reality, not one among others; and yet it cannot literally be numbered: it is the unique One without a second.[84]

When pressed, Hick acknowledges that something like a poly-Realism is logically possible, and cannot be ruled out *a priori*. However, he suggests that the postulation of (in human terms) *one, single* Real is the best hypothesis on several grounds.

Speaking the Singular Real? First, as noted above, one must, for better or worse, either speak of the Real in singular or plural terms. The problem of using some sort of less than literal designation is unavoidable, and to call it 'one' breeds fewer conceptual problems than to call it 'many.' Second, if one were to refer to it in the plural, the problem arises of how to delineate "the relationship between these different realities."[85] Third, to posit more than one Ultimate religious referent would be to necessarily relativize, and in this way violate, each of the various religions' claims to experiential relationship with the one "ultimate" Reality.[86] Since, for Hick, the essential "truthfulness" of each tradition has already been demonstrated by the fact of their apparent co-equal soteriological effectiveness, such a violation is unwarranted. And so, finally, Hick offers as the primary basis for his assumption that all the major religions are referring to the same ultimate Reality the:

striking similarity of the transformed human state described within the traditions as saved, redeemed, enlightened, wise, awakened, liberated. This similarity strongly suggests a common source of salvific transformation.[87]

From the very beginning of his pluralist probings, Hick has been challenged as to the problematic nature of what one can now refer to as his 'mono-Realist' presumption and the unitive, harmonizing impetus behind it.[88] Interestingly, this charge is leveled at Hick by both those within and outside of the pluralist camp.[89] Ninian Smart, for example, has noted that, by Hick's own account, "the upper noumenal has no number, like its lower [phenomenal] counterpart. It has to be utterly indeterminate. This is where using the locution 'the Real' represents a hostage to fortune." He goes on to argue that it would be more accurate to Hick's own thesis to speak of a "Noumenal Indeterminism" rather than a ('one') 'noumenal Real.' Here, one affirms "a noumenal Transcendent, but this is not specified either as a kind of substance or not. It is parallel to the notion of a this-cosmic noumenal described as Energy or Process rather than 'things-in-themselves.'"[90] Philip Quinn has posed the issue in a different fashion when he claims that Hick is "a polytheist at the phenomenal level and not a theist at all at the noumenal level."[91] While the latter half of this statement is an accurate description of Hick's ostensive claim, I will argue that to say Hick's treatment of the noumenal Reality is not theistic *at all* is, in fact— and despite Hick's best attempts—inaccurate.

The central question is this: given the radically divergent, even mutually contradictory, religious conceptions of ultimate reality, upon what basis does Hick maintain that each and every one of the conflictive phenomenal manifestations are perceptions of *one and the same* noumenal Reality? Does not a thesis involving *multiple* noumenal realities better account for the apparent phenomenal evidence?[92] Certainly this would be the case in the sensory realm. Thus, one would expect that only very strong evidence to the contrary could allow for Hick's apparently counter-factual claim.

Poly-Realism as Philosophical Conundrum I would argue that there is no such evidence forthcoming. His claim that to recognize a plurality of noumenal Realities would be to raise thorny conceptual problems regarding how they would be related to each other can hardly be an argument against doing so. Hick's very project is a pluralist response to taking seriously the diversity among the gods and absolutes within the world's religions. He has been willing to suggest that the religious traditions of the world revise their theological visions and philosophical self-understandings in order to acknowledge and accommodate the authenticity of these diverse (to his mind 'phenomenal') religious realities. With respect to their doctrines, Hick's suggestion asks a tradition to engage in any number of conceptual gymnastics and contortions necessary to recognize the pluralist implications of religious diversity. If the evidence of religious diversity points toward a plurality of realities at what Hick considers to be the noumenal level, he can hardly balk at being asked to wrestle with the philosophical difficulties this might raise. And, perhaps, just such considerations will suggest the need for the revision of certain elements of his hypothesis, namely ones that are imbedded in an all-too-often unexamined mono-realist paradigm that tends to drive the modern Western analytical (as opposed, even, to Continental) philosophical tradition. In any case, what is good for the traditional religionist is good for the modern liberal pluralist.[93]

Mono-Realism and Religious Ultimacy   Furthermore, Hick's justification of mono-Realism based upon an appeal to the various religions' claims to be in touch with the 'ultimate' is not compelling. Ironically, Hick himself provides the tools to undermine just such a claim. He has made a career out of explicating the manner in which traditional religious truth-claims can be mythologized—and in this way relativized—without (to his mind) doing violence to their essential (i.e., attitudinal) nature. When Hick is willing to detach any and all religious doctrines from their traditionally realist moorings, such as (to use Christian examples) the incarnation, the atonement, the Trinity, and even the ontological ultimacy of a personal God, what reason is there to recoil from similarly mythologizing the religious claim of experiencing the *single ultimate* Reality? In fact, given Hick's paradigm, this claim is most easily understood as just one more mythological religious affirmation *vis-à-vis* ultimate reality. It may be 'mythically true,' which, for Hick, means attitudinally appropriate. But such claims can in no way be used to support Hick's assertion that ultimate (noumenal) Reality itself is best conceptualized in singular terms.

Soteriocentrism and Mono-Realism   Finally, Hick's soteriologically-based argument for a single noumenal Reality remains unconvincing. As discussed in the previous chapter, his understanding of salvation—the human transformation from self-centeredness to Reality-centeredness—must be highly general in order to accommodate all religions, and so loses any real unitive force. Moreover, when one begins to analyze seriously the supposed common soteriological structure of the various religions, the presumed abstract unity quickly unravels. In the end then, soteriologically speaking, little remains upon which to base the notion of a single noumenal Real behind a supposed common and universal process.[94] However, even if Hick was able to make a convincing argument for a common soteriological experience, this would not solve the problem for him. To draw an analogy from the sensory realm: just because I share the same type of 'self to other-orientedness' experience within the bounds of a loving marriage as do numerous other husbands, there is nothing to suggest that we husbands are all loving the same noumenal wife, experienced in diverse phenomenal ways. Simply put, common *experience* does not necessarily entail a common *object of experience*.[95] To claim so, without any further reasons than Hick offers, is to beg the question at hand. George Mavrodes has also raised the question of how, within Kant's noumenal-phenomenal schema, one could suppose (as Hick does here) that *causal* relations pertain between the two realms: "...in the Kantian metaphysics the causal relations and the arguments that appeal to these relations have their place entirely within the phenomenal world. They do not provide a bridge from the phenomenal to the noumenal."[96] Thus, Hick's arguments for the plausibility of a mono-Realism over against a poly-Realism fail to convince, while the phenomenological evidence itself counts directly against the idea.

Locating Hick's 'Mono-' Impulse   In exploring the question of what it is that fuels Hick's monizing presumption, several points of interest arise. First, as alluded to above, there is the fact that Hick's own socio-cultural context in general, and his anglo-Western (e.g., British) philosophical tradition in particular, is indebted to a strong drive toward philosophical unification.[97] Hick reveals his penchant for philosophical unification in a recent article when he writes: "That humankind is one, the world one, and the divine reality one is a truth whose time has come."[98] It appears that this philosophical proclivity, in part, has kept Hick from seriously entertaining the truly pluralist—in some sense even polytheistic—implications of his own thesis.[99]

   Furthermore—and here we begin to move toward the second half of the compound charge under discussion—there is the issue of vestigial remnants of Hick's liberal Christian monotheism at play within his hypothesis. In this respect, it is worth noting that, while a number of additions and subtractions have occurred throughout the four editions of Hick's book, *Philosophy of Religion*—most of them occasioned by his pluralist shift, his opening chapter devoted to a monotheistic presentation of God has remained essentially unchanged. This is an important observation because it is precisely here, in a work ostensibly done in his philosophical, as opposed to Christian theological, mode, that one would expect to see evidence of a taming of his prior monotheistic commitments.[100] Given the extensive pluralist reworking Hick has done for this and other more recent editions of his earlier works, this can hardly be accounted for as an accidental oversight on his part.

Hick's unwillingness to seriously entertain the notion of multiple noumenal Realities behind the various religious phenomena is paralleled in the western liberal Christian tradition by the refusal to take seriously the idea of multiple entities in the spiritual world behind, say, the 'polytheism' of many traditional religions. Theologically speaking, this idea has often been resisted in the name of 'monotheism.' This sort of monotheism, what one could term 'philosophical' or 'absolute' monotheism, holds that the single God is the "only divine being."[101] Under this type of strict definition, the existence of other spiritual beings who are actual objects of religious worship is denied. But if this is the definition of 'monotheism' to be used, then, according to Peter Hayman, 'pure' monotheism is probably not seen in the Jewish tradition until the "philosophers of the Middle Ages."[102] For even the great 'monotheistic' prophets (i.e., Isaiah) would have acknowledged the existence of spiritual entities beyond Yahweh, whether 'gods,' 'angels,' or 'demons,' who are the objects—however unworthy—of human religious worship.[103]

Interestingly, Hick himself acknowledges the possible existence of Satan and other "disembodied minds," whether good or evil.[104] But as soon as Hick entertains this possibility, namely, the existence of a plurality of independently existing entities in a supernatural/spiritual—might one say 'noumenal'—realm, he is faced with the prospect of a plurality of noumenal Realities behind the various religions. His refusal to take this possibility more seriously, then, may well reflect the vestigial influence of the philosophical monotheism of his liberal Christian tradition. Thus, in sum, I would contend that Hick's unwillingness to seriously countenance the possibility of a plurality of ontological noumenal ultimates—each of which would correspond to one or more of the distinctive phenomenal religious ultimates—reveals a covert monotheism at the heart of his *mono*-Realist project.[105]

Hick's Hypothesis as Covert Mono-'Theism'

This final section will concentrate on the second half of the compound charge—namely, "*theism.*" My main contention here will focus on the inherent discrepancy that holds between Hick's claim (one that is vital to his pluralist project) that the Real is not personal, intentional, or purposive, and the equally solid commitments to his perennial religious epistemology and his eschatological scenario, both of which have been intimately—even necessarily, I shall argue— linked to a theistic understanding of ultimate Reality from their inception during his pre-pluralist days.[106]

Covert Theism and Hick's Religious Epistemology   First, a brief recap of the nature of Hick's religious epistemology is in order.[107] The essential structure of this epistemology has not changed since its formative days in the 1950s, as explicated in his first book, *Faith and Knowledge*. In short, Hick adopted early on the notion that the universe is 'religiously ambiguous.' That is, one cannot argue convincingly for the probability of—let alone demonstrate—either a religious or a naturalistic interpretation of the world over against the other. Again, this idea is central to his understanding of faith as a free act of interpretation, and, thus, the necessity of an "epistemic distance" between God and humanity if the latter are to retain their creaturely freedom as they respond to God's offer of relationship.[108] Fundamental to this understanding of religious experience and epistemology is the idea of a *personal God* who creates free creatures, and then invites them to freely enter into a personal love relationship. Prior to his pluralist move, Hick was always eminently clear on this point: "The reason why God reveals himself indirectly...is that only thus can the conditions exist for a *personal* relationship between God and man."[109]

Even after his pluralist shift, Hick explicitly retained this same epistemological framework.[110] In fact, Hick has made it quite clear that his move to a pluralist perspective is linked with the working out of the full and logical implications of his original religious epistemology.[111] Early on, he attempted to state it in terms that were equally applicable to non-theistic systems.[112] As time went on, the explicitly theistic elements of the system were either modified or, often, simply left implicit. Always, the notions of human "freedom," the fundamental religious ambiguity of the universe, the various religious traditions as functional "filters" that preserve human religious autonomy, etc., were at the fore.[113] In fact, even after his adoption of the neo-Kantian mechanism, Hick is found writing of our need for a high degree of "cognitive freedom and responsibility, without which we should not be personal beings, capable of a free response to the Eternal One."[114] To explicate this idea further, Hick shifts to "explicitly theistic terms"; he never does state the matter in terms understandable to a non-theistic tradition.[115]

Within Hick's current model, the "systematic [religious] ambiguity" of the universe continues to retain an important role.[116] And while the term "epistemic distance" is not used per se in *Interpretation of Religion*, Hick has indicated that the *idea* is still at work, particularly in his understanding of cognitive freedom.[117] Even more recently, in a 1993 publication, Hick affirms the same general view when he writes:

> But our relationship to the more ultimate environment of which the religions speak is importantly different [than to the sensory realm]. This latter confronts or surrounds or undergirds or envelops us as the bearer of ultimate value, and value differs from matter in leaving us free to recognize and respond to it or not. We are not forced to be aware of the Transcendent as we are forced to be aware of our physical surroundings.[118]

Although Hick has substituted religiously-neutral terms like "value" and "Transcendent" for the former idea of "personal God," in fact his general religious epistemology remains essentially unchanged. And such an epistemology, as noted above, presupposes a *personal* Reality in that only such a reality *could*—and/or *would care to*—'create' such a state of affairs. A non-personal/impersonal noumenal Reality simply could not account for this state of cognitive affairs, nor could it play the role required by ultimate Reality in Hick's epistemological system.[119] Unless Hick is willing to dismantle his longstanding religious epistemology, his thought will require at this point the presence of a personal or super-personal Real—but never anything less (i.e., non-personal/impersonal). It is telling that with two recent opportunities to address this specific criticism in published response form, Hick has not broached, let alone answered, the charges in either case.[120] It is important to note here that what is being identified is not simply vestigial traces of theism in Hick's *style* of presentation. Rather, I am suggesting that the problem lies in the very logic and content of his hypothesis itself. Thus, once again, one finds Hick clearly presupposing elements within his model that can only be attributable to a covert monotheism.

Covert Theism and Hick's Eschatological Scenario   Finally, I shall argue that Hick's most recent eschatological scenario remains inextricably linked to fundamentally monotheistic presuppositions. To begin with, there is the sense that, for Hick, the grand eschatological state of humanity remains under what must be something analogous to supervision by the divine presence. The problem, of course, is that anything like divine supervision demands qualities of the Real that are of a personal, or super-personal nature, such as purposiveness, fore-sight, etc. Mark Heim has noted this problem when he writes of "the assumption" in Hick's model that humanity's eschatological destiny is "administered in some way."[121] But this observation only points to a more fundamentally theistic—if subtly implicit—assumption in Hick's theory.

The more basic problem is this. In order for Hick's eschatological scenario to function in his philosophical system as it always has and presumably must— namely as providing the necessary *verificational* context for his religious realism—there must, on the other side of death, be some form of personal entity with identity ties to the prior terrestrial religious person.[122] In other words, Hick's theory requires some form of post-mortem *personal, self-conscious* existence which can 'verify' its prior realist claims via the eschatological experience. In his most recent explanation of how the eschatological state can establish a religious, as opposed to naturalistic, interpretation of religion, Hick writes: "If, then, we find after our bodily death that we still exist, our experience will have falsified the naturalistic hypothesis."[123] That this sort of eschatological experience remains a non-negotiable part of Hick's mature conception of religion is clear from the following comment found in a new Preface to the 1993 edition of his *Death and Eternal Life*:

> any religious understanding of human existence—not merely of one's own existence but of the life of humanity as a whole—positively requires some kind of immortality belief and would be radically incoherent without it.[124]

The problem here involves the implicit theistic privileging that such a notion entails. That is, the non-theistic religious traditions (e.g., Advaita Vedanta or Theravada Buddhism) whose post-mortem scenarios preclude the idea of individual conscious existence (whether in terms of a "pareschatological" stage, a "bardo" phase, or any other) find no place in Hick's eschatological verificationist schema, and thus run the risk of falling outside of Hick's realist model.

His more recent attempt to read the Advaita Vedanta scenario in terms of a single eternal eschatological Self composed of all individual human selves, and thus able to verify their past realist claims, raises some very real interpretive problems. It seems to me that Hick must posit a number of very questionable assumptions in this regard for his thesis to fly, including (1) the notion that Brahman, though traditionally understood in *impersonal* terms, can actually function very much like a self-conscious, personalistic super-mind, and (2) that this personalistic Brahman will serve to 'verify' as authentic the past experiences and general religious claims of individual consciousnesses which, according to the Advaitic system, are—and always were—nothing more than deceptive *maya*. Tellingly, when it comes to the question of correlating the post-mortem scenario of Theravada Buddhism with his eschatological verificationist schema, Hick essentially skirts the issue. Nirvana, after all, appears to leave little room for a final 'consciousness' of any kind, and thus a verificationist reinterpretation is out of the question.[125] And so, Hick's claim of a possible future verification of a religious, as opposed to a naturalistic, interpretation of religion for "all" the world's religions based upon "their common affirmation of continued personal existence beyond the present life" betrays a definite theistic presumption.[126]

One might offer the following rebuttal to this line of criticism.[127] An eschatological scenario requiring an actual conscious verification/falsification on the part of some (quasi) personal entity would privilege a theistic vision. However, viewed as a *formal category* (as opposed to a concrete conscious experience), eschatological verification/falsification could equally serve to authenticate a non-theistic, as well as a theistic, religious perspective. For example, it may be that Nirvana as understood by a Theravada Buddhist may be the final eschatological state. If so, there will be no conscious personal experience of any type that could verify it, or falsify, say, the Christian view. However, metaphysically speaking, such a state would, in fact, be the case nonetheless. Thus, Nirvana would have been 'verified' in a formal, if not an actual epistemological, sense.

In response, two observations will serve to undermine the force of this potential objection. First, it is noteworthy that Hick himself has not followed this line of thought. Again, although he raises the question of how Buddhist thought could fit his eschatological requirements, Hick never answers the question. Instead, he simply confirms one's natural suspicions that such an explanation is "elusive."[128] Second (and, I submit, the reason Hick does not pursue the line of thought under analysis), to reduce Hick's eschatological verification/ falsification principle to a formal category alone would be to render it ineffective for the very purpose for which it was originally designed. One might propose such a restructuring. But to do so would be to end up with a religious epistemology quite different from the one Hick has proffered for the last several decades. Hick has rejected this move. And so must anyone reject it who desires to remain faithful to Hick's basic epistemological approach to religion.

It is tempting at this point to pursue a detailed archaeological tracing of the roots of Hick's covert monotheism. It will suffice to say that the evidence suggests an obvious generative context: namely, Hick's decades-long commitment to the western liberal intellectual tradition—both in terms of rationality and religion. Don Cupitt has posed the issue quite bluntly when he writes that "John Hick is the platonic ideal of the liberal theologian who believes in the fatherhood of God and the brotherhood of man. He is sweet reasonableness incarnate...."[129] In any case, the above observations serve to elucidate the vestigial (one is tempted to add 'Christian') monotheism that attaches to, and thus undermines, what Hick would hope is a tradition-neutral model of religious pluralism.

Notes

1   I.e., much of this cataloging shall take the form of summary discussions in footnotes.

2   Alston, "Realism and the Christian Faith," 43 (emphasis in text). On religious realism and non-realism see Hick, "Religious Realism and Non-realism," in *Disputed Questions in Theology*, 3–16. My own use of these terms is similar to that of Hick's.

3   While various elements of the following critique are developed in an original fashion, the general charge that Hick's hypothesis contains the seeds of religious non-realism is not new. See e.g., Alston, "Realism and the Christian Faith," 37–60; L. Stafford Betty, "The Glitch in *An Interpretation of Religion*," in Hewitt, ed., *Problems in the Philosophy of Religion*, 100; Beverley J. Clack, "Leaving Things as They Are: A Response to John Hick and Paul Badham," *King's Theological Review* 13 (1990): 37–40; Hebblethwaite, "John Hick and the Question of Truth in Religion," in Sharma, ed., *God, Truth, and Reality*, 130–32; idem., review of *An Interpretation of Religion*, 332–3; Heim, "Pluralistic Hypothesis, Realism, and Post-Eschatology"; idem., *Salvations*, 35–43; Mavrodes, "God above the Gods"; C. S. Rodd, review of *An Interpretation of Religion*, *Expository Times* 101 (1989): 35. On related concerns see D. Z. Phillips, "Philosophers' Clothes," in *Relativism and Religion*, ed. Charles M. Lewis (New York: St. Martin's, 1995), 142–43; Quinn, "Towards Thinner Theologies."

4   See the discussion above in chapter four. Again, Hick ("Philosophy of World Religions," 232) has claimed that his hypothesis does not depend upon implications of the notion of divine infinity. However, he acknowledges that he does hold to such implications ("Religious Pluralism and the Divine: A Response to Paul Eddy," 418), and the fact that he continues to give it significant attention in the explication and defense of his theory (e.g., *Interpretation of Religion*, 237–9) justifies the following discussion.

5   *Interpretation of Religion*, 237.

6   Thomas Finger, *Christian Theology: an Eschatological Approach* (Scottdale, Pa.: Herald, 1985, 1989) II:502; see also Stephen Davis, "Why God Must be Unlimited," in Tessier, ed., *Concepts of the Ultimate*, 4–6.

7   See especially Raoul Mortley, *From Word to Silence*, Vol. 2: *The Way of Negation, Christian and Greek* (Bonn: Hanstein, 1986), 242–54. Also Deirdre Carabine, *The Unknown God: Negative Theology in the Platonic Tradition: Plato to Eriugena* (Grand Rapids: Eerdmans, 1995), 9; Mark Johnson, "Apophatic Theology's Cataphatic Dependencies," *The Thomist* 62 (1998): 519–31; Ward, "Truth and the Diversity of Religions," 6–11; Plantinga, *Does God Have a Nature?* (Milwaukee: Marquette University Press, 1980), 18–20.

8   E.g., see respectively Humphrey Palmer, *Analogy: A Study of Qualification and Argument in Theology* (New York: St. Martin's, 1973), especially ch. 13; David Burrell, *Aquinas, God and Action* (London: Routledge & Kegan, 1979). On Aquinas and negative theology see Gregory P. Rocca, "Analogy as Judgment and Faith in God's Incomprehensibility: A Study in the Theological Epistemology of Thomas Aquinas," (Ph.D. diss., Washington, D.C.: Catholic University of America, 1989).

9   See Gerard J. Hughes, "Aquinas and the Limits of Agnosticism," in *The Philosophical Assessment of Theology: Essays in Honour of Frederick C. Copleston*, ed. G. Hughes (Washington D. C.: Georgetown University Press, 1987), 37–63; Gregory P. Rocca, "Aquinas on God-Talk: Hovering Over the Abyss," *Theological Studies* 54 (1993): 641–61; George Lindbeck, "The *A Priori* in St. Thomas' Theory of Knowledge," in *The Heritage of Christian Thought: Essays in Honor of Robert Lowry Calhoun*, ed. R. E. Cushman and E. Grislis (New York: Harper & Row, 1965), 41–63.

10   See Philip A. Rolnick, *Analogical Possibilities: How Words Refer to God*, AARAS 18 (Atlanta: Scholars Press, 1993); Richard Swinburne, *The Coherence of Theism*, rev. ed. (Oxford: Clarendon, 1993), chs. 4 & 5; idem., "Analogy and Metaphor," in *Philosophical Assessment of Theology*, pp. 65–84; Patrick J. Sherry, "Analogy Today," *Philosophy* 51 (1976): 431–46; Barry Miller, "Analogy Sans Portrait: God-Talk as Literal but Non-anthropomorphic," *Faith and Philosophy* 7 (1990): 63–71. There are, of course, those who would argue that Aquinas has, in fact, given up far too much cognitive content vis-à-vis our knowledge of God by adopting a theory of religious language that is controlled by a divine simplicity doctrine. See e.g., William P. Alston, "Aquinas on Theological Predication: A Look Backward and a Look Forward," in Stump, ed., *Reasoned Faith*, 145–78.

11   "Infinity and the Absolute: Insights into Our World, Our Faith and Ourselves," *Christian Scholar's Review* 23 (1993): 179.

12   See Palmer's (*Analogy*, pp. 26–27) discussion in this regard. I am indebted at several points here to Peter Byrne's ("John Hick's Philosophy of World Religions," 296–99) critique of Hick's use of the concept of divine infinity.

13   So argues Jill Le Blanc; see her excellent discussion on these matters, "Infinity in Theology and Mathematics," *Religious Studies* 29 (1993): 51–62.

14   Ibid., 59–62.

15   Ferre, "In Praise of Anthropomorphism," in *God in Language*, Robert P. Scharlemann and Gilbert E. M. Ogutu, eds. (New York: Paragon, 1987), 192.

16   See e.g., D'Costa, "Christian Theology and Other Faiths," 295; Louw, "Theocentrism and Reality-centrism," 5; Netland, *Dissonant Voices*, 133–41, 215–21; Rose, "Knowing the Real," 132–6; Verkamp, "Hick's Interpretation," 106–7; Wiedenhofer, "Between Particularity and Universality," 8.

17   *Interpretation of Religion*, 239. Here Hick understands 'strong ineffability' to mean that absolutely *no* human concepts—substantive *or formal*—apply to the unknowable X. He

takes this definition from the discussion in Keith Yandell, "Some Varieties of Ineffability," *International Journal for Philosophy of Religion* 6 (1975): 167–79.

18   Ward, "Truth and the Diversity of Religions," 10.

19   *Interpretation of Religion*, 246.

20   Ward, "Truth and the Diversity of Religions," 10.

21   Ludwig Feuerbach, *The Essence of Christianity*, George Elliot, trans. (New York: Harper & Bros., 1957 [1841]), 14–5. See the similar challenge of David Hume, *Dialogues Concerning Natural Religion* (Indianapolis/New York: Bobbs-Merrill, 1947 [1779]), pt. IV, 158.

22   For readings of Kant's noumenal/phenomenal distinction in an anti-realist vein, see Hilary Putnam, *Reason, Truth, and History* (Cambridge: Cambridge University Press, 1981), ch. 3; Carl Posy, "Dancing to the Antinomy: A Proposal for Transcendental Idealism," *American Philosophical Quarterly* 20 (1983): 81–94.

23   For the purposes of this study, I shall not have to enter into the discussion of whether or not Kantianism itself offers an appropriate conceptual vehicle for theological thinking. Suffice to say that Christian thinkers have come out on both sides of this question. Contra Kant, see e.g., Alvin Plantinga, *The Twin Pillars of Christian Scholarship* (Grand Rapids, Mich.: Calvin College and Seminary, 1990); Nicholas Wolterstorff, "Is it Possible and Desirable for Theologians to Recover from Kant?," *Modern Theology* 14 (1998): 1–18; Hebblethwaite, "Hick and the Question of Truth," 132–3; Gregory A. Clark, "The Nature of Conversion: How the Rhetoric of Worldview Philosophy Can Betray Evangelicals," in *The Nature of Confession: Evangelicals and Postliberals in Conversation*, ed. Timothy R. Phillips and Dennis L. Okholm (Downers Grove, Ill.: InterVarsity, 1996), 201–18. Others, such as Merold Westphal, defend Kant at this point; see "Christian Philosophers and the Copernican Revolution," in Evans and Westphal, eds., *Christian Perspectives on Religious Knowledge*, 161–79; idem., "In Defense of the Thing in Itself," *Kant-Studien* 59 (1968): 118–41. For a helpful discussion of related matters see Terry F. Godlove, *Religion, Interpretation, and Diversity of Belief: The Framework Model from Kant to Durkheim to Davidson* (New York: Cambridge University Press, 1989).

24   Hick, *God Has Many Names*, 105.

25   E.g., see L. Philip Barnes, "Relativism, Ineffability, and the Appeal to Experience: A Reply to the Myth Makers," *Modern Theology* 7 (1990): 101–14.

26   See his "Hyper-Kantianism." Again, in this article, Forgie does not apply his critique to Hick.

27   *Interpretation of Religion*, 244.

28   See Ninian Smart, "A Contemplation of Absolutes," in Sharma, ed., *God, Truth and Reality*, 184–85.

29   Norman Kemp Smith notes that, for Kant, "the *a priori*, then, is merely relational, without inherent content"; *A Commentary to Kant's "Critique of Pure Reason,"* rev. ed. (Atlantic Highlands, N.J.: Humanities, 1992), xxxvi.

30   Forgie, "Hyper-Kantianism," 208.

31   See Michael Stoeber, "Constructivist Epistemologies of Mysticism: A Critique and Revision," *Religious Studies* 28 (1992): 107–16.

32   In regard to the various interpretations and criticisms of Kant at this point, see Karl Ameriks, "Recent Work on Kant's Theoretical Philosophy," *American Philosophical Quarterly* 19 (1982): 1–24; Richard E. Aquila, "Things in Themselves and Appearances: Intentionality and Reality in Kant," *Archiv für Geschichte der Philosophie* 61 (1979): esp. 293–5; Robert Adams,

"Things in Themselves," *Philosophy and Phenomenological Research* 57 (1997): 801–25.

33   *Interpretation of Religion*, 241 (emphasis added).

34   See the surveys cited at note #32 for problematic aspects of reading Kant in a purely 'one world'/perspectival manner. See also Philip Rossi, "The Final End of All Things: The Highest Good as the Unity of Nature and Freedom," in *Kant's Philosophy of Religion Reconsidered*, Philip Rossi and M. Wreen, eds. (Bloomington/Indianapolis: Indiana University Press, 1991), 133–64.

35   Stephen R. Palmquist, *Kant's System of Perspectives: An Architectonic Interpretation of the Critical Philosophy* (Lanham: University Press of America, 1993), 169–70, 176–7; see also Appendix 5: "The Radical Unknowability of the Thing in Itself."

36   Ibid., 178.

37   *Interpretation of Religion*, 166.

38   D'Costa, "John Hick and Religious Pluralism," 18.

39   Don Cupitt, "Thin-line Theism," *The Times Literary Supplement* (August 8, 1980): 902.

40   *Christian Theology of Religions*, 46, 58–60; "Response to Eddy," *Religious Studies* 31 (1995): 417–20. This response is to my article "Religious Pluralism and the Divine: Another Look at John Hick's Neo-Kantian Proposal," *Religious Studies* 30 (1994): 467–78.

41   "Response to Eddy," 417.

42   Ibid.; see also *Christian Theology of Religions*, 58–9.

43   Ibid., 418.

44   Aquinas, *On the Power of God*, English Dominican Fathers, trans. (Westminster: Newman, 1952), VII:5.

45   Netland, *Dissonant Voices*, 218. Ward ("Truth and Religious Diversity," 11) notes the problems that arise for Hick's thesis when, in the noumenal realm of the Real, the *via negativa* is entirely divorced from the *via eminentia*; see also Ward, *Religion and Revelation*, 311.

46   On which see Donald Bloesch, *God the Almighty: Power, Wisdom, Holiness, Love* (Downers Grove, Ill.: InterVarsity, 1995), 53.

47   On the pantheistic monist implications of paying God the well-intentioned metaphysical compliment of 'infinity' see Robert Oakes, "God and Cosmos: Can the 'Mystery of Mysteries' be Solved?," *American Philosophical Quarterly* 33 (1996): 315–23; William James, *The Works of William James: A Pluralistic Universe* (Cambridge, Mass.: Harvard University Press, 1977 [1903]): 140.

48   See "Response to Eddy," 418; *Christian Theology of Religions*, 60, n. 12.

49   "Response to Eddy," 418; see also *Christian Theology of Religions*, 59–60.

50   "Response to Eddy," 418.

51   Ward, "Truth and Religious Diversity," 10.

52   "Response to Eddy," 418.

53   Again, see Ward's incisive comments on this matter; "Truth and Religious Diversity," 10.

54   Actually, it is not always clear whether Hick says this or not, or, if he does, what he means by it. This issue will be addressed below. For now, I can proceed with my present concern given Hick's common statement regarding "the Real as humanly experienced"; *Interpretation of Religion*, 246.

55   Review of *Interpretation of Religion*, 262. At another point, Wainwright is more detailed as to just what content is involved: namely, "being a cause or necessary condition of finite substances and events"; "Religious Language, Religious Experience, and Religious

Pluralism," in Senor, ed., *The Rationality of Belief and the Plurality of Faith*, 179.

56   *Interpretation of Religion*, 351.

57   *Warranted Christian Belief*, 57.

58   See Ward ("Truth and Religious Diversity," 5) followed by Louw ("Theocentrism and Reality-centrism," 6).

59   "Truth and Religious Diversity," 5.

60   Ibid., 5–6.

61   "Knowing the Real," 133.

62   See Rose, "Knowing the Real," 136–7; Stephen Grover, review of *Interpretation of Religion*, *The Literary Times Supplement* (December 22–29, 1989), 1404; Mesle, review of *Interpretation of Religion*, 714; D'Costa, "Taking Other Religions Seriously," 526–7; Ward, *Religion and Revelation*, 311; Hebblethwaite, "Hick and the Question of Truth," 130.

63   See "Response to Eddy," 419. Hick offers a similar response to my argument in *Christian Theology of Religions*, 46.

64   "Response to Eddy," 419.

65   In a recent response article to Hick, George Mavrodes has reversed his earlier analysis (e.g., "Polytheism," in Senor, ed., *The Rationality of Belief and the Plurality of Faith*, 261–86) of Hick's hypothesis, and has now come to conclusions similar to mine when he questions the robust reality of both Hick's religious phenomenal entities and the noumenal Real itself; see "A Response to John Hick ['The Epistemological Challenge of Religious Pluralism']," *Faith and Philosophy* 14 (1997): 289–94.

66   See "Response to Eddy," 419–20.

67   Ibid., 419.

68   Ibid., 419, n. 8. Given Hick's definition of the term 'information' here, he would be less open to misunderstanding if he chose to use a term like 'stimulus.'

69   *Interpretation of Religion*, 242.

70   Ibid., 246. See Netland's (*Dissonant Voices*, 212–7) discussion of these two tensive strands of thought in Hick's work.

71   "Towards Thinner Theologies," 148–9; he quotes a paragraph from *Interpretation of Religion*, 246.

72   Ibid., 149.

73   Ibid.

74   "Realism and the Christian Faith," 54.

75   *Knowing the Real*, 107; see pp. 106–10. Rose claims that this criticism represents a new line of critique ("Knowing the Real," 146). While he may offer a novel nuance here, Netland has broached similar concerns; see *Dissonant Voices*, 215–17. For something of a defense of Hick against Netland's criticisms see Twiss, "Philosophy of Religious Pluralism," 553–7. In the light of an observation offered in his own article (555, n. 36) and Rose's critique respectively, Twiss's two points against Netland are to be judged ineffective.

76   "Response to Eddy," 419.

77   This is not to say that I agree with Hick's religious epistemology, and its (logically *a priori*) attendant claim of a finely-tuned religiously ambiguous universe. There are, I think, serious problems in this area of his thought as well.

78   Feuerbach, *Essence of Christianity*, 14–5.

79   "Response to Eddy," 419.

80   See e.g., Betty, "The Glitch," 100; Rose, "Knowing the Real," 170; Wainwright, review of *Christian Theology of Religions*, 125–6; Ward, *Religion and Revelation*, 311–12.

81   John C. Lyden, "Why Only 'One' Divine Reality?: A Critique of Religious Pluralism," *Dialogue & Alliance* 8 (1994): 63. See also Lipner, "At the Bend in the Road: A Story about Religious Pluralism," in *Problems in the Philosophy of Religion*, 224–7; Eliot Deutsch, review of *An Interpretation of Religion*, *Philosophy East and West* 40 (1990): 558–9, 562; Heim, *Salvations*, 29, n. 11; Mesle, review of *Interpretation of Religion*, 713; Slater, "Lindbeck, Hick, and the Nature of Religious Truth," 71–2.

82   Geivett and Phillips, "Response to Hick," 79. See also Geivett, "John Hick's Approach," 49–50; O'Leary, *Religious Pluralism and Christian Truth*, 20–1.

83   Netland, *Dissonant Voices*, 107; Ward, *Religion and Revelation*, 312.

84   *Interpretation of Religion*, 249. Hick has more recently emphasized that the "Real remains beyond the range of our human conceptuality, including the concept of number"; *Christian Theology of Religions*, 71.

85   *Christian Theology of Religions*, 70.

86   *Interpretation of Religion*, 248; see also *Christian Theology of Religions*, 69–70.

87   *Christian Theology of Religions*, 69; see also Hick, "A Religious Understanding of Religion," 132.

88   E.g., this type of concern is at least hinted at as early as 1970 in two responses, by William D. Nietmann and Margaret Chatterjee, to Hick's paper "Philosophy, Religions, and Human Unity"; see Mahadevan, ed., *Philosophy: Theory and Practice*, 473, 477.

89   This criticism has taken different forms. From those outside of the pluralist camp see Clayton, review of *An Interpretation of Religion*, 801–3; Clendenin, *Many Gods*, 101; Louw, "Theocentrism and Reality-centrism," 5–6; Schwöbel, "Particularity, Universality," 32; Luco J. van den Brom, "God, Gödel and Trinity," in *Christian Faith and Philosophical Theology: Essays in Honour of Vincent Brummer*, ed. G. van den Brink, L. J. van den Brom, and Marcel Sarot (Kampen, The Netherlands: Pharos, 1992), 66, n. 16. From those within the pluralist camp see: Kaufman, "Religious Diversity and Religious Truth," 163, n. 2; Panikkar, "The Jordan, the Tiber, and the Ganges," 109; Joseph Prabhu, "The Road Not Taken: A Story about Religious Pluralism, Part 2," in Hewitt, ed., *Problems in the Philosophy of Religion*, 239; Ninian Smart, "Responses," in *Hermeneutics, Religious Pluralism, and Truth*, 54–55; idem., "A Contemplation of Absolutes," in Sharma, ed., *God, Truth and Reality*, 177–79.

90   Smart, "Models for Understanding the Relations between Religions," in *Inter-Religious Models and Criteria*, Kellenberger, ed. (New York: St. Martin's, 1993), 62–3.

91   Quinn, "Toward Thinner Theologies," 164, n. 6.

92   Hick's "pluralism" is all about the phenomenal realm. When it comes to the noumenal realm of the Real, he seems to be guilty of a wide-spread "monotheist complacency" (on which see A. H. Armstrong, "Some Advantages of Polytheism," *Dionysius* 5 [1981] 181–88). Ward's (*Religion and Revelation*, 313) suggestion that Hick's thesis partakes of the 'quantifier shift' fallacy (discussed above) is also relevant here.

93   For some possible responses to philosophical problems raised by taking something like poly-Realism seriously, see Mavrodes, "Polytheism," 261–86.

94   Against the notion that one can easily understand the various religions under any harmonizing soteriological rubric see DiNoia, "Varieties of Religious Aims," in *Diversity of*

Religions, 34–64; Heim, *Salvations*; D'Costa, "John Hick and Religious Pluralism," 11–15; idem., "Taking Other Religions Seriously," 529. For similar criticisms (some of which would apply to Hick) with respect to a professedly "soteriocentric" model of religious pluralism see my "Paul Knitter's Theology of Religions," 242–43.

95   My criticism here has parallels to that of the charge that Hick falls into the 'quantifier-shift' fallacy, leveled by Ward and others.

96   "The God above the Gods," 200, n. 40.

97   Lyden ("Why Only 'One' Divine Reality?" 63) notes, "For Hick, the norm for truth is not the Christ, but a certain philosophical understanding of Reality as a single Absolute."

98   "On Wilfred Cantwell Smith," 20.

99   On taking some version of polytheism seriously, see Mavrodes, "Polytheism"; Armstrong, "Some Advantages of Polytheism"; William James, "Conclusions," in *A Pluralistic Universe*, 140; idem., Postscript in *Varieties of Religious Experience* (New York: Mentor, 1960 [1902]).

100   It is no secret that the concept of monotheism has always been a central category for both Hick the theologian and Hick the philosopher of religion. See for example: *Faith and Knowledge*, 128–29; *Philosophy of Religion* (all four eds.), ch. 1; "A Recent Development within Christian Monotheism."

101   Peter Hayman, "Monotheism—A Misused Word in Jewish Studies?," *Journal of Jewish Studies* 42 (1991): 15.

102   Ibid., 2.

103   N. T. Wright has proposed a more biblically accurate definition of monotheism, what he calls "creational monotheism," wherein one acknowledges one ontologically distinct Creator-God, as well as other created supernatural entities within the spiritual realm; see *The New Testament and the People of God*, 1992), 248–59. Others have proposed similar understandings of biblical monotheism that avoid mere henotheism, on one hand, and an absolute philosophical monotheism on the other. See e.g., Gregory A. Boyd, *God at War: The Bible and Spiritual Conflict* (Downers Grove, Ill.: InterVarsity, 1997), 119–29; Ulrich Mauser, "One God Alone: A Pillar of Biblical Theology," *Princeton Seminary Bulletin* 12 (1991): 255–65; N. H. Snaith, "The Advent of Monotheism in Israel," *The Annual of Leeds University Oriental Society* 5 (1963–5): 100–13.

104   *Interpretation of Religion*, 218.

105   Twiss ("Philosophy of Religious Pluralism," 557, n. 37), although generally appreciative of Hick's project, raises this very suspicion in passing. See also Apczynski, "Hick's Theocentrism," 42; Verkamp, "Hick's Interpretation," 114–6; Wells, "Taking Pluralism Seriously," 22–23; Clarke and Byrne, "A Religious Theory of Religion," 88–91; Joseph Prabhu, "The Road Not Taken: A Story about Religious Pluralism, Part 2" [a reply to Julius Lipner's "At the Bend in the Road: A Story about Religious Pluralism"] in Hewitt, ed., *Problems of the Philosophy of Religions*, 239.

106   This line of criticism has been suggested by a few other critics of Hick, although it has yet to be worked out to the degree, and in the manner, it is below. See Mesle, *John Hick's Theodicy*, 91–92; idem., "Humanism and Hick's Interpretation of Religion," 67; Rowe, "John Hick's Contribution to the Philosophy of Religion," 22. It follows upon the general observation of a number of Hick's critics who would argue, with Gavin D'Costa (*Hick's Theology of Religions*, 167), that "many of Hick's theological and epistemological assumptions in his *pre-Copernican* days uneasily remain firmly embedded within his Copernican framework."

107   The following is a summary review of the more detailed discussion offered above in chapter two.

108   *Faith and Knowledge*, esp. ch. 8.

109   Ibid., 184, also 186. For other relevant statements of the issue see: *Philosophy of Religion*, 1st ed., 70–3; *Evil and the God of Love*, ix, 17, 308–13; *Christianity at the Center*, 50–7; "God, Evil and Mystery," 540; *Arguments for the Existence of God*, 104–05, 114.

110   Thus, Byrne ("John Hick's Philosophy of World Religions," 295) is mistaken when he claims that Hick has abandoned the idea that ultimate reality must maintain an epistemic distance in order to preserve human freedom. The problem here is that he has identified a (possible) shift in Hick's assessment of *theistic proofs* in this regard, and apparently has falsely assumed that such a shift must also have occurred in Hick's thought concerning *religious experience* itself.

111   For a recent statement see Hick, "Religious Pluralism and the Rationality of Religious Belief."

112   See "Mystical Experience as Cognition," 50–1.

113   E.g., see *God Has Many Names*, 50–51, 86, 113; *Philosophy of Religion*, 3rd ed., 68–70; 4th ed., 64–7.

114   *God Has Many Names*, 50.

115   Ibid.

116   *Interpretation of Religion*, 124.

117   See Mesle, *John Hick's Theodicy*, 89.

118   Hick, "Religious Experience: Its Nature and Validity," in *Disputed Questions in Theology*, 31. See also Hick, "Afterword," in R. Douglas Geivett, *Evil and the Evidence for God: The Challenge of John Hick's Theodicy* (Philadelphia: Temple University Press, 1993), 234, where he writes "…for the limitlessly valuable divine reality must be responded to freely." Even more recently, in his 1995 "Response to Eddy" (419), Hick writes of the experience of "allow[ing] this impingement [of the Real] upon us to come to consciousness," a statement which signals the presence of the perennial concepts of 'epistemic distance' and faith as a free 'experiencing-as' response to the cognitively uncoercive divine presence.

119   There are a variety of ways one could pose the problem here. Lipner ("At the Bend in the Road," 224 [emphasis in text]) has put the question this way: "Does it make sense to speak of a *response* to the Transcendent without implying some sort of *initiative* on the part of the Transcendent in the first place?….[S]peaking properly, it only makes sense to talk of *persons* taking initiative, does it not?" Eliot Deutsch (review of *Interpretation of Religion*, 559) has summarized a similar concern: "Religious experience [for Hick] is thus always relational—and, therefore, essentially theistic, even if it appears to be otherwise."

120   Hick, "Response to Mesle" in *John Hick's Theodicy*, 115–34; Hick, "Reply" (to Mesle's "Humanism and Hick's Interpretation of Religion") in *Problems in the Philosophy of Religion*, 82–5.

121   *Salvations*, 29, n. 11.

122   More recently, in his defense of religious realism, Hick has shifted from using the term 'verification' to that of 'falsification'; see *Christian Theology of Religions*, 71–76. However, in *Interpretation of Religion* (178), he defends the use of the term 'verification' with regard to his eschatological thesis, if in a qualified sense.

123   *Christian Theology of Religions*, 73.

124   *Death and Eternal Life*, 15.

125   The most Hick can hope for here is to root religious realist claims in the earthly nirvanic

experience of enlightenment; see *Interpretation of Religion*, 183–8.

126   Hick, "On Religious Experience," 29.

127   I am indebted to Paul Griffiths and Paul Reasoner for raising the following issue during a discussion following the reading of my paper "John Hick's Religious Pluralism—Covert Monotheism?," at the midwest regional meeting of the Society of Christian Philosophers (April 7, 1995, Bethel College, St. Paul).

128   *Interpretation of Religion*, 183.

129   "Thin-Line Theism," 902.

Conclusion

John Hick's Religious Pluralism: The Promise and the Problem

John Hick's religious pluralism offers what is, to many in our religiously diverse world, an attractive promise. For almost three decades, he has aspired to provide a completely tradition-neutral account of religious diversity from a pluralist perspective that, at the same time, refuses to surrender to contemporary non-realist impulses. In conjunction with this attempt, Hick has wrestled admirably with the problem of conflicting conceptions of the divine within the religions. In fact, as I have suggested, no one has taken this problem more seriously than Hick, nor has anyone proposed a more conceptually ingenious and sophisticated attempt to solve this problem.

In spite of this remarkable attempt, I have argued that Hick's mature pluralist model—with its neo-Kantian hypothesis at the core—fails to achieve its intended goals. On one hand, it logically contains the constructivist seeds of the very religious non-realism he has so tirelessly resisted over the years. On the other hand (and possibly a reason that he does not recognize the presence of the implicit non-realist threat), Hick's religious theory ironically contains an incipient mono-theism that, by the nature of the case, is inextricably linked with his long-standing religious epistemology, with its notions of epistemic distance and eschatological verification. The irony here is composite: Hick's Christian theism gave birth to his religious epistemology in the 1940s. This, in turn, gave birth to his religious pluralism in the 1970s. His pluralism, ironically, has forced him to try to remove what is, in fact, its own original generative theistic impulse, while yet retaining the middle quotient: his foundational religious epistemology. Given the terms, this project, I submit, is simply not tenable. The twin threats—those of non-realism and covert monotheism—appear to be endemic to Hick's current model of religious pluralism.

It is no coincidence that those who have made suggestions to Hick regarding how to rectify his problem fall either into religious non-realism (e.g., Kaufman) or a position which privileges either a theistic (e.g., Ward, Wainwright, et al.) or a non-theistic religious worldview (e.g., Panikkar).[1] The recent critical analysis of Hick's thought by Kenneth Rose lays bare the problem. Rose wants to maintain with Hick religious realism and the cognitivity of religious language on one hand, and a robust religious pluralism on the other.

However, he argues that Hick's "quasi-Kantian pluralistic hypothesis" is ultimately unsuccessful, since it leads inevitably to the very religious non-realism and non-cognitivity of religious language that Hick wants to avoid.[2] This criticism of Rose parallels my own (in chapter six) by identifying a strand in Hick's thought that inherently pulls him toward a non-realist position.

Rose goes on to offer a proposal, constructed from other elements in Hick's thought (i.e., the cognitive ambiguity of the universe, epistemic distance, faith as interpretation, etc.) for a new pluralist model where "the possibility of increasing speculative and empirical knowledge of the causal role of the transcendent (not transcendental) Real in the production of human experience" is to be expected.[3] In fact, "[o]ne can always move more deeply into that transcendent dimension of the Real, though one can never exhaust it."[4] This will certainly enable Rose to avoid the trap of religious non-realism. However, what Rose appears to miss is that in rejecting the neo-Kantian hypothesis, he loses the mechanism by which Hick has sought to maintain tradition-neutrality within his pluralist model. Rose is left without any such mechanism. And the effects are glaring. Theoretically, Rose's model of pluralism is inherently destined to privilege either a theistic or a non-theistic vision of the divine. As soon as the door is opened to the possibility of even partial knowledge of the (what Hick would call noumenal) Real, it becomes an appropriate and open question as to which religious vision better represents the divine.

Practically, in Rose's case, it is the theistic vision that wins out over the non-theistic. For instance, in affirming Hick's notion of epistemic distance, Rose affirms the idea that divine "providence" is at work, and that human cognitive freedom has been "designed" to allow for non-coercive relationship with the divine.[5] Thus, Rose's model will hardly be attractive to those who seek a pluralism wherein the Advaita Vedanta or Theravada Buddhist understanding of ultimate Reality is as welcome as the Jewish or Christian vision. Tradition neutrality has not been achieved in Rose's reconstructed model, and to this extent its pluralist aspirations are undermined.

I submit that this type of dilemma is inevitable. Hick's decades-long project has done a great service to those exploring the philosophical problems of religious diversity. It has demonstrated that, in the end, a pluralist perspective that desires to maintain a finely-balanced tradition neutrality and, at the same time, a robust religious realism is simply not possible. To settle for one, it seems, is to lose the other. And, if Hick's project is any indicator, to attempt to maintain both is ultimately to gain neither.

John Hick's Religious Pluralism: The Christological Question

The focus of this study has been upon an 'immanent,' philosophical analysis of Hick's pluralist hypothesis. As a systematician within the Christian tradition, however, I cannot leave aside the question of theological implications. To this end, I have included in this study a series of 'Christological soundings' through the various developmental stages of Hick's project, as well as a fairly detailed summary of the types of criticisms that have been leveled at Hick's pluralist Christology. From this perspective, the question, 'Is Hick's religious pluralism Christian?' is as important a question—maybe more so—as is 'Does it work?'

Hick's own response to this question would likely be 'yes and no.' In one sense, he would admit his hypothesis is not 'Christian'; however, in other senses it certainly is. For Hick, this sort of response is possible because there are, to his mind, "two Christianities."[6] The first type, which Hick refers to as "conservative-evangelical" and which might more broadly be identified as historic traditional orthodoxy, will most naturally judge that Hick's pluralism falls outside of its bounds.[7] The second type, 'liberal' Christianity which is composed of "the more experimental forms of Christianity," would instead consider Hick's approach to be quite appropriate.[8] And so, not surprisingly, how one answers the question 'Is it Christian?' in regard to Hick's pluralism will be determined by just which form of Christianity one stands within while posing the question. That such radically different assessments are given by the 'two Christianities' leads Hick to the conclusion that "dialogue between the two Christianities is quite as important, and might well be both as difficult and as rewarding, as inter-religious dialogue."[9] As one who does self-consciously stand within the broad stream of historic orthodox Christianity, I am left with the theological conviction that, by denying the dogma of the deity of Jesus Christ, Hick has chosen to separate himself from 'Christianity' as traditionally understood. If this is what is meant by the term 'Christianity,' then both Hick and I would agree that his religious pluralism is not 'Christian.' This conclusion must have serious repercussions for any (historic) Christian response to religious diversity at the turn of the twenty-first century.

Beyond the question of purely dogmatic considerations, the present ferment in New Testament studies in general, and historical Jesus studies in particular, renders other aspects of Hick's Christological conclusions suspect. Unfortunately, the modern history of Jesus studies has tended toward a polarization between radical skepticism and conservative fideism, between Reimarus and Kähler.[10] However, with the arrival of the so-called 'Third Quest,' we are witness to a distinctive stream of scholarship that serves to break this trend.[11] Within this segment of the Quest, one can find scholars presenting concrete models of Jesus, rooted in serious historical investigation, that go some distance toward supporting aspects of a more traditional Christology.[12] Thus, the Christological conclusions that Hick has drawn (on the basis of the work of one sector of contemporary New Testament studies) can be subjected to questioning on both theological and historical bases.

John Hick's Religious Pluralism: The Lingering Challenge

I have argued that Hick's religious pluralism is ultimately unsuccessful with respect to its intended purpose. However, Hick's work nonetheless stands as a challenge, and this in several ways. On one hand, it stands as a challenge to those pluralists who would attempt to improve upon his model. A number of pluralists who have criticized Hick have demonstrated that they are less aware and/or sensitive than he to the delicate balance that must be struck if a pluralist model is ever to be successful. On the other hand, Hick's work stands as a challenge to those who would reject the pluralist paradigm as a response to religious diversity. He has often put this challenge along these lines:

> [My pluralist hypothesis] is an explanatory theory; and I suggest that critics who don't like it should occupy themselves in trying to produce a better one....And so the right response of someone who does not like my proposed explanation is not to complain that it is not proved but to work out a viable alternative.[13]

This study has been an assessment of Hick's pluralist hypothesis. And, again, it has found the hypothesis to be less than successful. Having come to this conclusion is an important step toward the larger project of arriving at a viable theology of religions. However, it is only one step toward that goal. As Hick suggests, it is the larger project that must be kept in mind. My own philosophical proclivities and theological convictions lead me to believe that this longer journey must lead one away from the pluralist paradigm and thus, so to speak, back over the Rubicon. In conclusion, this study may serve as one (among many that are necessary) ground-clearing exercise from which to launch out on a constructive quest for a viable Christian theology of religions.

Notes

1   Interestingly, in a recent discussion of *Advaita* (Sankara) and *Visistadvaita* (Ramanuja) *Vedanta* traditions, the ardent pluralist W. C. Smith has concluded that he 'prefers' Ramanuja because of his own 'theistic' predilections—and does so without apology; see "Vedanta and the Modern Age," *Religious Studies and Theology* 13 & 14 (1995): 12–20.

2   "Knowing the Real," 12–13.

3   Ibid., 170.

4   Ibid.

5   Ibid., 158.

6   *The Second Christianity*, 73.

7   Ibid., 74.

8   Ibid.

9   Ibid. Hick has recently entered into just such a dialogue with several different thinkers within the 'conservative-evangelical' tradition on the issue of Christian theology of religions; see *More than One Way? Four Views on Salvation in a Pluralistic World*.

10   Or, today, one could say between Robert Funk (*Honest to Jesus: Jesus for a New Millennium* [San Francisco: HarperSanFrancisco, 1996]) and Luke Timothy Johnson (*The Real Jesus: The Misguided Quest for the Historical Jesus and the Truth of the Traditional Gospels* [San Francisco: HarperSanFrancisco, 1995]).

11   Here I am following N. T. Wright's use of the term 'Third Quest'; see his *Jesus and the Victory of God*, ch. 3; idem, "Jesus, Quest for the Historical," in *Anchor Bible Dictionary*, ed. David N. Freedman (New York: Doubleday, 1992), III:796–802.

12   E.g., see Markus Bockmuehl, *This Jesus: Martyr, Lord, Messiah* (Edinburgh: T & T Clark, 1994); Craig Evans, "The Historical Jesus and the Christ of Faith: A Critical Assessment of a Scholarly Problem," *Christian Scholar's Review* 18 (1988): 48–63; Eduard Schweizer, *Jesus the Parable of God: What Do We Really Know about Jesus?* (Allison Park, Pa.: Pickwick, 1994); Ben Witherington, *The Christology of Jesus* (Minneapolis: Fortress, 1990); and especially Wright, *Jesus and the Victory of God*. It seems that Wright's work is coming to be recognized as the most formidable example of such a project. For a survey and assessment of the historical foundations and theological implications of his model of Jesus, see my "The (W)Right Jesus: Eschatological Prophet, Israel's Messiah, Yahweh Embodied," in *Jesus and the Restoration of Israel: A Critical Assessment of N. T. Wright's Jesus and the Victory of God*, Carey C. Newman, ed. (Downers Grove, Ill.: InterVarsity, 1999), 40–60.

13   *Christian Theology of Religions*, 50–51. Hick has posed this challenge many times over the years; e.g., see also "Theology of Religious Pluralism," 336; "Philosophy of World Religions," 236; "Straightening the Record," 195.

Bibliography

Works by John Hick

Books

Arguments for the Existence of God. London: Macmillan, 1970.
The Centre of Christianity, 2nd ed. London: SCM, 1977.
A Christian Theology of Religions: The Rainbow of Faiths. Louisville, Ky.: Westminster/John Knox, 1995.
Christianity at the Center. London: SCM, 1968; New York: Herder and Herder, 1970.
Death and Eternal Life. New York: Harper & Row, 1976.
Disputed Questions in Theology and the Philosophy of Religion. New Haven: Yale University Press, 1993.
Evil and the God of Love. London: Macmillan, 1966. Reprint, London: Collins-Fontana, 1968.
Faith and Knowledge: A Modern Introduction to the Problem of Religious Knowledge. Ithaca, N.Y.:
    Cornell University Press, 1957. Revised ed., 1966. Reprint, London: Collins-Fontana, 1974.
God and the Universe of Faiths, 2nd ed. London: Macmillan, 1973. Reprint, London: Collins-Fontana, 1977.
God Has Many Names. London: Macmillan, 1980; Philadelphia: Westminster, 1982.
An Interpretation of Religion: Human Responses to the Transcendent. New Haven: Yale University
    Press, 1989.
A John Hick Reader. Edited by Paul Badham. Philadelphia: Trinity, 1990.
The Metaphor of God Incarnate: Christology in a Pluralistic Age. Louisville, Ky.: Westminster/
    John Knox, 1993.
Philosophy of Religion. Englewood Cliffs, N.J.: Prentice-Hall, Inc., 1963.
Philosophy of Religion, 2nd ed. Englewood Cliffs, N.J.: Prentice-Hall, Inc., 1973.
Philosophy of Religion, 3rd ed. Englewood Cliffs, N.J.: Prentice-Hall, Inc., 1983.
Philosophy of Religion, 4th ed. Englewood Cliffs, N.J.: Prentice-Hall, Inc., 1990.
Problems of Religious Pluralism. New York: St. Martin's, 1985.
The Second Christianity, 3rd ed. London: SCM, 1983.
With Michael Goulder. *Why Believe In God?* London: SCM, 1983.

Edited Books

With Brian Hebblethwaite. *Christianity and Other Religions: Selected Readings.* Philadelphia:
    Fortress, 1980.
Classical and Contemporary Readings in the Philosophy of Religion, 2nd ed. Englewood Cliffs,
    N.J.: Prentice-Hall, 1970.
The Existence of God. New York: Macmillan, 1964.
With Hasan Askari. *The Experience of Religious Diversity.* Avebury, UK: Gower, 1985.
Faith and the Philosophers. New York: St. Martin's, 1964.
With Arthur C. McGill. *The Many-faced Argument: Recent Studies on the Ontological Argument
    for the Existence of God.* New York: Macmillan, 1967.
With Paul K. Knitter. *The Myth of Christian Uniqueness: Toward a Pluralistic Theology of Reli-
    gions.* Maryknoll, N.Y.: Orbis, 1987.

The Myth of God Incarnate. London: SCM, 1977; Philadelphia: Westminster, 1978.

With Edmund Meltzer. *Three Faiths—One God: A Jewish, Christian, Muslim Encounter*. Albany: SUNY, 1989.

Truth and Dialogue in World Religions: Conflicting Truth-Claims. Philadelphia: Westminster, 1974.

Articles, Essays, and Other Works

"The Buddha's Doctrine of the 'Undetermined Questions.'" In *Hermeneutics, Religious Pluralism and Truth*, 1–17. Edited by G. D. Pritchard. Winston-Salem: Wake Forest University, 1989.

"The Christian View of Other Faiths." *Expository Times* 84 (1972): 36–9.

"Christianity and Reincarnation." In *Sri Aurobindo: A Garland of Tributes*, 65–9. Edited by Arabinda Basu. Pondicherry: Sri Aurobindo Research Academy, 1973.

"Christology at the Crossroads." In *Prospect for Theology: Essays in Honour of H. H. Farmer*, 139–66. Edited by F. G. Healey. London: James Nisbet & Co., 1966.

"Christology in an Age of Religious Pluralism." *Journal of Theology for Southern Africa* 35 (1981): 4–9.

"The Christology of D. M. Baillie." *Scottish Journal of Theology* 11 (1958): 1–12.

"Comment on 'Jesus's Unsurpassable Uniqueness.'" *Horizons* 16 (1989): 121–4.

"A Concluding Comment." *Faith and Philosophy* 5 (1988): 49–55.

"Conclusion." In *More than One Way?: Four Views on Salvation in a Pluralistic World*, 81–91. Edited by Dennis L. Okholm and Timothy R. Phillips. Grand Rapids, Mich.: Zondervan, 1995.

"The Epistemological Challenge of Religious Pluralism." *Faith and Philosophy* 14 (1997): 277–86.

"Faith and Coercion." *Philosophy* 42 (967): 272–3.

"Five Misgivings." In *The Uniqueness of Jesus: A Dialogue with Paul F. Knitter*, 79–84. Edited by Leonard Swidler and Paul Mojzes. Maryknoll, N.Y.: Orbis, 1997.

Forward to *The Meaning and End of Religion*, 2nd ed., by Wilfred Cantwell Smith. San Francisco: Haper & Row, 1978.

"God, Evil and Mystery." *Religious Studies* 3 (1968): 539–46.

"Incarnation." Letter to the editors. *Theology* 80 (1977): 204–6.

"Incarnation and Atonement: Evil and Incarnation." In *Incarnation and Myth: The Debate Continued*, 77–84. Edited by Michael Goulder. Grand Rapids, Mich.: Eerdmans, 1979.

"An Inspiration Christology for a Religiously Plural World." In *Encountering Jesus: A Debate on Christology*, 5–22. Edited by Stephen Davis. Atlanta: John Knox Press, 1988.

"Interpretation and Reinterpretation in Religion." In *The Making and Remaking of Christian Doctrine: Essays in Honor of Maurice Wiles*, 57–72. Edited by Sarah Coakley and David Pailin. Oxford: Clarendon, 1993.

"An Irenaean Theodicy." In *Encountering Evil: Live Options in Theodicy*, 39–52. Edited by Stephen Davis. Atlanta: Knox, 1981.

"Is the Doctrine of Atonement a Mistake?" In *Reason and the Christian Religion: Essays in Honour of Richard Swinburne*, 247–63. Edited by Alan G. Padgett. Oxford: Clarendon, 1994.

"Is There a Doctrine of the Incarnation?" In *Incarnation and Myth: The Debate Continued*, 47–50. Edited by Michael Goulder. Grand Rapids, Mich.: Eerdmans, 1979.

"Is There Only One Way to God?" *Theology* 85 (1982): 4–7.

"Jesus and Mohammad." In *Islam in a World of Diverse Faiths*, 114–18. Edited by Dan Cohn-Sherbok. New York: St. Martin's, 1991.

"Jesus and the World Religions." In *The Myth of God Incarnate*, 167–85. Edited by John Hick. Philadelphia: Westminster, 1977.

"John Hick on Religion, Philosophy and Related Issues." *Journal of Theology for Southern Africa* 35 (1981): 3–9.

"Learning from Other Faiths: The Christian View of Other Faiths." *Expository Times* 84 (1972): 36–9.

"Letter to the Editors: Incarnation." *Theology* 80 (1977): 204–6.

"Letter to the Editors: Only One Way to God?." *Theology* 86 (1983): 128–9.

"Letter to the Editors: World Religions." *Theology* 92 (1989): 297.

"A Liberal Christian View." *Free Inquiry* (Fall 1985): 40–2.

"Living in a Multi-cultural Society: Practical Reflections of a Theologian." *Expository Times* 89 (1978): 100–4.

"The Logic of God Incarnate." *Religious Studies* 25 (1989): 409–23.

"Mystical Experience as Cognition." In *Mystics and Scholars: The Calgary Conference on Mysticism 1976*, 41–56. Edited by Harold Coward and Terence Penelhum. Calgary: Canadian Corporation for Studies in Religion, 1977.

"The Nature of Religious Faith." *Proceedings of the International Congress on Philosophy* 11 (1953): 57–62.

"The Non-Absoluteness of Christianity." In *The Myth of Christian Uniqueness: Towards a Pluralistic Theology of Religions*, 16–36. Edited by John Hick and Paul F. Knitter. Maryknoll, N.Y.: Orbis, 1987.

"A Non-Substance Christology?" *Colgate-Rochester Divinity School Bulletin* (1959): 41–54.

"Oman, John Wood." In *The Encyclopedia of Philosophy*, v–vi:537. Edited by Paul Edwards. New York: Macmillan, 1967.

"On Conflicting Religious Truth-Claims." *Religious Studies* 19 (1983): 485–91.

"On Grading Religions." *Religious Studies* 17 (1981): 451–67.

"On Religious Experience." In *Faith, Scepticism and Personal Identity: A Festschrift for Terence Penelhum*, 17–29. Edited by J. J. MacIntosh and H. A. Meynell. Calgary: University of Calgary Press, 1994.

"On Wilfred Cantwell Smith: His Place in the Study of Religion." *Method and Theory in the Study of Religion* 4 (1992): 5–20.

"Only One Way to God?" Letter to the Editors. *Theology* 86 (1983): 128–9.

"The Outcome: Dialogue into Truth." In *Truth and Dialogue in World Religions: Conflicting Truthclaims*, 140–55. Edited by John Hick. Birmingham: University of Birmingham, 1974.

"A Philosophy of Religious Pluralism." In *The World's Religious Traditions: Essays in Honour of Wilfred Cantwell Smith*, 147–64. Edited by Frank Whaling. Edinburgh: Clark, 1984.

"The Philosophy of World Religions." *Scottish Journal of Theology* 37 (1984): 229–36.

"Philosophy, Religions, and Human Unity." In *Philosophy: Theory and Practice*, 462–77. Edited by T. Mahadevan. Madras: University of Madras, 1974.

"Pluralism and the Reality of the Transcendent." *Christian Century* 98 (January 21, 1981): 45–48.

"A Pluralist View." In *More than One Way?: Four Views on Salvation in a Pluralistic World*, 29–59. Edited by Dennis L. Okholm and Timothy R. Phillips. Grand Rapids, Mich.: Zondervan, 1995.

"The Possibility of Religious Pluralism: A Reply to Gavin D'Costa." *Religious Studies* 33 (1997): 161–66.

"The Problem of Evil in the First and Last Things." *Journal of Theological Studies* 19 (1968): 519–602

"The Real and Its Personae and Impersonae." In *Concepts of the Ultimate*, 143–76. Edited by Linda Tessier. New York: St. Matrin's, 1989.

"A Recent Development within Christian Monotheism." *The Concept of Monotheism in Islam and Christianity*, 60–70. Edited by Hans Koechler. Vienna: Braumueller, 1982.

"The Reconstruction of Christian Belief for Today and Tomorrow" [Parts 1 & 2]." *Theology* 73 (1970): 339–45, 399–405.

"Religion as 'Skilful Means': A Hint from Buddhism." *International Journal for Philosophy of Religion* 30 (1991): 141–58.

"Religious Diversity as Challenge and Promise." In *The Experience of Religious Diversity*, 3–24. Edited by John Hick and Hasan Askari. Aldershot, UK: Avebury/Gower, 1985.

"Religious Pluralism." In *The Encyclopedia of Religion*, XII:331–3. 16 vols. Edited by Mircea Eliade. New York: Macmillan, 1987.

"Religious Pluralism." In *The World's Religious Traditions: Current Perspectives in Religious Studies, Essays in Honour of Wilfred Cantwell Smith*, 147–64. Edited by Frank Whaling. Edinburgh: Clark, 1984.

"Religious Pluralism and Absolute Claims." In *Religious Pluralism*, 193–213. Edited by Leroy Rouner. Notre Dame: University of Notre Dame Press, 1984.

"Religious Pluralism and Salvation." *Faith and Philosophy* 5 (1988): 365–77.

"Religious Pluralism and the Divine: A Response to Paul Eddy." *Religious Studies* 31 (1995): 417–20.

"Religious Pluralism and the Rationality of Religious Belief." *Faith and Philosophy* 10 (1993): 242–9.

"A Religious Understanding of Religion: A Model of the Relationship Between Traditions." In *Many Mansions: Interfaith and Religious Intolerance*, 122–36. Edited by Dan Cohn-Sherbok. London: Bellew, 1992.

"A Religious Understanding of Religion: A Model of the Relationship Between Traditions." In *Inter-Religious Models and Criteria*, 21–36. Edited by J. Kellenberger. New York: St. Martin's, 1993.

"A Remonstrance in Concluding." In *Jesus in History and Myth*, 211–7. Edited by R. Joseph Hoffmann and Gerald A. Larue. Buffalo: Prometheus, 1986.

"Reply [to Gillis]." In *Problems in the Philosophy of Religion: Critical Studies of the Work of John Hick*, 51–3. Edited by Harold Hewitt. New York: St. Martin's, 1991.

"Reply [to Loughlin]." In *Problems in the Philosophy of Religion: Critical Studies of the Work of John Hick*, 206–9. Edited by Harold Hewitt. New York: St. Martin's, 1991.

"Reply [to Mesle]." In *Problems in the Philosophy of Religion: Critical Studies of the Work of John Hick*, 82–5. Edited by Harold Hewitt. New York: St. Martin's, 1991.

"Response to Alister E. McGrath." In *More than One Way?: Four Views on Salvation in a Pluralistic World*, 181–6. Edited by Dennis L. Okholm and Timothy R. Phillips. Grand Rapids, Mich.: Zondervan, 1995.

"A Response to Brian Hebblethwaite." In *Incarnation and Myth: The Debate Continued*, pp. 192–4. Edited by Michael Goulder. Grand Rapids, Mich.: Eerdmans, 1979.

"Response to Clark H. Pinnock." In *More than One Way?: Four Views on Salvation in a Pluralistic World*, 124–8. Edited by Dennis L. Okholm and Timothy R. Phillips. Grand Rapids, Mich.: Zondervan, 1995.

"A Response to Gerard Loughlin." *Modern Theology* 7 (1990): 57–66.

"Response to Mesle." In C. Robert Mesle. *John Hick's Theodicy: A Process Humanist Critique*, 115–34. New York: St. Martin's 1991.

"Response to R. Douglas Geivett and W. Gary Phillips." In *More than One Way?: Four Views on Salvation in a Pluralistic World*, 246–50. Edited by Dennis L. Okholm and Timothy R. Phillips. Grand Rapids, Mich.: Zondervan, 1995.

"Response to Robert Cook." *Themelios* 19 (1994): 20.

"Rethinking Christian Doctrine in the Light of Religious Pluralism." In *Christianity and the Wider Ecumenism*, 89–102. Edited by Peter Phan. New York: Paragon, 1990.

"Straightening the Record: Some Response to Critics." *Modern Theology* 6 (1990): 187–95.
"Theology and Verification." *Theology Today* 17 (1960): 12–31.
"The Theology of Religious Pluralism." *Theology* 86 (1983): 335–40.
"Theology's Central Problem." *Expository Times* 80 (1969): 228–32.
"Towards a Philosophy of Religious Pluralism." *Neue Zeitschrift für Systematische Theologie und Religionsphilosophie* 22 (1980): 131–49.
"Trinity and Incarnation in the Light of Religious Pluralism." In *Three Faiths—One God: A Jewish, Christian, Muslim Encounter*, 197–210. Edited by John Hick and Edmund Meltzer. Albany: SUNY, 1989.
"Transcendence and Truth." In *Religion without Transcedence?* 41–59. Edited by D. Z. Phillips. New York: St. Martin's, 1997.
"Whatever Path Men Choose is Mine." *Modern Churchman* 18 (1974): 8–17.
"The Will to Believe: William James's Theory of Faith." *London Quarterly and Holborn Review* 127 (1952): 290—95.

Works on John Hick's Thought

Almond, Philip. "John Hick's Copernican Theology." *Theology* 86 (1983): 36–41.
Alston, William P. "Realism and the Christian Faith." *International Journal for Philosophy of Religion* 38 (1995): 37–60.
———. "Religious Diversity and Perceptual Knowledge of God." *Faith and Philosophy* 5 (1988): 440–52.
———. "Response to Hick ['The Epistemological Challenge of Religious Pluralism']" *Faith and Philosophy* 14 (1997): 287–8.
Anderson, Norman. *The Mystery of the Incarnation*. London: Hodder & Stoughton, 1978.
Apczynski, John V. "John Hick's Theocentrism: Revolutionary or Implicitly Exclusivist?" *Modern Theology* 8 (1992): 39–52.
Arens, Edmund. "Perspektiven und Problematik pluralistischer Christologie." *Münchener Theologische Zeitschrift* 46 (1995): 329–43.
Arulampalam, Sriganda E. M. "Toward an Exclusivistic Model of Dialogue in a Religiously Pluralistic World." Ph.D. diss. Southern Baptist Theological Seminary, 1994.
Ashdown, Lance Spencer. "Anonymous Skeptics: Swinburne, Hick and Alston." Ph.D. diss. Claremont Graduate University, 1997.
Badham, Paul. "John Hick and Human Response to Transcendent Reality." *Dialogue and Alliance* 5 (1991): 43–51.
———. "The Philosophical Theology of John Hick." In *A John Hick Reader*, 1–14. Edited by Paul Badham. Philadelphia: Trinity, 1990.
Ball, David M. "'I am…': The 'I am' Sayings of Jesus and Religious Pluralism." In *One God, One Lord: Christianity in a World of Religious Pluralism*, 2nd ed., 65–84. Edited by Andrew D. Clarke and Bruce W. Winter. Grand Rapids: Baker, 1992.
Barnes, L. Philip. "Continuity and Development in John Hick's Theology." *Studies in Religion/Sciences Religieuses* 21 (1992): 395–402.
———. "Towards a Theology of World Religions: An Outline and Assessment of the Work of John Hick." *Churchman* 97 (1983): 216–31.
Begley, John. "Philosophy of the World Religions: The Views of John Hick." *Australian Catholic Record* 72 (1995): 306–15.
Betty, L. Stafford. "The Glitch in *An Interpretation of Religion*." In *Problems in the Philosophy of*

Religion: Critical Studies of the Work of John Hick, 98–103. Edited by Harold Hewitt. New York: St. Martin's, 1991.

Byrne, Peter. "John Hick's Philosophy of World Religions." Scottish Journal of Theology 35 (1982): 289–301.

———. Prolegomena to Religious Pluralism: Reference and Realism in Religion. New York: St. Martin's, 1995.

Carey, George. God Incarnate. Downers Grove, Ill.: InterVarsity, 1977.

Carruthers, Gregory H. The Uniqueness of Jesus Christ in the Theocentric Model of the Christian Theology of World Religions: An Elaboration and Evaluation of the Position of John Hick. Lanham, Md.: University Press of America, 1990.

Christian, William. Review of Faith and Knowledge. Religion in Life 27 (1958): 627–8.

Clack, Beverley J. "Leaving Things as They Are: A Response to John Hick and Paul Badham." King's Theological Review 13 (1990): 37–40.

Clark, David K. "Can Apologists Enter Genuine Dialogue?" In The Challenge of Religious Pluralism: An Evangelical Analysis and Response, 152–62. Edited by David K. Clark, et al. Proceedings of the Wheaton College Theology Conference 1. Wheaton, Ill.: Wheaton Theology Conference, 1992.

Clark, Kelly James. "Perils of Pluralism." Faith and Philosophy 14 (1997): 303–20.

Clarke, Peter, and Peter Byrne. Religion Defined and Explained. New York: St. Martin's, 1993.

Clayton, John. Review of An Interpretation of Religion. Journal of Theological Studies 43 (1992): 800–4.

Clendenin, Daniel B. Many Gods, Many Lords: Christianity Encounters World Religions. Grand Rapids: Baker, 1995.

Cobb, Jr., John B. "Beyond 'Pluralism'." In Christian Uniqueness Reconsidered: The Myth of a Pluralistic Theology of Religions, 81–95. Edited by Gavin D'Costa. Maryknoll, N.Y.: Orbis, 1990.

Cook, Robert. "Postmodernism, Pluralism and John Hick." Themelios 19 (1993): 10–12.

———. "Response to John Hick." Themelios 19 (1994): 20–1.

Coventry, John. "The Myth and the Method." Theology 81 (1978): 252–61.

Coward, Harold. Pluralism: Challenge to World Religions. Maryknoll, N.Y.: Orbis, 1985.

Cupitt, Don. "Thin-line Theism [review of God Has Many Names]." The Times Literary Supplement (August 8, 1980): 902.

Davis, Caroline Franks. The Evidential Force of Religious Experience. Oxford: Clarendon, 1989.

D'Costa, Gavin. "An Answer to Mr. Loughlin." New Blackfriars 66 (1985): 135–7.

———. "Christian Theology and Other Faiths." In Companion Encyclopedia of Theology, 291–313. Edited by Peter Byrne and Leslie Houlden. New York: Routledge, 1995.

———. "Christian Theology and Other Religions: An Evaluation of John Hick and Paul Knitter." Studia Missionalia 42 (1993): 161–78.

———. "Elephants, Ropes and a Christian Theology of Religions." Theology 88 (1985): 259–67.

———. "'Extra Ecclesiam nulla Salus' Revisited." In Religious Pluralism and Unbelief: Studies Critical and Comparative, 130–47. Edited by Ian Hamnett. London: Routledge, 1990.

———. "The Impossibility of a Pluralist View of Religions." Religious Studies 32 (1996): 223–32.

———. "John Hick and Religious Pluralism: Yet Another Revolution." In Problems in the Philosophy of Religion: Critical Studies of the Work of John Hick, 3–27. Edited by Harold Hewitt, Jr. New York: St. Martin's, 1991.

———. "John Hick's Copernican Revolution: Ten Years After." New Blackfriars 65 (1984): 323–31.

———. John Hick's Theology of Religions: A Critical Evaluation. Lanham, Md.: University Press of America, 1987.

————. "The New Missionary: John Hick and Religious Pluralism." *International Bulletin of Missionary Research* (1991): 66–9.

————. "The Pluralist Paradigm in the Christian Theology of Religions." *Scottish Journal of Theology* 39 (1986): 211–24.

————. "Revelation and World Religions." In *Divine Revelation*, 112–39. Edited by Paul Avis. Grand Rapids, Mich.: Eerdmans, 1997.

————. Review of *The Metaphor of God Incarnate. Religious Studies* 31 (1995): 136–8.

————. "Taking Other Religions Seriously: Some Ironies in the Current Debate on a Christian Theology of Religions." *The Thomist* 54 (1990): 519–29.

————. *Theology and Religious Pluralism.* Oxford: Blackwell, 1986.

————. "Theology of Religions." In *The Modern Theologians*, ii:274–90. Edited by David Ford. Oxford: Blackwell, 1989.

Del Colle, Ralph. *Christ and the Spirit: Spirit-Christology in Trinitarian Perspective.* New York: Oxford University Press, 1994.

Deutsch, Eliot. Review of *An Interpretation of Religion. Philosophy East and West* 40 (1990): 557–62.

DiNoia, J. A. *The Diversity of Religions: A Christian Perspective.* Washington, D.C.: Catholic University of America Press, 1992.

————. "Pluralist Theology of Religions: Pluralistic or Non-Pluralistic?." In *Christian Uniqueness Reconsidered: The Myth of a Pluralistic Theology of Religions*, 119–34. Edited by Gavin D'Costa. Maryknoll, N.Y.: Orbis, 1990.

Dupuis, Jacques. *Toward a Christian Theology of Religious Pluralism.* Maryknoll, N.Y.: Orbis, 1997.

Eddy, Paul R. "John Hick and the Historical Jesus." In *The Convergence of Theology: A Festschrift in Honor of Gerald O'Collins*, 304–19. Edited by Stephen T. Davis and Daniel Kendall. New York: Paulist Press, 2001.

————. "John Hick's Theological Pilgrimage." In *The Challenge of Religious Pluralism: An Evangelical Analysis and Response*, 26–38. Edited by David K. Clark, et al. Proceedings of the Wheaton College Theology Conference 1. Wheaton, Ill.: Wheaton Theology Conference, 1992.

————. "Religious Pluralism and the Divine: Another Look at John Hick's Neo-Kantian Proposal." *Religious Studies* 30 (1994): 467–78.

Edwards, David L. "John Hick and the Uniqueness of Jesus.'" In his *Tradition and Truth: The Challenge of England's Radical Theologians 1962–1989*, 212–53. London: Hodder and Stoughton, 1989.

Erickson, Millard J. *How Shall They be Saved? The Destiny of Those Who Do Not Hear of Jesus.* Grand Rapids: Baker, 1996.

Ernst, Carl W. "From Philosophy of Religion to History of Religion." In *Problems in the Philosophy of Religion: Critical Studies of the Work of John Hick*, 46–50. Edited by Harold Hewitt, Jr. New York: St. Martin's, 1991.

Forrester, Duncan. "Professor Hick and the Universe of Faiths." *Scottish Journal of Theology* 29 (1976): 65–72.

Franck, Olof. *The Criteriological Problem: A Critical Study with Special Regard to Theories Presented by Antony Flew, D.Z. Phillips, John Hick, Basil Mitchell, Anders Jeffner, and Hans Hof.* Stockholm: Almqvist & Wiksell, 1988.

Fredericks, James L. "A Universal Religious Experience? Comparative Theology as an Alternative to a Theology of Religions." *Horizons* 22 (1995): 67–87.

Gnanakan, Ken. *The Pluralistic Predicament.* Bangalore, India: Theological Book Trust, 1992.

Geivett, R. Douglas. "John Hick's Approach to Religious Pluralism." In *The Challenge of Reli-*

gious Pluralism: An Evangelical Analysis and Response, 39–55. Edited by David K. Clark, et al. Proceedings of the Wheaton College Theology Conference 1. Wheaton, Ill.: Wheaton Theology Conference, 1992.

———, and W. Gary Phillips. "Response to John Hick." In *More than One Way?: Four Views on Salvation in a Pluralistic World*, 71–80. Edited by Dennis L. Okholm and Timothy R. Phillips. Grand Rapids, Mich.: Zondervan, 1995.

Gilkey, Langdon. "Plurality and Its Theological Implications." In *The Myth of Christian Uniqueness: Towards a Pluralistic Theology of Religions*, 37–50. Edited by John Hick and Paul F. Knitter. Maryknoll, N.Y.: Orbis, 1987.

Gillis, Chester. "An Interpretation of *An Interpretation of Religion*." In *Problems in the Philosophy of Religion: Critical Studies of the Work of John Hick*, 28–45. Edited by Harold Hewitt, Jr. New York: St. Martin's, 1991.

———. "John Hick as Philosopher of Religion." Unpublished paper, 20 pp.

———. "John Hick's Christology." *Bijdragen* 49 (1988): 41–57.

———. *Pluralism: A New Paradigm for Theology*. Grand Rapids: Eerdmans, 1993.

———. *A Question of Final Belief: John Hick's Pluralistic Theology of Salvation*. London: Macmillan, 1989.

Green, Garrett. Review of *An Interpretation of Religion*. *Theology Today* 46 (1990): 461–62.

Green, Michael, ed. *The Truth of God Incarnate*. Grand Rapids: Eerdmans, 1977.

Griffiths, Paul J. *An Apology for Apologetics: A Study in the Logic of Interreligious Dialogue*. Maryknoll, N.Y.: Orbis, 1991.

———. "The Uniqueness of Christian Doctrine Defended." In *Christian Uniqueness Reconsidered: The Myth of a Pluralistic Theology of Religions*, 157–73. Edited by Gavin D'Costa. Maryknoll, N.Y.: Orbis, 1990.

———, and Delmas Lewis. "On Grading Religions, Seeking Truth, and Being Nice to People." *Religious Studies* 19 (1983): 75–80.

Grover, Stephen. Review of *Interpretation of Religion*. *The Literary Times Supplement* (December 22–29, 1989): 1404.

Heaney, James J. "Faith and the Logic of Seeing-as." *International Journal for Philosophy of Religion* 10 (1979): 189–98.

Hebblethwaite, Brian. "John Hick and the Question of Truth in Religion." In *God, Truth, and Reality: Essays in Honour of John Hick*, 124–34. Edited by Arvind Sharma. New York: St. Martin's, 1993.

———. Review of *An Interpretation of Religion*. *Zygon* 26 (1991): 328–33.

Heim, S. Mark. "Pluralism and the Otherness of World Religions." *First Things* #25 (August–September 1992): 29–35.

———. "The Pluralistic Hypothesis, Realism, and Post-Eschatology." *Religious Studies* 28 (1992): 207–19.

———. "Salvations: A More Pluralistic Hypothesis." *Modern Theology* 10 (1994): 341–60.

———. *Salvations: Truth and Difference in Religion*. Maryknoll, N.Y.: Orbis, 1995.

Heron, Alasdair. "Article Review: Doing Away with the Incarnation?" *Scottish Journal of Theology* 31 (1978): 51–71.

Hewitt, Harold, ed. *Problems in the Philosophy of Religion: Critical Studies of the Work of John Hick*. New York: St. Martin's, 1991.

Huang, Yong. "Religious Pluralism and Interfaith Dialogue: Beyond Universalism and Particularism." *International Journal for Philosophy of Religion* 37 (1995): 127–44.

Hunt, Anne. "No Other Name? A Critique of Religious Pluralism." *Pacifica* 3 (1990): 45–60.

Hurtado, Art. "The 'Real', the Incarnation and Myth in John Hick's Pluralistic Hypothesis." Paper presented at the 1998 Southwest Regional meeting of the American Academy of Religion, Dallas, Tex. 15 pp.

Jeffner, Anders. "The Difficult Limits of Logic." In *God, Reality and Truth: Essays in Honor of John Hick*, 135–42. Edited by Arvind Sharma. New York: St. Martin's, 1993.

Kaufman, Gordon D. "Religious Diversity and Religious Truth." In *God, Reality and Truth: Essays in Honor of John Hick*, 143–64. Edited by Arvind Sharma. New York: St. Martin's, 1993.

———. "Religious Diversity, Historical Consciousness, and Christian Theology." In *The Myth of Christian Uniqueness: Towards a Pluralistic Theology of Religions*, 3–15. Edited by John Hick and Paul F. Knitter. Maryknoll, N.Y.: Orbis, 1987.

Kennick, W. E. Review of *Faith and Knowledge*. *Philosophical Review* 67 (1958): 407–9.

Knitter, Paul F. *No Other Name? A Critical Survey of Christian Attitudes Toward the World Religions*. Maryknoll, N.Y.: Orbis, 1985.

Kraft, James. "What Constitutes a Distinctively Christian Approach to Interfaith Dialogue?" *Dialog* 37 (1998): 282–90.

Kubias, Craig. "John Hick's Epistemology: A Viable Basis for World Theology?" In *Church Divinity, 1983*, 55–68. Edited by John H. Morgan. Notre Dame: Foundations, 1983.

LaFargue, Michael. "Radically Pluralist, Thoroughly Critical: A New Theory of Religions." *Journal of the American Academy of Religion* 60 (1992): 693–716.

Lash, Nicholas. "Interpretation and Imagination." In *Incarnation and Myth: The Debate Continued*, 19–26. Edited by Michael Goulder. Grand Rapids, Mich.: Eerdmans, 1979.

Lewis, Hywel D. "Appendix B: A Note on Professor Hick's Views." In *Jesus in the Faith of Christians*, 107–10. London: Macmillan, 1981.

Lillegard, Norman. "Philosophers, Theologians, and the Pluralism Problem." *Philosophy and Theology* 7 (1993): 381–403.

Lipner, Julius J. "At the Bend in the Road: A Story about Religious Pluralism." In *Problems in the Philosophy of Religion: Critical Studies of the Work of John Hick*, 213–34. Edited by Harold Hewitt. New York: St. Martin's, 1991.

———. "Christians and the Uniqueness of Christ." *Scottish Journal of Theology* 28 (1975): 359–68.

———. "Does Copernicus Help? Reflections for a Christian Theology of Religions." *Religious Studies* 13 (1977): 243–58.

———. "Truth-claims and Inter-religious Dialogue." *Religious Studies* 12 (1976): 217–30.

Londis, James J. "God, Probability and John Hick." *Religious Studies* 16 (1980): 457–63.

Loughlin, Gerard. "Myths, Signs and Significations." *Theology* 89 (1986): 268–75.

———. "Noumenon and Phenomena." *Religious Studies* 23 (1987): 493–508.

———. "Paradox and Paradigms: Defending the Case for a Revolution in Theology of Religions." *New Blackfriars* 66 (1985): 127–35.

———. "Prefacing Pluralism: John Hick and the Mastery of Religion." *Modern Theology* 7 (1990): 29–55.

———. "See-Saying / Say-Seeing." *Theology* 91 (1988): 201–8.

———. "Squares and Circles: John Hick and the Doctrine of the Incarnation." In *Problems in the Philosophy of Religion: Critical Studies of the Work of John Hick*, 181–205. Edited by Harold

Hewitt. New York: St. Martin's, 1991.

Louw, Dirk J. "The Soteriocentrism of John Hick." *South African Journal of Philosophy* 14 (1995): 19–23.

————. "Theocentrism and Reality-centrism: A Critique of John Hick and Wilfred Cantwell Smith's Philosophy of Religious Pluralism." *South African Journal of Philosophy* 13 (1994): 1–8.

Lyden, John C. "Why Only 'One' Divine Reality?: A Critique of Religious Pluralism." *Dialogue and Alliance* 8 (1994): 60–74.

Mackie, Beth. "Concerning 'Eschatological Verification Reconsidered.'" *Religious Studies* 23 (1987): 129–35.

Macquarrie, John. "Postscript: Christianity without Incarnation? Some Critical Comments." In *Truth of God Incarnate*, 140–4. Edited by Michael Green. Grand Rapids: Eerdmans, 1977.

Marshall, Molly Truman. *No Salvation Outside the Church? A Critical Inquiry*. Lewiston, N.Y.: Mellen, 1993.

Mathis, Terry Richard. *Against John Hick: An Examination of His Philosophy of Religion*. New York: University Press of America, 1985.

Mavrodes, George I. "The God above the Gods: Can the High Gods Survive?" In *Reasoned Faith: Essays in Philosophical Theology in Honor of Norman Kretzmann*, 179–203. Edited by Eleonore Stump. Ithaca: Cornell University Press, 1993.

————. "Polytheism." In *The Rationality of Belief and the Plurality of Faith: Essays in Honor of William P. Alston*, 261–86. Edited by Thomas D. Senor. Ithaca: Cornell University Press, 1995.

————. "A Response to John Hick ['The Epistemological Challenge of Religious Pluralism']." *Faith and Philosophy* 14 (1997): 289–94.

McCabe, Herbert. "The Myth of God Incarnate." *New Blackfriars* 58 (1977): 350–7.

McCord Adams, Marilyn. "Chalcedonian Christology: A Christian Solution to the Problem of Evil." In *Philosophy and Theological Discourse*, 173–98. Edited by Stephen D. Davis. New York: St. Martin's, 1997.

McCready, Douglas. "The Disintegration of John Hick's Christology." *Journal of the Evangelical Theological Society* 39 (1996): 257–70.

McCutcheon, Russell T. *Manufacturing Religion: The Discourse on Sui Generis Religion and the Politics of Nostalgia*. New York: Oxford University Press, 1997.

————. "'My Theory of the Brontosaurus': Postmodernism and 'Theory' of Religion." *Studies in Religion* 26 (1997): 3–23.

McGrath, Alister E. "Response to John Hick." In *More than One Way?: Four Views on Salvation in a Pluralistic World*, 65–70. Edited by Dennis L. Okholm and Timothy R. Phillips. Grand Rapids, Mich.: Zondervan, 1995.

Mesle, C. Robert. "Humanism and Hick's Interpretation of Religion." In *Problems in the Philosophy of Religion: Critical Studies of the Work of John Hick*, 54–85. Edited by Harold Hewitt. New York: St. Martin's, 1991.

————. *John Hick's Theodicy: A Process Humanist Critique*. New York: St. Martin's 1991.

————. Review of *An Interpretation of Religion. Journal of the American Academy of Religion* 58 (1990): 710–14.

Miller, Ed L. Review of *Disputed Questions in Theology and the Philosophy of Religion. Journal of the American Academy of Religion* 59 (1996): 884–6.

Min, Anselm. "Christology and Theology of Religions: John Hick and Karl Rahner." *Louvain Studies* 11 (1986): 3–21.

Mitchell, Basil. "A Summing Up of the Colloquy: Myth of God Debate." In *Incarnation and Myth: The Debate Continued*, 233– 40. Edited by Michael Goulder. Grand Rapids, Mich.: Eerdmans, 1979.

Moule, Charles. "Incarnation and Atonement: A Comment on Professor Hick's Critique of Atonement Doctrine." In *Incarnation and Myth: The Debate Continued*, 85–6. Edited by Michael Goulder. Grand Rapids, Mich.: Eerdmans, 1979.

Nash, Ronald H. *Is Jesus the Only Savior?* Grand Rapids: Zondervan, 1994.

Neill, Stephen. "Jesus and Myth." In *The Truth of God Incarnate*, 58–70. Edited by Michael Green. Grand Rapids: Eerdmans, 1977.

Netland, Harold A. *Dissonant Voices: Religious Pluralism and the Question of Truth*. Grand Rapids, Mich.: Eerdmans, 1991.

———. "Professor Hick on Religious Pluralism." *Religious Studies* 22 (1986): 249–61.

Newbigin, Lesslie. *The Gospel in a Pluralist Society*. Grand Rapids, Mich.: Eerdmans, 1989.

———. "Religion for the Marketplace." In *Christian Uniqueness Reconsidered: The Myth of a Pluralistic Theology of Religions*, 135–48. Edited by Gavin D'Costa. Maryknoll, N.Y.: Orbis, 1990.

O'Collins, Gerald. "The Incarnation Under Fire." *Gregorianum* 76 (1995): 263–80.

Ogden, Schubert M. "Problems in the Case for a Pluralistic Theology of Religions." *Journal of Religion* 68 (1988): 493– 507.

Okholm, Dennis L., and Timothy R. Phillips, eds. *More than One Way? Four Views on Salvation in a Pluralistic World*. Grand Rapids, Mich.: Zondervan, 1995.

O'Leary, Joseph Stephen. *Religious Pluralism and Christian Truth*. Edinburgh: Edinburgh University Press, 1996.

Orteza y Miranda, Evelina. "Religious Pluralism and Tolerance." *British Journal of Religious Education* 17 (1994): 19–34.

Panikkar, Raimundo. "The Jordan, the Tiber, and the Ganges: Three Kairological Moments of Christic Self-Consciousness." In *The Myth of Christian Uniqueness: Towards a Pluralistic Theology of Religions*, 89–116. Edited by John Hick and Paul F. Knitter. Maryknoll, N.Y.: Orbis, 1987.

Pannenberg, Wolfhart. "Religious Pluralism and Conflicting Truth Claims: The Problem of a Theology of the World Religions." In *Christian Uniqueness Reconsidered: The Myth of a Pluralistic Theology of Religions*, 96–106. Edited by Gavin D'Costa. Maryknoll, N.Y.: Orbis, 1990.

Penelhum, Terence. "Reflections on the Ambiguity of the World." In *God, Truth, and Reality: Essays in Honour of John Hick*, 165–75. Edited by Arvind Sharma. New York: St. Martin's, 1993.

Pentz, Rebecca. "Hick and Saints: Is Saint-Production a Valid Test?" *Faith and Philosophy* 8 (1991): 96–103.

Perrett, Roy W. "John Hick on Faith: A Critique." *International Journal for Philosophy of Religion* 15 (1984): 57–66.

Peters, Ted. "Confessional Universalism and Inter-Religious Dialogue." *Dialog* 25 (1986): 145–9.

Phillips, D. Z. "Philosophers' Clothes." In *Relativism and Religion*, 135–53. Edited by Charles M. Lewis. New York: St. Martin's, 1995.

Pinnock, Clark H. "Conclusion." In *More than One Way?: Four Views on Salvation in a Pluralistic World*, 141–8. Edited by Dennis L. Okholm and Timothy R. Phillips. Grand Rapids, Mich.: Zondervan, 1995.

———. "Response to John Hick." In *More than One Way?: Four Views on Salvation in a Pluralistic World*, 60–4. Edited by Dennis L. Okholm and Timothy R. Phillips. Grand Rapids, Mich.: Zondervan, 1995.

Plantinga, Alvin. "Ad Hick." *Faith and Philosophy* 14 (1997): 295–98.

————. "Pluralism: A Defense of Religious Exclusivism." In *The Rationality of Belief and the Plurality of Faith: Essays in Honor of William P. Alston*, 191–215. Edited by Thomas D. Senor. Ithaca: Cornell University Press, 1995.

————. *Warranted Christian Belief*. New York: Oxford University Press (forthcoming).

Prabhu, Joseph. "The Road Not Taken: A Story about Religious Pluralism, Part 2." In *Problems in the Philosophy of Religion: Critical Studies of the Work of John Hick*, 235–41. Edited by Harold Hewitt. New York: St. Martin's, 1991.

Quinn, Philip L. "Religious Pluralism and Religious Relativism." *Scottish Journal of Religious Studies* 15 (1994): 69–84.

————. "Towards Thinner Theologies: Hick and Alston on Religious Diversity." *International Journal for Philosophy of Religion* 38 (1995): 145–64.

Ratzinger, Cardinal Joseph. "Relativism: The Central Problem for Faith Today." *Origins* 26 (1996): 309–17.

Rodd, C. S. Review of *An Interpretation of Religion*. *Expository Times* 101 (1989): 33–35.

Rodwell, John. "Myth and Truth in Scientific Enquiry." In *Incarnation and Myth: The Debate Continued*, 64–73. Edited by Michael Goulder. Grand Rapids, Mich.: Eerdmans, 1979.

Rose, Kenneth Thomas. "Knowing the Real: John Hick on the Cognitivity of Religions and Religious Pluralism." Ph.D. diss. Harvard University, 1992.

————. *Knowing the Real: John Hick on the Cognitivity of Religions and Religious Pluralism*. TSR 20. New York: Lang, 1996.

Rowe, William. "John Hick's Contribution to the Philosophy of Religion." In *God, Truth and Reality: Essays in Honour of John Hick*, 18–23. Edited by Arvind Sharma. New York: St. Martin's, 1993.

Runzo, Joseph, "God, Commitment, and Other Faiths: Pluralism Vs. Relativism." *Faith and Philosophy* 5 (1988): 343–61.

Russell, Stanley H. "The Finality of Christ and Other Religions." *Epworth Review* 4 (1977): 77–84.

Sanders, John. *No Other Name: An Investigation into the Destiny of the Unevangelized*. Grand Rapids: Eerdmans, 1992.

Schilbrack, Kevin Edward. "The Metaphysical Interpretation of Religions." Ph.D. diss. University of Chicago, 1995.

Schwöbel, Christoph. "Particularity, Universality, and the Religions: Toward a Christian Theology of Religions." In *Christian Uniqueness Reconsidered: The Myth of a Pluralistic Theology of Religions*, 30–46. Edited by Gavin D'Costa. Maryknoll, N.Y.: Orbis, 1990.

Segal, Robert A. "A Review Essay: Religion as Interpreted Rather than Explained." Review of *An Interpretation of Religion*. *Soundings* 74 (1991): 275–88.

Sharma, Arvind. *The Philosophy of Religion and Advaita Vedanta: A Comparative Study in Religion and Reason*. University Park, Pa.: Pennsylvania State University Press, 1995.

Sharma, Arvind, ed. *God, Truth and Reality: Essays in Honour of John Hick*. New York: St. Martin's, 1993.

Sinkinson, Chris. *John Hick: An Introduction to His Theology*. Leicester: RTSF, 1995.

Slater, Peter. "Lindbeck, Hick and the Nature of Religious Truth." *Studies in Religion* 24 (1995): 59–75.

Smart, Ninian. "A Contemplation of Absolutes." In *God, Truth, and Reality: Essays in Honour of John Hick*, 176–88. Edited by Arvind Sharma. New York: St. Martin's, 1993.

————. "Models for Understanding the Relations between Religions." In *Inter-Religious Models and Criteria*, 58–67. Edited by J. Kellenberger. New York: St. Martin's, 1993.

Stetson, Brad. *Pluralism and Particularity in Religious Belief.* Westport, Conn.: Praeger, 1994.

Stinnett, Timothy R. "John Hick's Pluralistic Theory of Religion." *Journal of Religion* 70 (1990): 569–88.

Stiver, Dan R. Review of *The Metaphor of God Incarnate. International Journal for Philosophy of Religion* 40 (1996): 180–2.

Stoeber, Michael. *Theo-Monistic Mysticism: A Hindu-Christian Comparison.* New York: St. Martin's, 1994.

Streiker, Lowell D. "John Hick." In *Modern Theologians: Christian and Jews,* 152–68. Edited by Thomas E. Bird. Notre Dame: University of Notre Dame Press, 1967.

Sugirtharajah, R. S. "A Professor of Pluralism." *One World* 76 (May 1982): 19–20.

Surin, Kenneth. "A 'Politics of Speech': Religious Pluralism in the Age of the McDonald's Hamburger." In *Christian Uniqueness Reconsidered: The Myth of a Pluralistic Theology of Religions,* 192–212. Edited by Gavin D'Costa. Maryknoll, N.Y.: Orbis, 1990.

———. "Revelation, Salvation, the Uniqueness of Christ and Other Religions." *Religious Studies* 19 (1983): 323–43.

———. "Towards a 'Materialist' Critique of 'Religious Pluralism': An Examination of the Discourse of John Hick and Wilfred Cantwell Smith." In *Religious Pluralism and Unbelief: Studies Critical and Comparative,* 114–29. Edited by Ian Hamnett. New York: Routledge, 1990.

Tan, Wyle. "Religious Pluralism Revisited." *Asia Journal of Theology* 2 (1988): 342–9.

Thomas, Owen. Review of *Interpretation of Religion. Anglican Theological Review* 73 (1991): 501–4.

Tilley, Terrence W. Review of *Interpretation of Religion. Theological Studies* 51 (1990): 137–9.

Tinker, Melvin. "Truth, Myth and Incarnation." *Themelios* 14 (1988): 11–17.

Tune, Anders S. Review of *The Metaphor of God Incarnate. Dialog* 35 (1996): 155–7.

Twiss, Sumner B. "The Philosophy of Religious Pluralism: A Critical Appraisal of Hick and His Critics." *Journal of Religion* 70 (1990): 533–68.

Van Inwagen, Peter. "*Non Est* Hick." In *The Rationality of Belief and the Plurality of Faith: Essays in Honor of William P. Alston,* 216–41. Edited by Thomas D. Senor. Ithaca: Cornell University Press, 1995.

———. "A Reply to Professor Hick ['The Epistemological Challenge of Religious Pluralism']." *Faith and Philosophy* 14 (1997): 299–302.

Van Ness, Peter H. "Conversion and Christian Pluralism." *Philosophy and Theology* 7 (1993): 337–53.

Verkamp, Bernard J. "Hick's Interpretation of Religious Pluralism." *International Journal for Philosophy of Religion* 30 (1991): 103–24.

Vroom, Hendrik. *No Other Gods: Christian Belief in Dialogue with Buddhism, Hinduism, and Islam.* Translated by Lucy Jansen. Grand Rapids, Mich.: Eerdmans, 1996.

Wainwright, William J. "Religious Language, Religious Experience, and Religious Pluralism." In *The Rationality of Belief and the Plurality of Faith: Essays in Honor of William P. Alston,* 170–88. Edited by Thomas D. Senor. Ithaca, N.Y.: Cornell University Press, 1995.

———. Review of *A Christian Theology of Religions. International Journal for Philosophy of Religion* 42 (1997): 124–8.

———. Review of *An Interpretation of Religion. Faith and Philosophy* 9 (1992): 259–65.

Ward, Keith. "Divine Ineffability." In *God, Truth and Reality: Essays in Honour of John Hick,* 210–20. Edited by Arvind Sharma. New York: St. Martin's, 1993.

———. *Religion and Revelation.* New York: Oxford University Press, 1994.

———. "Truth and the Diversity of Religions." *Religious Studies* 26 (1990): 1–18.

Warren, Max. "The Uniqueness of Christ." *Modern Churchman* 18 (1974): 55–65.

Wells, Harry L. "Taking Pluralism Seriously: The Role of Metaphorical Theology within Inter-religious Dialogue." *Journal of Ecumenical Studies* 30 (1993): 20–33.

Werbick, Jürgen. "Heil durch Jesus Christus allein? Die 'Pluralistische Theologie' und ihr Plädoyer für einen Pluralismus der Heilswege." In *Der einzige Weg zum Heil?* 11–61. Edited by Michael von Brück and Jügen Werbick. Freiburg: Herder, 1993.

Wiedenhofer, Siegfried. "Between Particularity and Universality: A Christian View of the Possibility of Ensuring the Identity and Communicability of Cultural and Religious Traditions." Unpublished paper, 1995.

Yandell, Keith E. "Some Varieties of Religious Pluralism." In *Inter-Religious Models and Criteria*, 187–211. Edited by J. Kellenberger. New York: St. Martin's, 1993.

Other Works

Adams, Robert. "Things in Themselves." *Philosophy and Phenomenological Research* 57 (1997): 801–25.

Aleaz, K. P. "Religious Pluralism and Christian Witness: A Biblical-Theological Analysis." *Bangalore Theological Forum* 21 (1990): 48–67.

Alston, William P. *Perceiving God: The Epistemology of Religious Experience.* Ithaca: Cornell University Press, 1991.

Amaladoss, Michael. *Making All Things New: Dialogue, Pluralism and Evangelism in Asia.* Maryknoll, N.Y.: Orbis, 1990.

Ameriks, Karl. "Recent Work on Kant's Theoretical Philosophy." *American Philosophical Quarterly* 19 (1982): 1–24.

Anderson, Gerald H., and Thomas F. Stransky, eds. *Christ's Lordship and Religious Pluralism.* Maryknoll, N.Y.: Orbis, 1981.

Aquila, Richard E. "Things in Themselves and Appearances: Intentionality and Reality in Kant." *Archiv für Geschichte der Philosophie* 61 (1979): 293–307.

Armstrong, A. H. "Some Advantages of Polytheism." *Dionysius* 5 (1981): 181–88.

Barnes, L. Philip. "Relativism, Ineffability, and the Appeal to Experience: A Reply to the Myth Makers." *Modern Theology* 7 (1990): 101–14.

Barnes, Michael. *Religions in Conversation.* London: SPCK, 1989.

Beilby, James. "Rationality, Warrant, and Religious Diversity." *Philosophia Christi* 17 (1994): 1–14.

Bloesch, Donald. *God the Almighty: Power, Wisdom, Holiness, Love.* Downers Grove, Ill.: InterVarsity, 1995.

Bongmba, Elias K. "Two Steps Forward, One Step Backward: Schleiermacher on Religion." *Journal of Theology for Southern Africa* 97 (1997): 81–96.

Boyd, Gregory A. *God at War: The Bible and Spiritual Conflict.* Downers Grove, Ill.: InterVarsity, 1997.

Burrell, David. *Aquinas, God and Action.* London: Routledge & Kegan, 1979.

———. "God, Religious Pluralism, and Dialogic Encounter." In *Reconstructing Christian Theology*, 49–78. Edited by Rebecca S. Chopp and Mark Lewis Taylor. Minneapolis: Fortress, 1994.

———. Review of *The Diversity of Religions*, by J. A. DiNoia. *Modern Theology* 10 (1994): 107–9.

Carabine, Deirdre. *The Unknown God: Negative Theology in the Platonic Tradition: Plato to Eriugena.* Grand Rapids: Eerdmans, 1995.

Carson, D. A. *The Gagging of God: Christianity Confronts Pluralism.* Grand Rapids: Zondervan, 1996.

Chubb, Jehangir. "Presuppositions of Religious Dialogue." *Religious Studies* 8 (1972): 289–310.

Clark, Andrew D., and Bruce W. Winter, eds. *One God, One Lord: Christianity in a World of Religious Pluralism*, 2nd ed. Grand Rapids, Mich.: Baker, 1992.

Clark, Gregory A. "The Nature of Conversion: How the Rhetoric of Worldview Philosophy Can Betray Evangelicals." In *The Nature of Confession: Evangelicals and Postliberals in Conversation*, 201–18. Edited by Timothy R. Phillips and Dennis L. Okholm. Downers Grove, Ill.: InterVarsity, 1996.

Cobb, Jr., John B. *Beyond Dialogue: Toward a Mutual Transformation of Christianity and Buddhism*. Philadelphia: Fortress, 1982.

———. *Christ in a Pluralistic Age*. Philadelphia: Westminster, 1975.

Cobb, Jr., John B., and Christopher Ives, eds. *The Emptying God: A Buddhist-Jewish-Christian Conversation*. Maryknoll, N.Y.: Orbis, 1990.

Compson, Jane. "The Dalai Lama and the World Religions: A False Friend?" *Religious Studies* 32 (1996): 271–9.

Contreras, C. A. "Christian Views of Paganism." In *Aufstieg und Niedergang der Römischen Welt*, II:23, 2, 974–1022. Edited by H. Temporini and W. Haase. New York: de Gruyter, 1980.

Copeland, E. Luther. "Christian Theology and World Religions." *Review and Expositor* 94 (1997): 423–35.

Cowdell, Scott. "Hans Küng and World Religions: The Emergence of a Pluralist." *Theology* 92 (1989): 85–92.

Cragg, Kenneth. *The Christian and Other Religion*. London: Mowbrays, 1977.

Davies, Douglas. "Salvation in Preliterate Societies." In *Meaning and Salvation in Religious Studies*, 101–20. SHR 46. Leiden: Brill, 1984.

Davis, Stephen T. "Why God Must be Unlimited." In *Concepts of the Ultimate*, 3–22. Edited by Linda J. Tessier. New York: St. Martin's, 1989.

D'Costa, Gavin. "Christ, the Trinity, and Religious Plurality." In *Christian Uniqueness Reconsidered: The Myth of a Pluralistic Theology of Religions*, 16–29. Edited by Gavin D'Costa. Maryknoll, N.Y.: Orbis, 1990.

———, ed. *Christian Uniqueness Reconsidered: The Myth of a Pluralistic Theology of Religions*. Maryknoll, N.Y.: Orbis, 1990.

———. "Creating Confusion: A Response to Markham." *New Blackfriars* 74 (1993): 41–7.

———. "Karl Rahner's Anonymous Christian—A Reappraisal." *Modern Theology* 1 (1985): 131–48.

———. "Whose Objectivity? Which Neutrality? The Doomed Quest for a Neutral Vantage Point from which to Judge Religions." *Religious Studies* 29 (1993): 79–95.

Dean, William. *History Making History: The New Historicism in American Religious Thought*. Albany: SUNY, 1988.

———. "The Persistence of Experience: A Commentary on Gordon Kaufman's Theology." In *New Essays in Religious Naturalism*, 67–81. Edited by W. Creighton Peden and Larry E. Axel. Macon: Mercer University Press, 1993.

Donovan, Peter. "The Intolerance of Religious Pluralism." *Religious Studies* 29 (1993): 217–29.

Driver, Tom F. "The Case for Pluralism." In *Myth of Christian Uniqueness: Towards a Pluralistic Theology of Religions*, 203–18. Edited by John Hick and Paul F. Knitter. Maryknoll, N.Y.: Orbis, 1987.

Eck, Diana L. *Encountering God: A Spiritual Journey from Bozeman to Banaras*. Boston: Beacon, 1993.

Eddy, Paul R. "Paul Knitter's Theology of Religions: A Survey and Evangelical Response." *Evangelical Quarterly* 65 (1993): 225–45.

————. "The (W)Right Jesus: Eschatological Prophet, Israel's Messiah, Yahweh Embodied." In *Jesus and the Restoration of Israel: A Critical Assessment of N. T. Wright's Jesus and the Victory of God.* Edited by Carey Newman. Downers Grove, Ill.: InterVarsity, 1999.

Farmer, H. H. *Revelation and Religion: Studies in the Theological Interpretation of Religious Types.* London: Nisbet, 1954.

Feuerbach, Ludwig. *The Essence of Christianity.* Translated by George Elliot. New York: Harper & Bros., 1957 [1841].

Finger, Thomas. *Christian Theology: an Eschatological Approach,* 2 vols. Scottdale, Pa.: Herald, 1985, 1989.

Ford, James E. "Systematic Pluralism: Introduction to an Issue." *The Monist* 73 (1990): 335–49.

Forgie, William. "Hyper-Kantianism in Recent Discussions of Mystical Experience." *Religious Studies* 21 (1985): 205–18.

Garver, Eugene. "Why Pluralism Now?" *The Monist* 73 (1990): 388– 410.

Geivett, R. Douglas, and W. Gary Phillips. "A Particularist View: An Evidentialist Approach." In *More than One Way?: Four Views on Salvation in a Pluralistic World,* 213–45. Edited by Dennis L. Okholm and Timothy R. Phillips. Grand Rapids, Mich.: Zondervan, 1995.

Gellman, Jerome. "God and Theoretical Entities: Their Cognitive Status." *International Journal for Philosophy of Religion* 13 (1982): 131–41.

Gilkey, Langdon. "The Pluralism of Religions." In *God, Truth and Reality: Essays in Honour of John Hick,* 111–23. Edited by Arvind Sharma. New York: St. Martin's, 1993.

————. *Through the Tempest: Theological Voyages in a Pluralistic Culture.* Edited by Jeff Pool. Minneapolis: Fortress, 1991.

Godlove, Terry F. *Religion, Interpretation, and Diversity of Belief: The Framework Model from Kant to Durkheim to Davidson.* New York: Cambridge University Press, 1989.

Grant, Colin. *A Salvation Audit.* Scranton: University of Scranton Press, 1994.

————. "The Threat and Prospect in Religious Pluralism." *Ecumenical Review* 41 (1989): 50–63.

Griffiths, Paul J. "Denaturalizing Discourse: Abhidharmikas, Propositionalists, and the Comparative Philosophy of Religion," *Myth and Philosophy,* 57–91. Edited by Frank Reynolds and David Tracy. Albany: SUNY, 1990.

————. "Doctrines and the Virtue of Doctrine: The Problematic of Religious Plurality." In *Religions and the Virtue of Religion,* 29–44. Edited by Thérèse-Anne Druart and Mark Rasevic. Washington, D.C.: Catholic University of America, 1992.

————. "Encountering Buddha Theologically." *Theology Today* 47 (1990): 39–51.

————. "Modalizing the Theology of Religions." *Journal of Religion* 73 (1993): 382–9.

————. "Philosophizing Across Cultures: Or, How to Argue with a Buddhist." *Criterion* (Winter 1987): 10–14.

————. "The Properly Christian Response to Religious Plurality." *Anglican Theological Review* 79 (1997): 3–26.

————. "Review Symposium: Religious Diversity." *The Thomist* 52 (1988): 319–27.

————. "Why We Need Interreligious Polemics." *First Things* #44 (June–July, 1994): 31–7.

Griffiths, Paul J., ed. *Christianity through non-Christian Eyes.* Maryknoll, N.Y.: Orbis, 1990.

Guelzo, Allen C. "First Church of Historical Relativism: Ernst Troeltsch and the Intellectual Sources of Pluralism." In *The Challenge of Religious Pluralism: An Evangelical Analysis and Response,* 9–25. Edited by David K. Clark, et al. Proceedings of the Wheaton College Theology Conference 1. Wheaton, Ill.: Wheaton Theology Conference, 1992.

Guthrie, Shirley C. "The Way, the Truth, and the Life in the Religions of the World." *Princeton Seminary Bulletin* 17 (1996): 45–57.

Hanson, R. P. C. "The Christian Attitude to Pagan Religions up to the Time of Constantine the Great." In *Aufstieg und Niedergang der Römischen Welt*, II:23, 2, 910–73. Edited by H. Temporini and W. Haase. New York: de Gruyter, 1980.

Hart, Ray L. "Religious and Theological Studies in American Higher Education: A Pilot Study." *Journal of the American Academy of Religion* 59 (1991): 715–82.

Hasker, William. "Proper Function, Reliabilism, and Religious Knowledge: A Critique of Plantinga's Epistemology." In *Christian Perspectives on Religious Knowledge*, 66–86. Edited by C. Stephen Evans and Merold Westphal. Grand Rapids: Eerdmans, 1993.

Hayman, Peter. "Monotheism — A Misused Word in Jewish Studies?" *Journal of Jewish Studies* 42 (1991): 1–15.

Heim, S. Mark. *Is Christ the Only Way? Christian Faith in a Pluralistic World*. Valley Forge: Judson, 1985.

———, ed. *Grounds for Understanding: Ecumenical Resources for Responses to Religious Pluralism*. Grand Rapids: Eerdmans, 1998.

———. "Pluralisms: Toward a Theological Framework for Religious Diversity." *Insights* 107 (1991): 17–25.

Hocking, William Ernest. *The Coming World Civilization*. New York: Harper, 1956.

———. *Living Religions and a World Faith*. New York: Macmillan, 1940.

Hogan, Kevin. "The Experience of Reality: Evelyn Underhill and Religious Pluralism." *Anglican Theological Review* 74 (1992): 334–47.

Holden, Michael David. "The Place of Exclusivist Religion in the Contemporary World." Ph.D. diss. Claremont Graduate School. 1985.

Hughes, Gerard J. "Aquinas and the Limits of Agnosticism." In *The Philosophical Assessment of Theology: Essays in Honour of Frederick C. Copleston*, 37–63. Edited by Gerard Hughes. Washington, D. C.: Georgetown University Press, 1987.

Hume, David. *Dialogues Concerning Natural Religion*. Indianapolis/New York: Bobbs-Merrill, 1947 [1779].

———. *An Inquiry Concerning Human Understanding*. Edited by Charles W. Hendel. Indianapolis: Bobbs-Merrill, 1955 [1748].

James, William. *The Works of William James: A Pluralistic Universe*. Camrbidge, Mass.: Harvard University Press, 1977 (1903):.

———. *Varieties of Religious Experience*. New York: Mentor, 1960 (1902).

Jaspers, Karl. *The Origin and Goal of History*. Translated by Michael Bullock. London: Routledge & Kegan Paul, 1953 [1949].

Johnson, Mark. "Apophatic Theology's Cataphatic Dependencies." *The Thomist* 62 (1998): 519–31.

Kant, Immanuel. *The Critique of Pure Reason*, abridged ed. Translated by Norman Kemp Smith. London: Macmillan, 1952.

Kaufman, Gordon D. "Christian Theology and the Modernization of the Religions." In *The Theological Imagination: Constructing the Concept of God*, 172–206. Philadelphia: Westminster, 1981.

———. "Religious Diversity and Religious Truth." In *God, Truth and Reality: Essays in Honour of John Hick*, 143–64. Edited by Arvind Sharma. New York: St. Martin's, 1993.

———. "Religious Diversity, Historical Consciousness, and Christian Theology." In *The Myth of Christian Uniqueness: Toward a Pluralistic Theology of Religions,* 3–15. Edited by J. Hick and P. Knitter. Maryknoll, N.Y.: Orbis, 1987.

Keith, Graham. "Justin Martyr and Religious Exclusivism." *Tyndale Bulletin* 43 (1992): 57–80.

Knitter, Paul F. "Can Our 'One and Only' also be a 'One among Many'? A Response to Responses." In *The Uniqueness of Jesus: A Dialogue with Paul F. Knitter,* 145–82. Edited by Leonard Swidler and Paul Mojzes. Maryknoll, N.Y.: Orbis, 1997.

———. "Five Theses on the Uniqueness of Jesus." In *The Uniqueness of Jesus: A Dialogue with Paul F. Knitter,* 3–16. Edited by Leonard Swidler and Paul Mojzes. Maryknoll, N.Y.: Orbis, 1997.

———. "Key Questions for a Theology of Religions." *Horizons* 17 (1990): 92–102.

———. "The Pluralist Move and Its Critics." *The Drew Gateway* 58 (1988): 10–16.

———. "Toward a Liberation Theology of Religions." *The Myth of Christian Uniqueness: Toward a Pluralistic Theology of Religions,* 3–15. Edited by John Hick and Paul F. Knitter. Maryknoll, N.Y.: Orbis, 1987.

Küng, Hans. "The World Religions in God's Plan of Salvation." In *Christian Revelation and World Religions,* 25–66. Edited by Joseph Neuner. London: Burns and Oates, 1967.

Labuschagne, C. J. *The Incomparability of Yahweh.* Leiden: Brill, 1966.

Lampe, G. W. H. *God As Spirit: The Bampton Lectures, 1976.* Oxford: Clarendon Press, 1977.

———. "The Holy Spirit and the Person of Christ." In *Christ, Faith and History: Cambridge Studies in Christology,* 111–30. Edited by S. W. Sykes and J. P. Clayton. Cambridge: Cambridge University Press, 1972.

Lindbeck, George. "The *A Priori* in St. Thomas' Theory of Knowledge." In *The Heritage of Christian Thought: Essays in Honor of Robert Lowry Calhoun,* 41–63. Edited by R. E. Cushman and E. Grislis. New York: Harper & Row, 1965.

———. *The Nature of Doctrine: Religion and Theology in a Postliberal Age.* Philadelphia: Westminster, 1984.

Markham, Ian. "Creating Options: Shattering the 'Exclusivist, Inclusivist, and Pluralist' Paradigm." *New Blackfriars* 74 (1993): 33–41.

Martinson, Paul Varo. *A Theology of World Religions: Interpreting God, Self, and World in Semitic, Indian, and Chinese Thought.* Minneapolis: Augsburg, 1987.

Mauser, Ulrich. "One God Alone: A Pillar of Biblical Theology." *Princeton Seminary Bulletin* 12 (1991): 255–65.

McGrath, Alister E. "The Challenge of Pluralism for the Contemporary Christian Church." In *The Challenge of Religious Pluralism: An Evangelical Analysis and Response,* 229–57. Edited by David K. Clark, et al. Proceedings of the Wheaton College Theology Conference 1. Wheaton, Ill.: Wheaton Theology Conference, 1992.

———. "The Challenge of Pluralism for the Contemporary Christian Church." *Journal of the Evangelical Theological Society* 35 (1992): 361–73.

———. "The Christian Church's Response to Pluralism." *Journal of the Evangelical Theological Society* 35 (1992): 487–501.

———. "A Particularist View: A Post-Enlightenment Approach." In *More than One Way?: Four Views on Salvation in a Pluralistic World,* 151–80. Edited by Dennis L. Okholm and Timothy R. Phillips. Grand Rapids, Mich.: Zondervan, 1995.

McKenzie, David E. "Kant, a Moral Criterion, and Religious Pluralism." *American Journal of Theology and Philosophy* 6 (1985): 47–56.

McWilliams, Warren. "Spirit Christology and Inclusivism: Clark Pinnock's Evangelical Theology of Religions." *Perspective in Religious Studies* 24 (1997): 325–36.

Mead, Sidney E. *The Nation with the Soul of a Church*. New York: Harper & Row, 1975.

Merrigan, Terrence. "Religious Knowledge in the Pluralist Theology of Religions." *Theological Studies* 58 (1997): 686–707.

Milbank, John. "The End of Dialogue." In *Christian Uniqueness Reconsidered: The Myth of a Pluralistic Theology of Religions*, 174–91. Edited by Gavin D'Costa. Maryknoll, N.Y.: Orbis, 1990.

Min, Anselm Kyongsuk. "Towards a Dialectic of Pluralism." Paper presented at the Christian Theological Research Fellowship annual meeting, Philadelphia, Pa., November 18, 1995. 32 pp.

Mortley, Raoul. *From Word to Silence*, Vol. 2: *The Way of Negation, Christian and Greek*. Bonn: Hanstein, 1986.

Mouw, Richard, and Sander Griffioen. *Pluralisms and Horizons: An Essay in Christian Public Philosophy*. Grand Rapids: Eerdmans, 1993.

Neusner, Jacob. "Can You Be 'Religious' in General?" *Religious Studies and Theology* 12 (1992): 69–73.

North, John. "The Development of Religious Pluralism." In *The Jews among Pagans and Christians in the Roman Empire*, 174–93. Edited by Judith Lieu, John North, and Tessa Rajak. New York: Routledge, 1992.

Oakes, Robert A. "God and Cosmos: Can the 'Mystery of Mysteries' be Solved?" *American Philosophical Quarterly* 33 (1996): 315–23.

———. "Noumena, Phenomena, and God." *International Journal for Philosophy of Religion* 4 (1973): 30–8.

Ogden, Schubert M. *Is There Only One True Religion or Are There Many?* Dallas: Southern Methodist University Press, 1992.

———. "Religious Studies and Theological Studies: What is Involved in the Distinction between the Two?" *Council of Societies for the Study of Religion Bulletin* 24 (1995): 3–4.

Oman, John W. *Grace and Personality*. New York: Association, 1961 [1919].

———. *The Natural and the Supernatural*. Cambridge: Cambridge University Press, 1931.

Palmer, Humphrey. *Analogy: A Study of Qualification and Argument in Theology*. New York: St. Martin's, 1973.

Palmquist, Stephen R. *Kant's System of Perspectives: An Architectonic Interpretation of the Critical Philosophy*. Lanham: University Press of America, 1993.

Panikkar, Raimundo. "The Invisible Harmony: A Universal Theory of Religion or a Cosmic Confidence in Reality?." In *Towards a Universal Theology of Religion*, 118–53. Edited by Leonard Swidler. Maryknoll, N.Y.: Orbis, 1987.

Penelhum, Terence. "Parity is Not Enough." In *Faith, Reason, and Skepticism*, 98–120. Edited by Marcus Hester. Philadelphia: Temple University Press, 1992.

Peters, Ted. "Culture Wars: Should Lutherans Volunteer or be Conscripted?" *Dialog* 32 (1993): 37–52.

———. *God—the World's Future: Systematic Theology for a Postmodern Era*. Minneapolis: Fortress, 1992.

Pinnock, Clark H. *Flame of Love: A Theology of the Holy Spirit*. Downers Grove, Ill.: InterVarsity, 1996.

Plantinga, Alvin. *Does God Have a Nature?* Milwaukee: Marquette University Press, 1980.

———. "Is Belief in God Properly Basic?" *Nous* 15 (1981): 41–51.

———. "Is Belief in God Rational?" In *Rationality and Religious Belief*, 7–27. Edited by C. F. Delaney. Notre Dame: University of Notre Dame Press, 1979.

———. "Pluralism: A Defense of Religious Exclusivism." In *The Rationality of Belief and the Plurality of Faith: Essays in Honor of William P. Alston*, 191–215. Edited by Thomas D. Senor. Ithaca: Cornell University Press, 1995.

———. "Reason and Belief in God." In *Faith and Rationality: Reason and Belief in God*, 16–93. Edited by Alvin Plantinga and Nicholas Wolterstorff. Notre Dame: University of Notre Dame, 1983.

————. *The Twin Pillars of Christian Scholarship*. Grand Rapids, Mich.: Calvin College and Seminary, 1990.

Posy, Carl. "Dancing to the Antinomy: A Proposal for Transcendental Idealism." *American Philosophical Quarterly* 20 (1983): 81–94.

Race, Alan. "Christianity and Other Religions: Is Inclusivism Enough?" *Theology* 89 (1986): 178–86.

————. *Christians and Religious Pluralism*. Maryknoll, N.Y.: Orbis, 1983.

Ramachandra, Vinoth. *The Recovery of Mission: Beyond the Pluralist Paradigm*. Grand Rapids: Eerdmans, 1996.

Reck, Andrew J. "An Historical Sketch of Pluralism." *The Monist* 73 (1990): 367–87.

Rocca, Gregory P. "Analogy as Judgment and Faith in God's Incomprehensibility: A Study in the Theological Epistemology of Thomas Aquinas." Ph.D. diss. Catholic University of America, 1989.

————. "Aquinas on God-Talk: Hovering Over the Abyss." *Theological Studies* 54 (1993): 641–61.

Rose, Kenneth. "Keith Ward's Exceptionalist Theology of Religions." *New Blackfriars* 79 (1998): 164–76.

Rossi, Philip. "The Final End of All Things: The Highest Good as the Unity of Nature and Freedom." In *Kant's Philosophy of Religion Reconsidered*, 133–64. Edited by Philip Rossi and M. Wreen. Bloomington/Indianapolis: Indiana University Press, 1991.

Runzo, Joseph. *Reason, Relativism and God*. New York: St. Martin's, 1986.

————. "Perceiving God, World-Views and Faith: Meeting the Problem of Religious Pluralism." In *World Views and Perceiving God*, 219–39. Edited by Joseph Runzo. New York: St. Martin's, 1993.

Saler, Benson. *Conceptualizing Religion: Immanent Anthropologists, Transcendent Natives, and Unbounded Categories*. New York: Brill, 1993.

Schineller, J. Peter. "Christ and Church: A Spectrum of Views." *Theological Studies* 37 (1976): 545–66.

Schleiermacher, Friedrich. *On Religion: Speeches to Its Cultured Despisers*. Translated by Richard Crouter. New York: Cambridge University Press, 1988.

————. *On Religion: Speeches to Its Cultured Despisers*. Translated by John Oman. London: Kegan Paul, Trench & Trubner, 1893.

Schrotenboer, Paul. "Varieties of Pluralism." *Evangelical Review of Theology* 13 (1989): 110–24.

Schüssler Fiorenza, Francis. "Christian Redemption between Colonialism and Pluralism." In *Reconstructing Christian Theology*, 269–302. Edited by Rebecca S. Chopp and Mark Lewis Taylor. Minneapolis: Fortress, 1994.

Seager, Richard Hughes, ed. *The Dawn of Religious Pluralism: Voices from the World's Parliament of Religions, 1893*. LaSalle, Ill.: Open Court, 1993.

Sharpe, Eric J. *Comparative Religion: A History*, 2nd ed. La Salle, Ill.: Open Court, 1986 [1975].

Smith, Norman Kemp. *A Commentary to Kant's "Critique of Pure Reason"*, rev. ed. Atlantic Highlands, N.J.: Humanities, 1992.

Smith, Steven G. "Bowl Climbing: The Logic of Religious Question Rivalry." *International Journal for Philosophy of Religion* 36 (1994): 27–43.

Smith, Wilfred Cantwell. "A Human View of Truth." *Studies in Religion* 1 (1971): 6–24.

————. *The Meaning and End of Religion: A New Approach to the Religious Traditions of Mankind*. New York: Mentor/New American Library, 1964 [1962].

————. *Questions of Religious Truth*. New York: Scribner's Sons, 1967.

———. *Towards a World Theology: Faith and the Comparative History of Religion*. Maryknoll, N.Y.: Orbis, 1981.

———. "Vedanta and the Modern Age." *Religious Studies and Theology* 13 & 14 (1995): 12–20.

Snaith, N. H. "The Advent of Monotheism in Israel." *The Annual of Leeds University Oriental Society* 5 (1963–5): 100–13.

Swinburne, Richard. *The Existence of God*. New York: Oxford University Press, 1979.

Thomas, M. M. "A Christ-Centered Humanist Approach to Other Religions in the Indian Pluralistic Context." In *Christian Uniqueness Reconsidered: The Myth of a Pluralistic Theology of Religions*, 49–62. Edited by Gavin D'Costa. Maryknoll, N.Y.: Orbis, 1990.

———. *Risking Christ for Christ's Sake: Towards an Ecumenical Theology of Pluralism*. Geneva: WCC, 1987.

Thomas, Owen C. *Attitudes Towards Other Religions: Some Christian Interpretations*. New York: Harper & Row, 1969.

———. "Religious Plurality and Contemporary Philosophy: A Critical Survey." *Harvard Theological Review* 87 (1994): 197– 213.

Tillich, Paul. *Christianity and the Encounter of the World Religions*. New York: Columbia University Press, 1963.

Tracy, David. *Dialogue with the Other: The Inter-Religious Dialogue*. Grand Rapids, Mich.: Eerdmans, 1990.

Tracy, David, and John B. Cobb, Jr. *Talking about God: Doing Theology in the Context of Modern Pluralism*. New York: Seabury, 1981.

Troeltsch, Ernst. "The Place of Christianity among the World Religions." In *Christianity and Other Religions: Selected Readings*, 11–31. Edited by John Hick and Brian Hebblethwaite. Philadelphia: Fortress, 1980.

Van Beeck, Frans. "Christian Faith and Theology in Encounter with Non-Christians: Profession? Protestation? Self-Maintenance? Abandon?" *Theological Studies* 55 (1994): 46–65.

Watson, Walter. *The Architectonics of Meaning: Foundations of the New Pluralism*. Albany: SUNY, 1985.

———. "Types of Pluralism." *The Monist* 73 (1990): 350–66.

Wenty, Richard. *The Culture of Religious Pluralism*. Boulder, Colo.: Westview, 1998.

Westphal, Merold. "Christian Philosophers and the Copernican Revolution." In *Christian Perspectives on Religious Knowledge*, 161–79. Edited by C. Stephen Evans and Merold Westphal. Grand Rapids: Eerdmans, 1993.

———. "In Defense of the Thing in Itself." *Kant-Studien* 59 (1968): 118–41.

Wilken, Robert L. "Religious Pluralism and Early Christian Thought." *Pro Ecclesia* 1 (1992): 89–103.

Winter, Bruce W. "In Public and in Private: Early Christians and Religious Pluralism." *One God, One Lord: Christianity in a World of Religious Pluralism*, 2nd ed., 125–48. Grand Rapids, Mich.: Baker, 1992.

Wolterstorff, Nicholas. "Is it Possible and Desirable for Theologians to Recover from Kant?" *Modern Theology* 14 (1998): 1–18.

Wright, N. T. *Jesus and the Victory of God*. Minneapolis: Fortress, 1996.

———. *The New Testament and the People of God*. Minneapolis: Fortress, 1992.

Yandell, Keith E. "Some Varieties of Ineffability." *International Journal for Philosophy of Religion* 6 (1975): 167–79.

Index